THE MENORAH CODE

ISBN: 978-0-578-27330-3

Dedication

To יהוה [YHWH], my Elohim, and my Salvation. It is by and through HIS inspiration that the fullness of HIS gospel, hidden within the Menorah, has come to be written within the pages of this book.

May the credit for the light and wisdom in HIS Menorah Code be attributed to the incomprehensible intelligence of the Most High.

May the people forgive my weak attempt to reveal thy greatness.

Note : **This book does not insert Hebrew words into the text without translation, so you don't need to know any Hebrew words in order to understand.**

Acknowledgements

יהוה (YHWH) : Thank you for answering my prayers, and revealing treasures which have been hidden form those who are wise in their own eyes, and prudent in their own sight. Even those treasures which have been hidden from the beginning.

To my wife : For coming with me to this deaf, dumb, and blind planet. I love you.

A COMPREHENSIVE ETYMOLOGICAL DICTIONARY OF THE HEBREW LANGUAGE FOR READERS OF ENGLISH, by ERNEST KLEIN.

A CONCISE HEBREW AND ARAMAIC LEXICON OF THE OLD TESTAMENT, by WILLIAM L. HOLLADAY

The Hebrew word search on biblehub.com

Preface

Welcome to the knowledge of the eternal.

The Tree of Knowledge and the Tree of Eternal Life are made one in the Menorah. It is a coded message hidden in symbols, sent into the future, to shed light on a world filled with darkness.

I will give an abridged version of what brought me to this point in time... I had hypothesized that the 22 knops (buds) and 22 bowls (flowers) of the Menorah were the 22 letters of the Hebrew Aleph–Bet.

I made a matrix based on the Menorah and intended to try writing in the letters in the order I saw fit. I had tried this a few times before, but this time was different. I was unable to write what "I" wanted in the matrix. My hand was being controlled by someone else. I would try to write one letter, and my hand was forced to write another.

Now, I knew the odds of creating the intended pattern were huge, but there seemed to be no pattern in what I was being forced to write. I had taken the time to learn the Hebrew Aleph-Bet before beginning, so I could see the order of Aleph-Bet appeared to be completely random.

When the matrix of 22 letters (plus the ע Ayin on top) was finished, I was shown that the key to unlocking the grid was found in the sign of the Aaronic blessing.

I had a travel dictionary, which turned out to be enough to see that there was something there, but I still needed a good Biblical Hebrew Dictionary.

In researching the "Tree of Life", I came across images of the Kabbalah tree of life. Though it did not have the letters filling in the center of the tree that I had, I saw that applying the tools in the center actually gave me some of the words which they had in those places.

It took me a long time just playing with these tools to begin noticing patterns. That's not to say I didn't receive dreams, visions, and a still small voice whispering in my ear, showing and telling me things. I did, but as I did not know Hebrew, and had to look up every word, I felt bogged down in the data.

When the patterns began to appear, I noticed layers. I was shown that flipping the center pipe of the Menorah creates the Tree of Life, and I began to stumble across one ancient symbol after another. If that wasn't enough, I was shown letters from which the main letters were made being used in the cypher.

Here is a list of what I have been shown or found:

1. Definitions for Hebrew words appear to be based on letter definitions which the tools assign to each letter.
2. The Hebrew language with the Aramaic-Hebrew letters must have been "created" at the same time as the Tree of Life / Knowledge. *(The only way the "code" will work properly is to use the Biblical Hebrew dating back to 500 BC. This is when, according to the book of 2nd Ezdras, the scriptures were re-given through Ezra and his scribes were forced to write in a character which they had not formerly known.)* The odds of any other explanation are beyond the number of Atoms in the known universe.
3. From what I have seen so far, it appears that "letter overlays" contain prophecies from the beginning to the end.
4. Symbols found : Tree of Life, Tree of Knowledge [the Kabbalah Tree of Life is a neutered subset of this], The Star of David, The "Sun" of Righteousness, The Ankh (The Seraph), The Ouroboros [Nehushtan], The Swastikas [two sets of 4 small carpenters squares in center], and the Flower of Life.
5. The Eternal Ordinances of the Kingdom of YHWH [being drawing forth from the water, being kindled with fire, a garden of Eden play, being clothed in a garment reaching to the palms of the hands and ankles of the feet, the veil, and becoming one].

I know that there are many among you that believe you have a Bible which contains everything you need to know. If this is so, you do not know the Bible.

Do you know how many books have been removed?
How about the Book of 2nd Esdras (Ezra)?
Chapter 14:
44 In forty days they wrote two hundred and four books.
45 And it came to pass, when the forty days were filled, that the Highest spake, saying, The first that thou hast written publish openly, that the worthy and unworthy may read it:
46 But keep the seventy last, that thou mayest deliver them only to such as be wise among the people:
47 For in them is the spring of understanding, the fountain of wisdom, and the stream of knowledge.
// Hidden knowledge, wisdom, and understanding, reserved for those who were worthy and wise. We also see "secret" teachings mentioned in early Christian texts.

Oh the lament, "My people are destroyed for lack of knowledge. Because you have rejected knowledge, I will also reject you." (Hosea 4:6)

Oh the lament, Isaiah 28:
8 "For all tables are full of vomit and filthiness, so there is no place clean.
9 "Whom shall he teach knowledge? And whom shall he make to understand doctrine? Them that are weaned from milk, and drawn from the breasts.

10 "For precept must be upon precept, precept upon precept; line upon line, line upon line; here a little and there a little:

11 For with stammering lips and another tongue will he speak to this people.

12 To whom he said, this is the rest where with ye may cause the weary to rest; and this is the refreshing: yet they would not hear."

We see ancient religious symbols found everywhere on the earth. Ancient traces of the original tree which proves that most "Pagan" religions, were using long revered symbols found in the Tree of Life to give them an heir of mystic knowledge, or ancient authenticity.

Many of these symbols continue to be used today. However, if the people worshiping in these churches understood how to read the Tree of Life, they would know that they were being misled by pretenders, liars, and the blind leading the blind.

The great whore, her harlots, and the synagogues of Satan cast a veil of darkness over the earth. These have an appearance of divinity, yet their cacophony of doctrines bear the mark of Babel. Wide is the way and narrow the gate.

Understand this; I am not writing this to say, "follow me". I am merely a tool in the master's hand revealing the light and life of the world in the Menorah, and I shall place it upon a mountain for all to see. It is time to look to that light and life.

Forget the babbling deaf, dumb, and blind voices of men. I'll show you a sign in bronze, a prophecy revealed. Look to your creator and cast off the venom of the serpent which has blinded you. No man, preacher, Rabbi, or religious leader can do this for you. **You must do it yourself.**

I fully expect that the Jews will understand these things more than any other people. However, the prophecies in the tree, had from the beginning, may be too much for them to bear. I tell you plainly, trusting that your salvation is sure because a man tells you so is a whoredom. You must seek your betrothed and follow HIM. HE is your Salvation.

Ask יהוי YHWH if these things are true. Ask as sons of the Most High. Receiving answers directly is part of your birth-right. Then ask what you must do.

His sheep will hear his voice and follow HIM. As for the rest, they are not his sheep, and I will loose no sleep over their choices, for judgment lies in the court of the creator.

So call upon HIS name. Seek your betrothed, and follow HIM.

"... Would God that all YHWH'S people were prophets, and that the YHWH would put his spirit upon them!" Numbers 11: 29

Abbreviations

TOL = Tree of Life
TOK = Tree of Knowledge

Atbash : This word pertains to a well known ancient Hebrew code wherein the first letter [the א Aleph] is paired with the last letter [the ת Taw] . . . then, the second letter [the ב Bet] is paired with the second to last [the ש Shin]. The sequence continues from the beginning to the end of the Aleph-Bet, but you can see how the A,T,B,Sh became known as Atbash.

   To make referencing this easier, you should understand that the 22 knops [buds] and bowels [flower petals] of the Menorah are assigned a letter [in the flower petal], and an Atbash letter [in the bud]. As the buds are below the flower petals, they will all be referred to as Atbash letters.

An **Atbash "pair"** will consist of the top letter [in the flower petals] and the letter in the bud which holds the petals in place.

YOU WILL NEED TO REMEMBER THIS ONE :
{} Set Symbol : A Hebrew letter inserted between these brackets will indicate that the *following letter is a subset of a composite letter.

   Example : ר{ה} : This indicates that the Hebrew Letter ר Reish is pulled from a composite letter. In this case, the ה Hei is made from a י Yud [hand, forearm, or foreleg], and a Reish [head]. This symbol will tell you that the ה Hei has been de-constructed, and the component letter *following the {} bracket is being used.

*[Following because Hebrew is read from right to left.]

Table of Contents

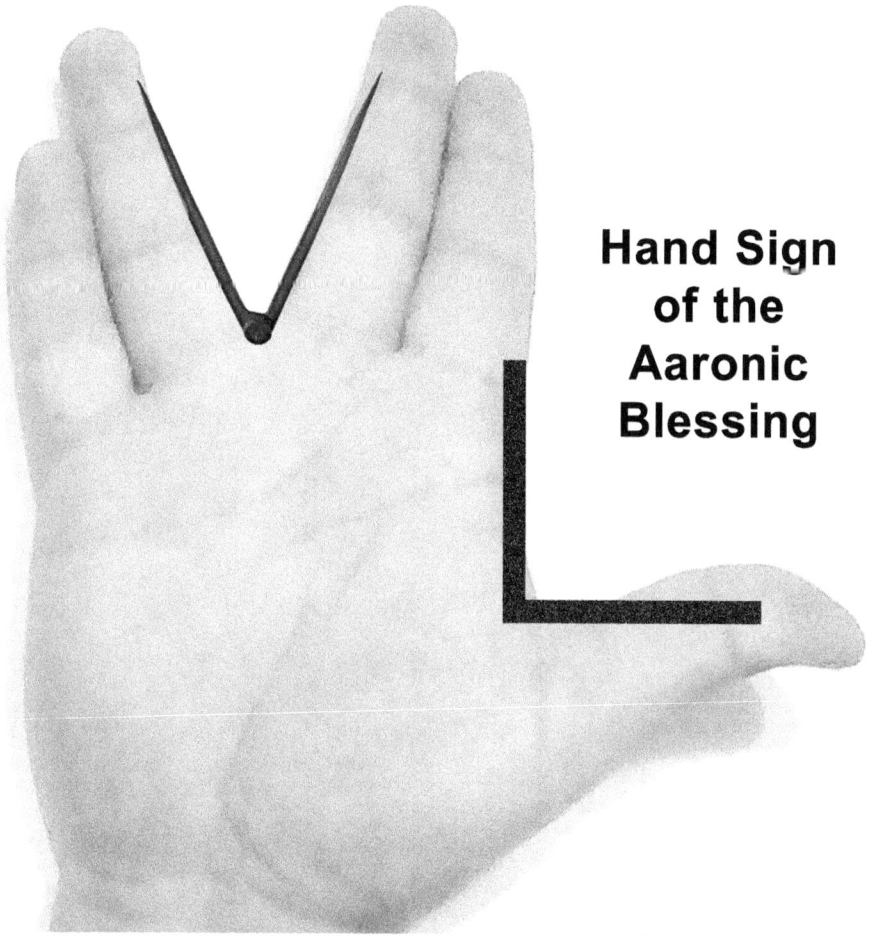

**Hand Sign
of the
Aaronic
Blessing**

While one may receive a blessing to live long and prosper, one should go back further in time to discover the origin and meaning behind this symbol.

Chapter 1 : Line Upon Line

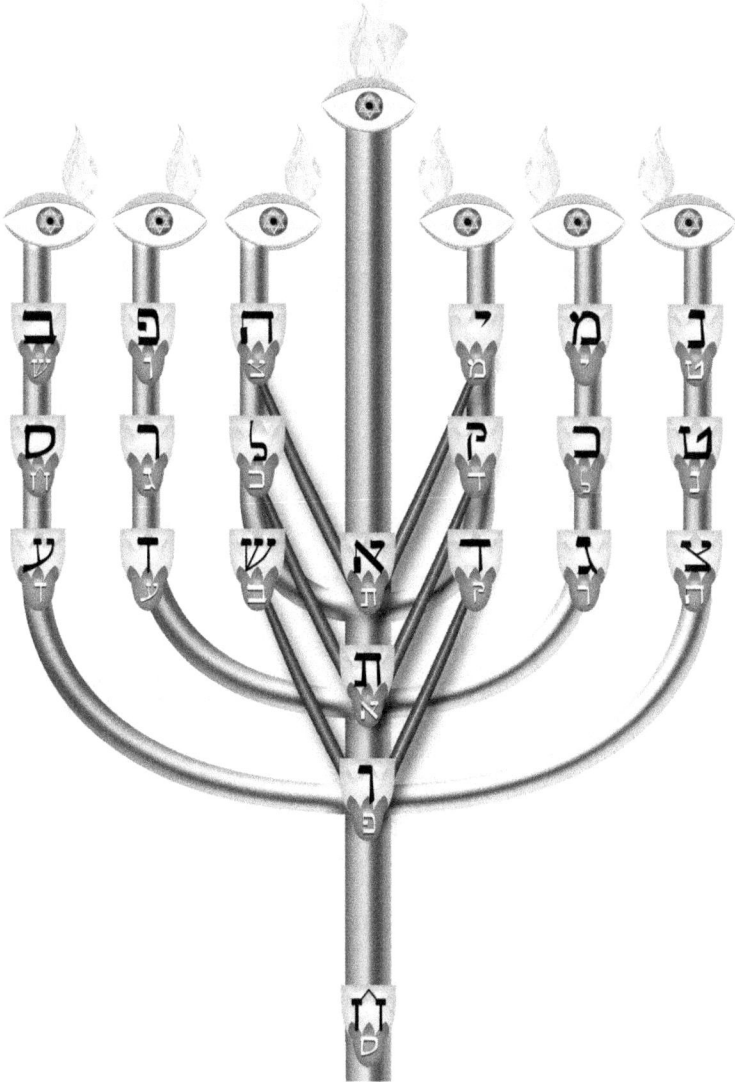

Take a mental note that the "eyes" which you see on top are the Almond shaped lamps of the Menorah. These are ע="Ayin" [the letter ע means "eye"], and that letter will be counted as filling that layer of the grid.

Now take note of the three compass placements. We are going to transform this symbol into a matrix.

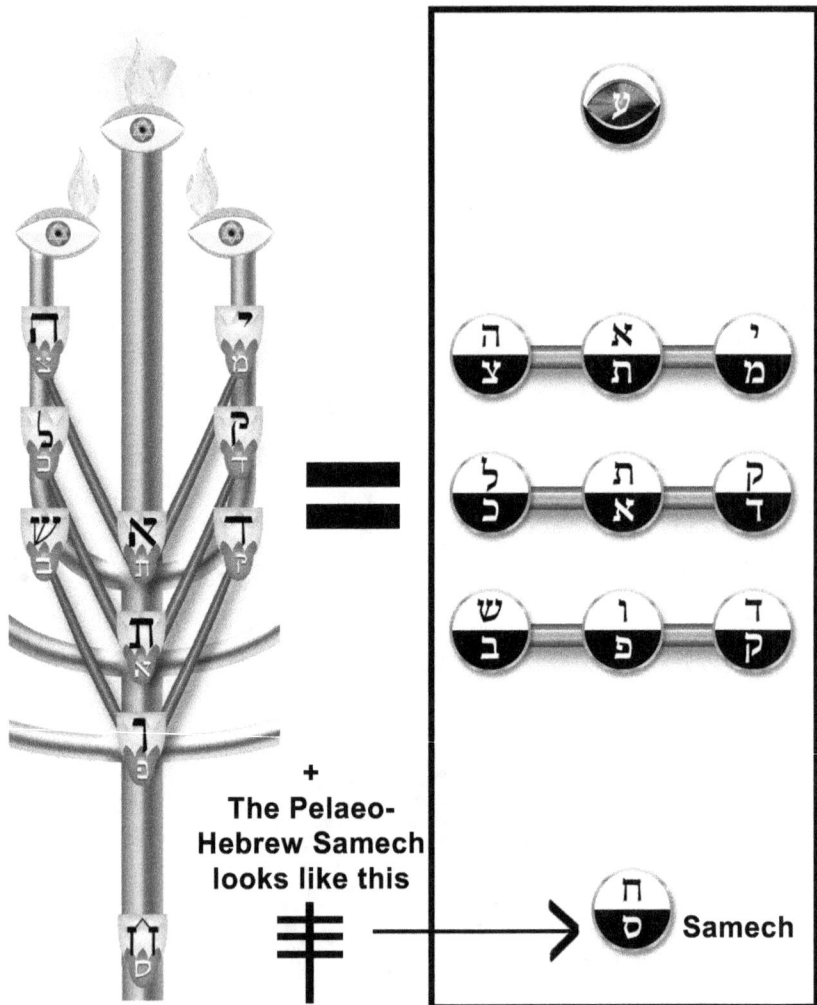

The Pelaeo-
Hebrew Samech
looks like this

Samech

Do you see how bringing the center pipe of the Menorah up gives us another symbol?

Consider the similarity to the Kabbalah Tree of Life (opposite page).

Some readers may understand enough Hebrew to question why these grids are mirror opposites. The ה Hei and the צ Tzaddi are known to represent the woman and the righteous respectively, yet they are shown as a reflections.

The answer to this lies behind a veil and a perspective which the reader is unable to comprehend without furthering their knowledge, so we will cover this a little later.

This background information leading to the full matrix will allow us to look at the א Aleph and begin to understand, line upon line.

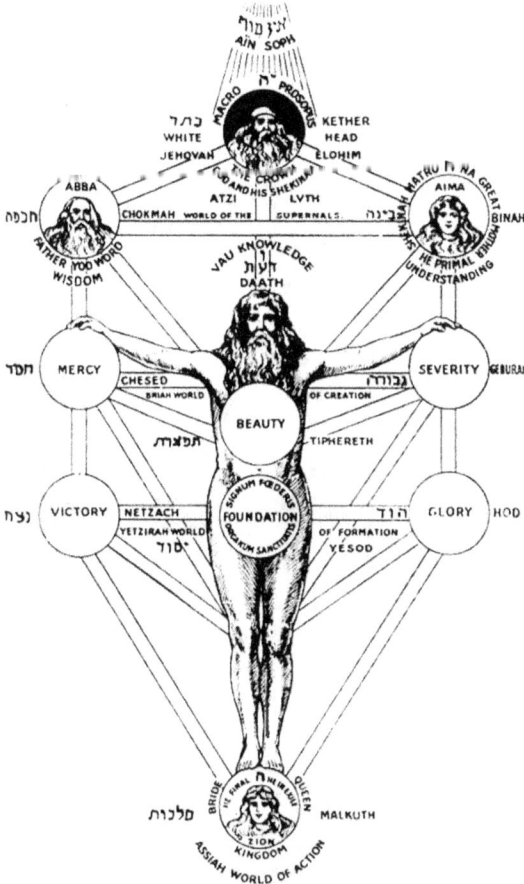

Place the man's right hand on your right.
Like looking into a mirror

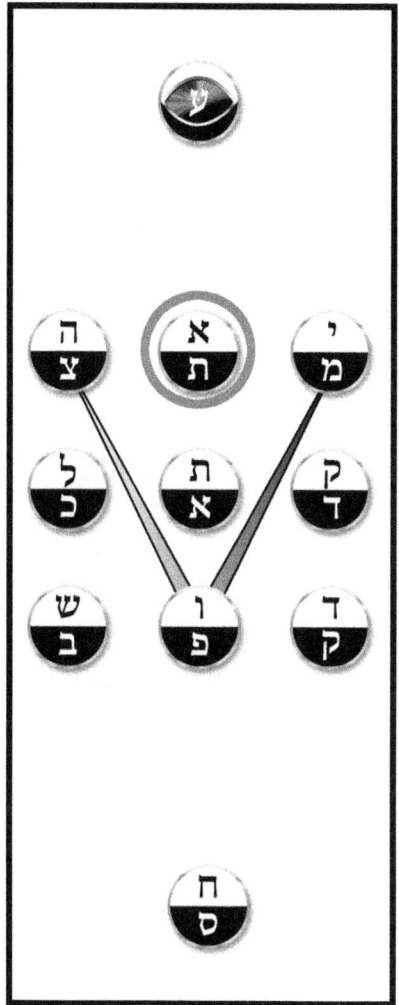

Looking only at the "Almond Petals" (letters with white background) of the Menorah, a compass **targeting the א Aleph** gives us the Holy Name of יהוה **YHWH**.

This is your first lesson: *The letters at each of the three points of the compass combine to give definitions to the target letter.* That target is the א Aleph at the open end of the compass.

Your next lesson is to note that the א Aleph itself is *made from part of each of these three letters.* The letter א has a י Yud in the upper right corner, a ו Waw dividing the center diagonally, and a י Yud which it has taken out of the ה Hei. That's right. The "foreleg" of the ה Hei is by definition, a י Yud [forearm, hand, foreleg].

This means that the other part of the ה Hei, the ר Reish, is there as well.

I found these things out rather recently, but teaching it from the beginning is best.

Place the man's right hand on your right.
Like looking into a mirror

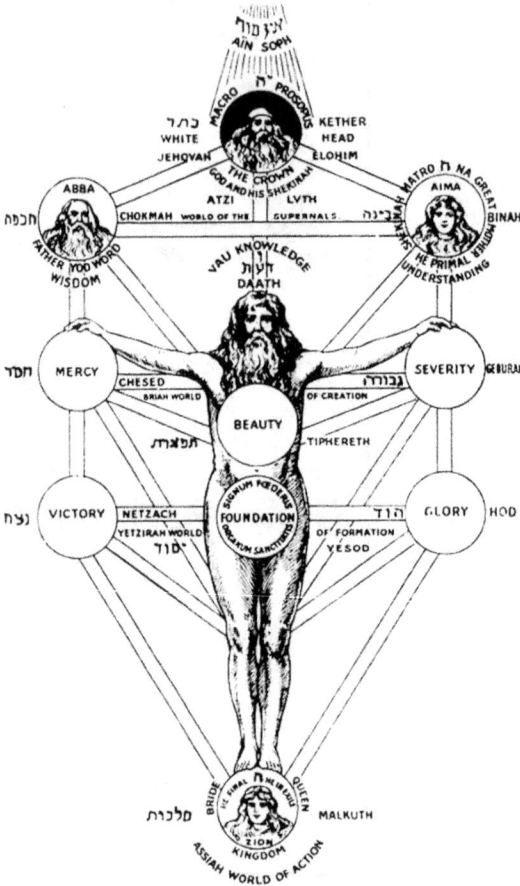

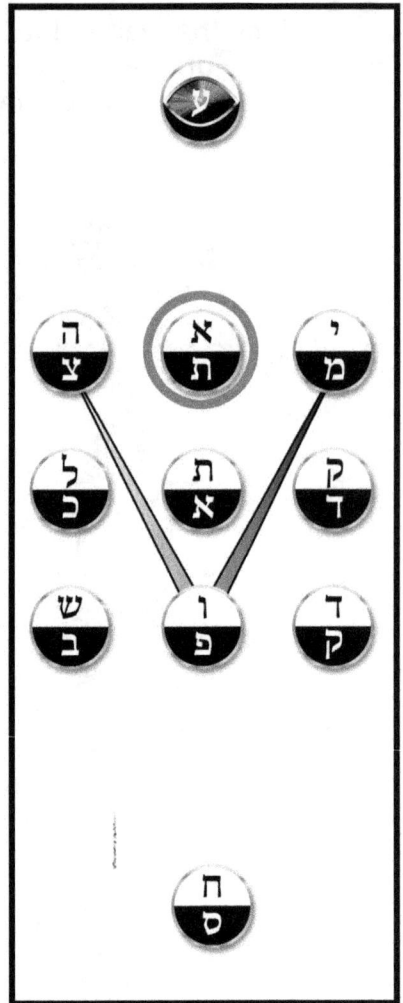

Now take note of the titles יה Yah and יהוה YHWH associated with the א Aleph position being targeted. It is identical to what is shown in the Menorah Code.

Do you see the female Mother figure associated with the ה Hei, and the male Father figure associated with the י Yud? Remember this. We will examine their identities in more detail later.

I will write a chapter just on the rules, *and it will help anyone willing to skip to that chapter to learn them.* However, most people are going to get bored, so I will continue to teach the rules as we go.

For now, I'm going to zip through a couple more examples from the Kabbalah Tree of Life to show that it is a fragment which came from the Menorah Code. Yet it will soon become obvious that without all the letters, it is just a fragment, whose value lays in authenticating the existence of the original, complete, tree.

Place the man's right hand on your right.
Like looking into a mirror

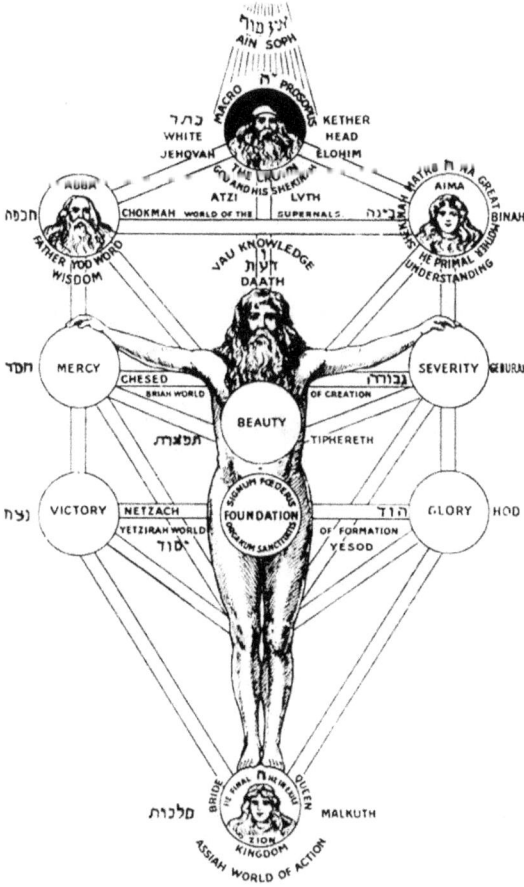

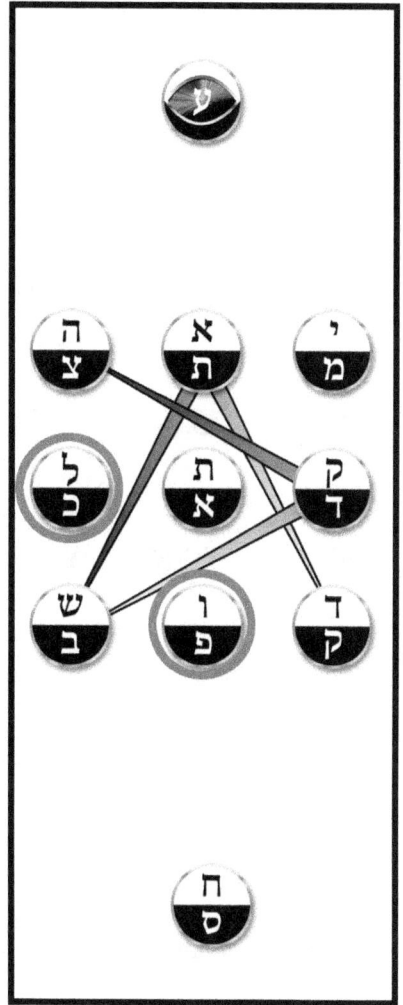

The ל Lamed target shows קשה "Severe" (note that the spelling is different). The ו Waw shows אש which is not just fire, Strongs 787 is "foundation".

I'm going to remind you of a couple of things before moving on :
1. Only Biblical Hebrew may be used. If you cannot verify that, don't use it.
2. Masoretic vowel points did NOT exist in the pure Hebrew language. In my opinion, the Masoretic vowel points are the greatest crime ever perpetrated against the writings dictated by the Almighty. The Hebrew words are supposed to be full and rich with concepts, not just the narrow definitions the Masoretic vowel points have assigned them. That is what makes Hebrew the divine language and superior to Greek or English.

So let's try another lesson...

Most of us know that Yeshua "Jesus" was a Jew, so don't be surprised at how many times he was quoting doctrine found in the Menorah Code.

"And the Jews marveled, saying, How knows this man letters, having never learned?" John 7:15

Your new target is the מ Mem [white background]. There is a "ruler of 2" which connects the ב Bet on the top left to the other side of the "cylinder", the נ Nun on the top right. בן Ben, or Son. Now observe the י Yud [white background] targeted giving us אדם Adam, or Man. Put these together and we have "Son of Man". Note that the מ Mem is seated on the right hand of מאד Power. Also note that the main target, the מ Mem (see bottom of Compass), is a גר "foreigner, alien, sojourner, stranger". See Luke 22:69; and Hebrews 11:13.

The "Ruler of 2" ends on the target letter & "Definitions given to letters" may be applied within another tool which touches that letter.

Now let's show you the Two Trees hidden within the one. This is your introduction to the Temple.

Left square belonging to (ע) left 'pillar' בעז (Boaz) in strength, quickly

Top compass החיימ : of Life

יכין Jachin small square belonging to נ right 'pillar', "he will establish"

בעז (Boaz)

[bottom corners] = עץ : Tree

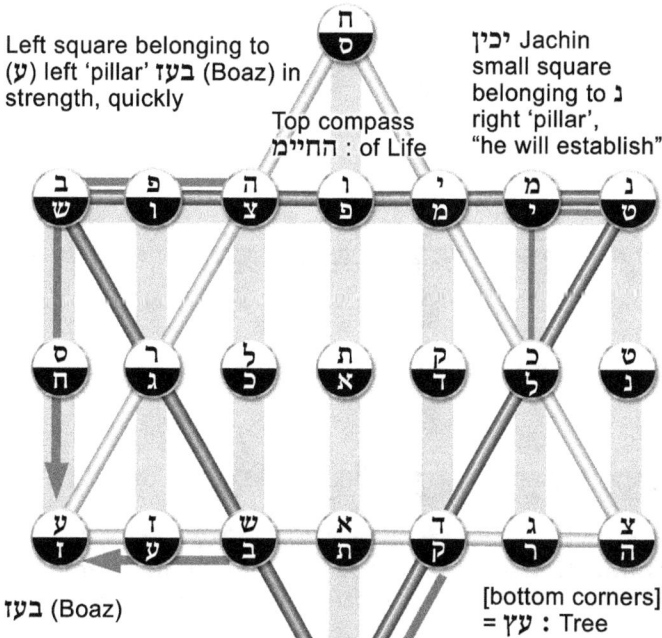

Reading the top compass : The ע Eye of יה Yah is a subset of Tree of Knowledge with evil on the left, and the righteous on the right

דע : Ruler of 2, gives the ע [Ayin] (eye) the definition "knowledge"

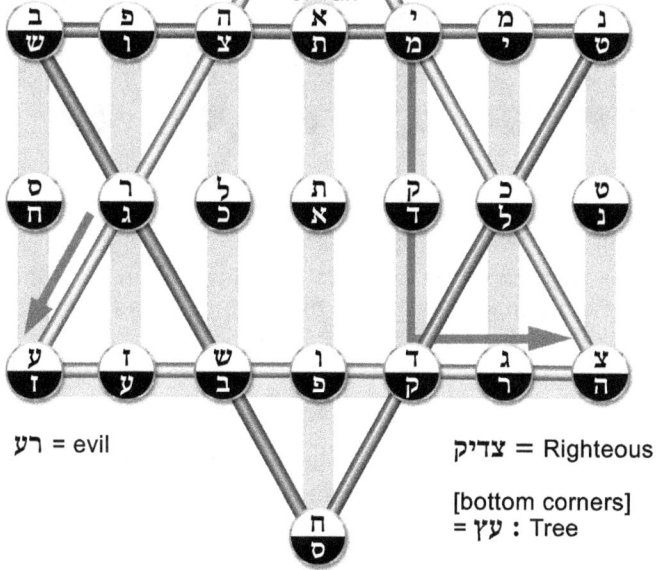

יה+ע means Knowledge of Yah

רע = evil

צדיק = Righteous

[bottom corners] = עץ : Tree

You need to understand that the two trees are אחד ONE in the Menorah. This is the Temple. The center א/ת is the Holy of Holies. (Pay attention to the squares)

The Mother :

Target is the ה Hei
Within חוה Eve, we separate
the ה Hei into a י Yud and a
ר Reish. (רוח) Ghost. Now add
הקדוש = The Holy Ghost

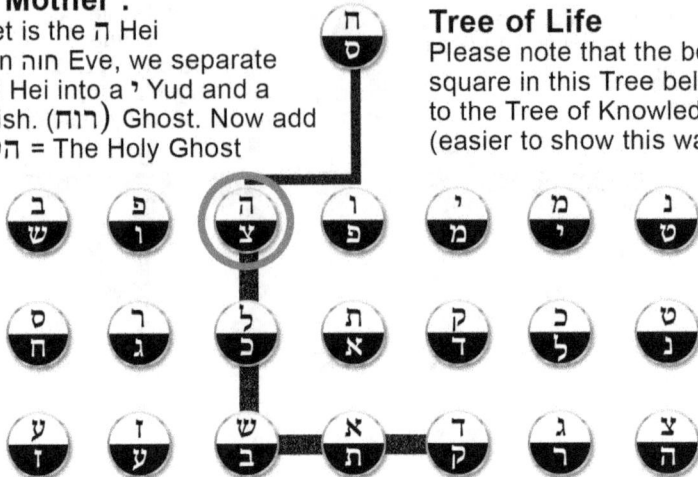

Tree of Life

Please note that the bottom
square in this Tree belongs
to the Tree of Knowledge.
(easier to show this way)

*Yes, you are seeing Adam and Eve in the same places as the
Father and Mother in the Kabbalah tree of life. Remember that
there are many layers, stories, and symbols in the trees.*

A Name of the Father :

Target for both tools is the י Yud
(אדם) Adam or Man
(קדוש) Holy or Holiness
(אדם קדוש) Man of Holiness

Tree of Knowledge

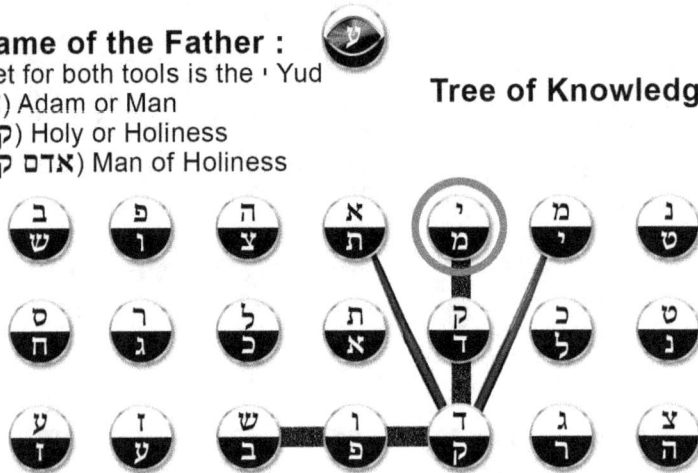

Now pay attention to the word מקדוש "Temple" in the square. We
are going to examine the "SUN" of Righteousness with the 4 squares
which belong to the Holy of Holies next.

How many of you have wondered at what "The **SUN** of Righteousness" in Malachi
4: 2 is all about? Isn't this thought related to some type of "SUN GOD" worship?

As it turns out, this is just one of many symbols used by apostate cults and
religions to imply that they had a higher knowledge linked to symbols which the
people were already used to seeing [and accepted as sacred], long after they lost
the true meaning.

The Sun of Righteousness in Malachi 4:2

carpenters square

Temple Door

The square which you see below is made by four carpenters squares, and would overlap. Note how the opposing squares share the same words.

Sun   of righteousness

Bottom Left & Top Right corners שמש : "Sun" is reflected in both squares.	Top Left & Bottom Right corners צדקה : "of righteousness" is reflected.

Sun   of righteousness

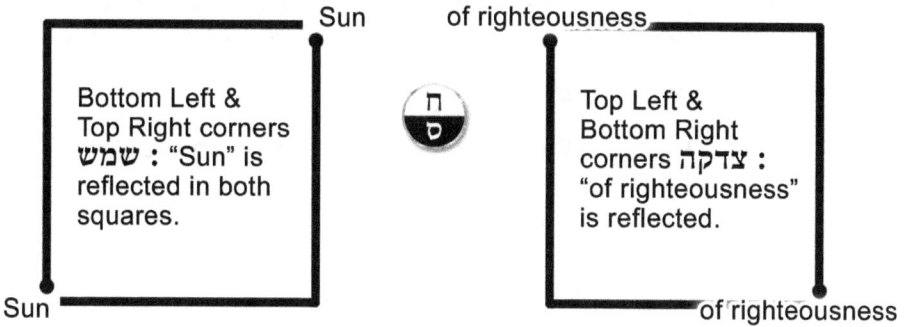

I find the task of conveying the knowledge which I have been given a formidable one. You are but babes. Little children who have not yet been weaned from your mothers breast. So how can I feed you a giant, dense, loaf of bread? I can't. All I can do is to feed you a trail of bread crumbs.

Some of you may feel as if the things which I am showing you are insignificant. However, for those who have finished this book, and returned for round two, these symbols will become more transparent.

Raise your right hand to the square _|, look into the combined trees (p. 25), see the natural words within the square and my father's house, the temple, becomes clear. Then add the tools which assign words within that square and say, "destroy this temple, and in three days I will raise it up again". See the unleavened bread land on "my body", and wine on the blood . . . look for a sacrament.

Be patient. This may seem incomprehensible, but it is not. Once you can firmly grasp the rules, and translate words into Biblical Hebrew, you can follow the scriptures and see their full meanings appear in the Menorah.

The א Aleph Overlay :

Pay attention to the ו Waw Crossing the Center of the א Aleph Diagonally.

(אלף) Aleph : ONE
(אלוף) Aloph : Bull, Chief of a tribe

Tree of Life

There is a story of Adam and Eve in here. While working on it I literally saw the ה Hei (Eve) fall through the ו Waw and morph into the שׁ Shin. It was years before I understood the metaphor.

The ל Lamed Overlay :

Letter definitions include (צלע) Rib

Tree of Knowledge

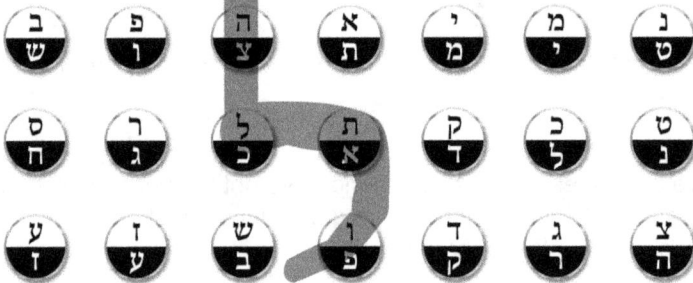

The story of Eve being made from Adam's rib just became a lesson for you to ponder. Was it literal, or just a way of conveying information waiting to be found in the tree?

Are you beginning to understand why it is necessary to flip the perspective we originally saw in the Kabbalah Tree of Life, like looking into a mirror? The letter overlays REQUIRE this. More to the point, you can see why the scriptures were re-given to Ezra, in the Book of 2nd Esdras (around 500 B.C.), and why the scribes were forced to write in a character which they had not formerly known (block-letter Aramaic Hebrew). The original Hebrew language MUST have been co-created with the coding in the Trees of Life and Knowledge.

The א Aleph Overlay :

Pay attention to the ו Waw
Crossing the Center of the
(יתד) Tent peg, Nail
Remember that the י Yud and the ר Reish are in the ה Hei

Tree of Knowledge

Consider the (איש) husband and (אשה) wife found within the א Aleph.
It will bring you one step closer to understanding.

(אחד) ONE :

Please note that the words husband
and wife belong to the
(ש/Shin) on the bottom.

Tree of Knowledge

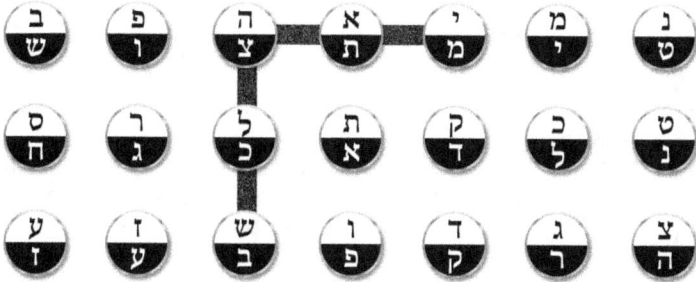

Remember that in the story of Adam and Eve, they were married,
and became (אחד) one flesh. This will be covered later, in the
bridal chamber.

So, Eve comes from (השמים) the Heavens (same square) and lands in a spot
which includes a husband and a wife.

Just getting you familiar with looking at squares.

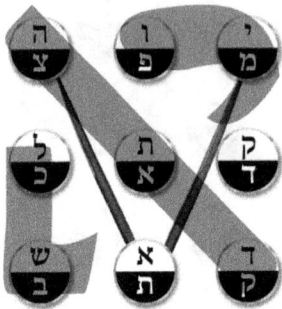

Identity of the ו Waw in יהוה YHWH

TOL \/ אהיה I AM

TOK /\ בר SON deconstruct ת Taw (ו+ר)

TOK /\ דבר WORD deconstruct ת Taw

TOK /\ ברא CREATE, SON decon-ב (ו+ר)

ח
ס

Tree of Life

Identity of the י Yud in יהוה YHWH

Remember that we have already identified the Father as אדם קדוש Man of Holiness. Now add TOK |_ שדי Almighty.

Identity of the ה Hei in יהוה YHWH

Remember that we have already identified the Mother as רוח הקדוש Holy Ghost.

These שלש 3 are אחד united as א 1 in the א Aleph and יהוה YHWH.

Now let's examine some of the letters around the "Temple".

Knowledge
Hand pointing
אית to spell a word.

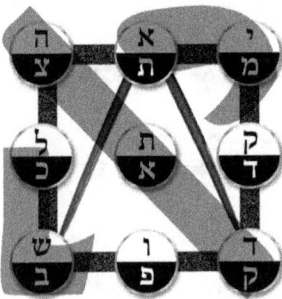

Begin on the right with the ק Kuf and go clockwise, reserving that which is on the top (in heaven) for last.

קדוש ליהוה Holiness to the Lord (for the gentiles) Holiness to YHWH (Holy Name)

A little further into the book, you will see that יהוה YHWH, and אחד ONE meet in the Dalet beneath the overlay. The overlays themselves will also have stories made from the letters beneath.

For now, just remember that I am giving you pieces. More words will be added which you can place in these locations.

I will probably say it more times than I should, but all codes should be read with both trees together. I just need you to know how to Separate them to look at details in the letters.

ח
ס

I am still trying to teach you as we go, so if there is anything you are not following, please stop and find it in the "RULES" section.

I'm not going to spoon feed you. I am showing you the tools, but the true manna must come from the source.

Let's continue the lesson by looking at words assigned to letters connected to the [2 sets] 4 carpenters squares which surround the תא "room" in the Temple.

Learning requires practice. There are some who will prefer to skim the information, but those who wish to understand will seek knowledge in prayer.

Here is a lesson to practice : Find the letters which own these words, and determine if or where they fit into the "incomplete" story being told in the 2 sets of large squares. This is designed to help you "begin" to recognize patterns.

שא to forgive, lift up; שדה a beautiful woman; שהד to bear witness; עץ wood, beam, or tree; קתל to slay; אל EL short form of Elohim; שה lamb; של to put off, loose, error, offense, crime, that belongs to; in you [Atbash of של]; אהיה I AM; יהוה YHWH; חוש to feel pain, to feel anxious, to feel afraid; שלש throo; צלב to hang, impale, crucify; שב gray, old man, one who returns; son, word, and creator - see opposite page; מצה unleavened bread, and חמץ leavened [risen bread]; יתד nail or tent peg [big nail]; גוי, "my body"; מצה unleavened bread; דק this is a veil; דם blood; ילד son; דל door; יד hand; קד to rend, tear [note that rending the veil takes place within the temple]; דם blood, מים water; אדם Adam, or man; יום day, ימים days; חיים life [in the plural]; חי life; יהוה YHWH; מת dead; תפלה prayer; קום Arise; שדד destroy.

Two Trees Made One

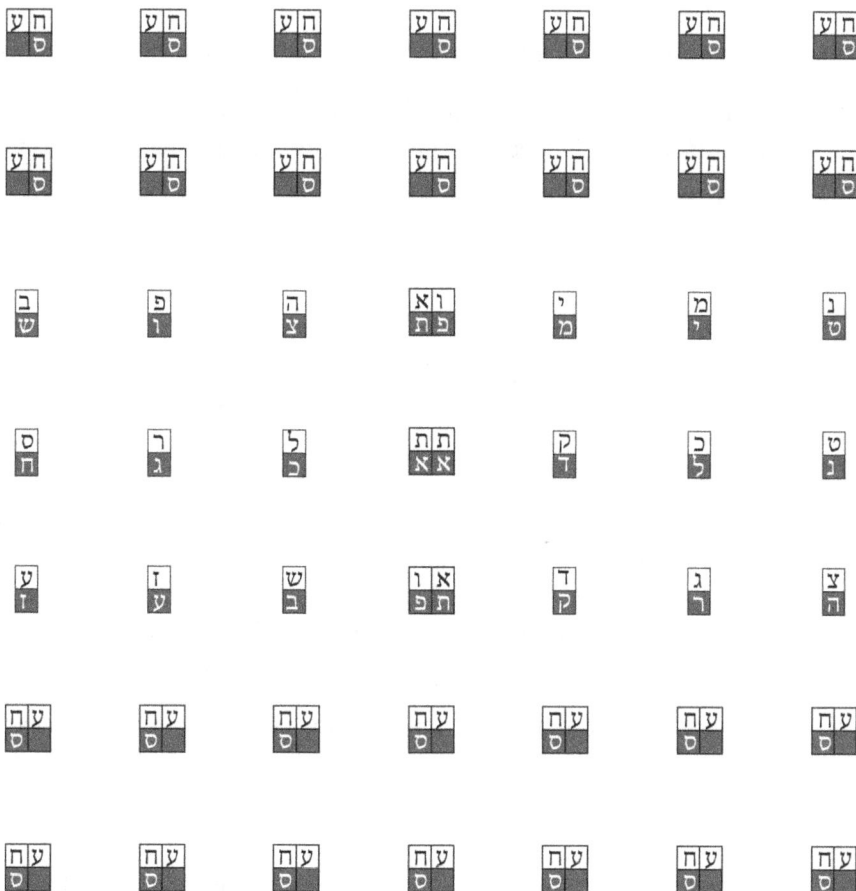

Row 1 (seven squares, each):
ח	ע
ס	

Row 2 (seven squares, each):
ח	ע
ס	

Row 3 (seven squares):
| ב / ש | פ / ו | ה / צ | ו א / פ ת | י / מ | מ / י | נ / ט |

Row 4 (seven squares):
| ס / ח | ר / ג | ל / כ | ת ת / א א | ק / ד | כ / ל | ט / נ |

Row 5 (seven squares):
| ע / ז | ז / ע | ש / ב | א ו / ת פ | ד / ק | ג / ר | צ / ה |

Row 6 (seven squares, each):
ע	ח
ס	

Row 7 (seven squares, each):
ע	ח
ס	

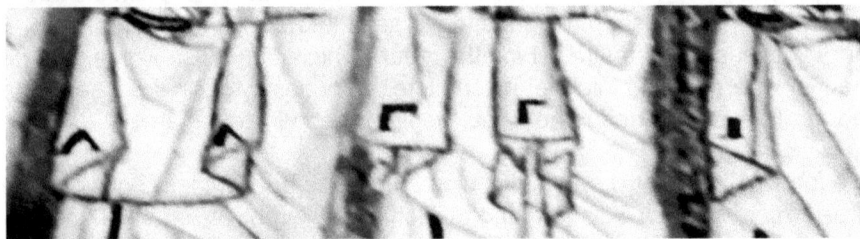

Now, I am going to dispel some illusions which some of you may have.

I was born and raised in the LDS church. I began this quest inquiring of YHWH because I saw things within the church which I associated with the Masons. So I asked, and received all of my answers, and more.

The Image above comes from an early Christian church fresco. The marks which you see in the clothing of these people are called "Gammadia". Search this topic and you will find many examples. Far too many to include here.

I created a graphic which has a connection to burial clothing belonging to a first century "Christian" sect found in Fayum Egypt (opposite page). In reality, the symbols which go into the tree of life are broken up a little so that the laces are up further towards the neck. I'll go through that graphic and its symbols more in another chapter.

So, here is my point. Is it more likely that the Masons are using ancient religious symbols, or that the 1st century Christian church which fled from the Romans and settled in Egypt were all Masons? How about the fresco above?

We are going to see many symbols which predate Israel. Are we to believe that the Masons are responsible for this too? . . . Only if you are missing your logic circuits.

The problem with Archaeology is that it is a religion unto itself. They are unwilling to consider anything which lies beyond the accepted orthodox historical narrative which was [re]written by the powers that be.

When you learn the TRUTH which has been hidden within the Menorah (Tree of Life and Tree of Knowledge made אחד ONE), you will realize that your secular sages, and religious leaders are either liars or blind. Now guess who the blind following the blind is? If you are metaphorically the bride, seeking other men instead of your betrothed, that makes you guilty of whoredoms, doesn't it?

This being said, I will tell you again . . . I'm just the messenger. I am going to show you the trees and how to read them. Those who truly seek this knowledge will find it for themselves. No "man or woman" can secure your connection to Salvation. You must do this yourself. Seek the light if you are the children of light. Seek the

LEFT SIDE   RIGHT SIDE

compare with
Early Christian Textile Markings
found in Fayum Egypt

waters of eternal lives in the heavens and know the truth.

I have been trying to feed you a trail of bread crumbs to prepare you to decrypt the "Sun of Righteousness" yourself.

If I were to do the whole thing for you, you would say that it was just the worthless words of a man, another lying poser. . . but I could not have invented the Tree of Life. Just the fact that Hebrew letters are named and defined by the decryption rules proves that whoever invented this code invented the language itself. I am, and have been, trying to decrypt this treasure for years. Though it would be so much easier if I did not need to research every word (I don't speak Hebrew).

Now, I am going to show you a *composite symbol* which is found **everywhere in the world**. This symbol is most often found on old synagogues, religious centers, and in depictions of the Tree of Life. . . Thousands of years ago, the Greeks called it the **Tetra-Gammadia** (four Greek letters [Gamma] that look like carpenters squares), while others called it **Swastika**.

Tetra-Gammadia :

Take 4 small squares with targets going out to the 4 corners (bottom graphic). these intersect 4 large squares which surround the circle.

That which came from the center (א/ת) joins the 4 corners of the square shape, and returns in the other direction to the center like 4 loops going counter-clockwise.

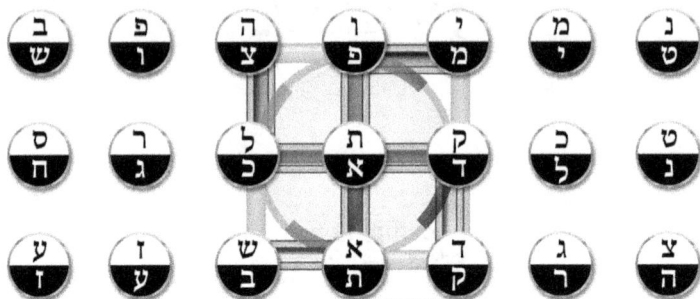

There are many sayings within the Bible which are direct clues telling us how to read the trees. Consider YHWH is ONE.
The only way to see אחד+יהוה in the ד Dalet is to join both trees.

Continuing your lesson :
Look at the small square which has (אדם) Adam or Man ending on the י Yud. The < ק Kuf means (ילד) Son, and the (ruler of 2) (את) or (אות) is a sign. This small square is saying "Sign of the Son of Man".

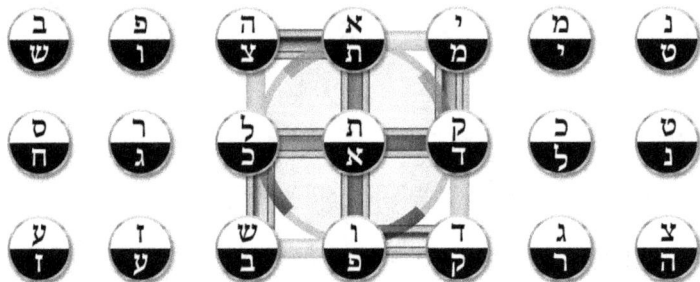

Look at the small square (bottom left) which has צלב "to crucify", owned by the (ב) Bet; קתל to slay, owned by the ל Lamed; של to put off, loose, crime which belongs; בך in you. More will become visable later.

You will need a good "Biblical Hebrew" dictionary. Stay away from sites such as Do it in Hebrew because it MUST be Biblical Hebrew. I would suggest using biblehub.com. Just add a keyboard which you can use your mouse to click on, in your screen, and add a Hebrew keyboard setting. There are sites which can help you configure your computer to type in Hebrew characters.

ALL TOOLS must include letters in BOTH trees, as if they were ONE.

Tree of Life :

The ילד, ב{מ}ן Son, שמש Sun מת dead (TOK), שלש three ימים days now receives חיים Life, the מצה bread of חיים Life, becomes חמץ leavened, _| to קום Arise.

When we go from the TOK to the TOL, the ו Waw moves from its position to become the target of the compass. Remember, the compass coming up from below? This is : אהיה I AM.

Now rip a ז{מ}, a ר{ה}, & watch the מ ו ג Sun rise in the East.

There is a lot more here than you see, but I'm just feeding you crumbs as you learn the code.

I find most early "Christian" church floor plans are similar to this shape. Some with domes which match the "Sun" in the code.

Nauvoo Sunstone

Religious symbols, whether past, or present, are meant to convey knowledge.

Unfortunately, when the knowledge of what these symbols mean is lost, there is no shortage of "opinion".

Are you beginning to see how symbols can make perfect sense if you know what it means? Can you see the origins of pagan "Sun god" cults? The Sun dies for 3 days, then rises?

I think that before we see the rest of the "Sun of Righteousness", we should digress into the ALL SEEING EYE. There are some interesting things there which may help you to understand the connections we are about to make.

Please be patient, once we get to the Seraph, things will begin to go deeper and faster. Just try to begin grasping the concepts.

Coincidence?

Is Noah using the Tree of Life to name his children?

שם Shem (large square)
חם Ham (ruler of 2)
יפת Japeth (ruler of 2 add ת from TOK)

2 of these names are placed in the hand of our Father in שמים Heaven, and יפת Japeth is in the light of YHWH.

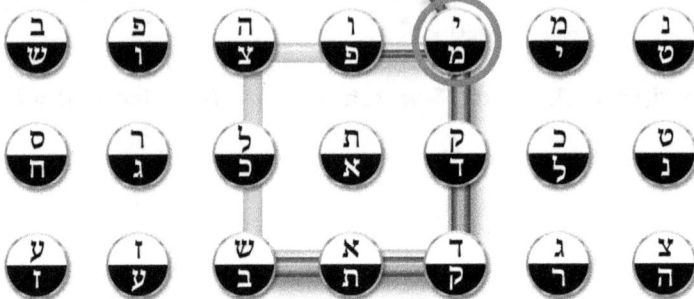

Below you see the letter ע, or Ayin, which means EYE. This is connected by the compass (shape of a triangle) to יה Yah (short for YHWH). The eye of Yah.

Unfortunately, this was turned into the eye of Ra - ה{רע by those wo like the רע="evil" side of the עץ tree of דע knowledge

Now we look into the pyramid shaped compass and see מצרים Egypt!

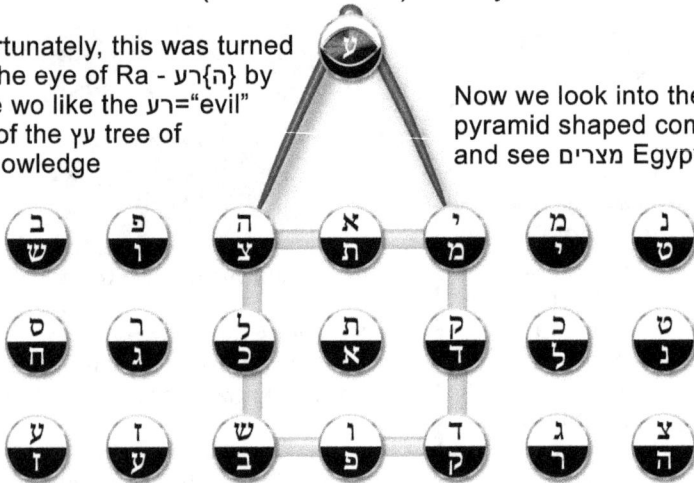

What is going on here? Is somebody using the Tree the way Noah did to name his sons, is this part of a story, or a little of both?

By the way . . . just the FACT that Noah had this knowledge means that the attempt by my brethren, the Jews, to impose "Noahide Laws" on the world is a lie. We will see that our forefathers knew far more than you, and they actually had eyes to see.

Now, what other Egyptian coincidences do we see handed down from נח Noah to his sons, חם Ham in this case, as his name, is the ancient name for Egypt.

Pharaoh claims to be the א Aleph :

Below you see the ruler of 3 אלף Aleph (which we have identified as YHWH).

פרעה Pharaoh
(the ר Reish is part of the ה)
(the ע Ayin is in the TOK)
is a name linking him to the
א Aleph in the large square.

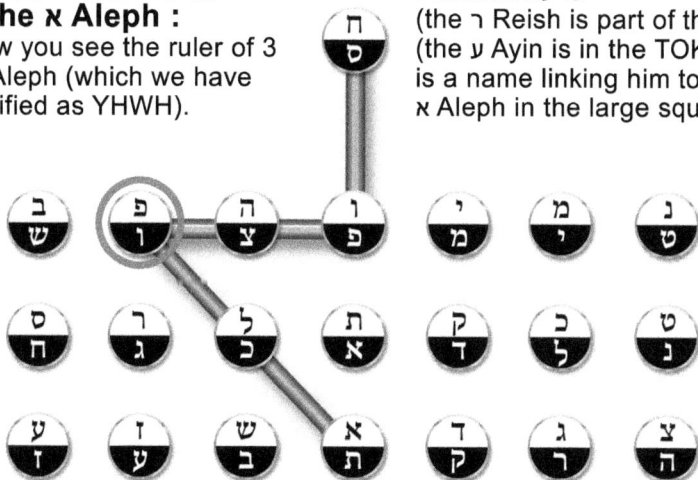

Since we know that Pharaoh claimed to be a god, it appears the name was intended to be a claim.

The square below is accessing the other side of the cylinder to give us the word נחש Serpent.

Bird of Prey עיט

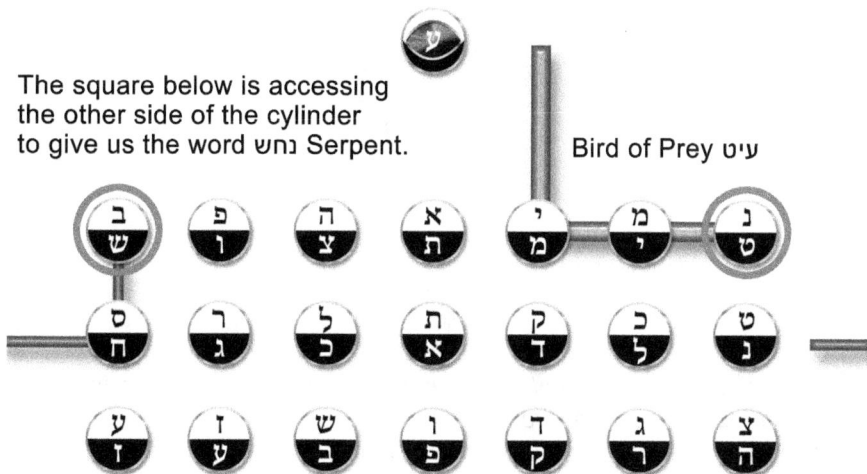

Now recall Pharaoh's crown. By wearing the Bird of Prey on one side, and the Serpent on the other, he was claiming to be the Tree of Life.

I hope we remember that the two trees are actually made ONE in the Menorah. Yet I want you to remember what happens when you split the two.

There are too many uses in Egypt to believe that this knowledge wasn't passed down. Consider that the נ Nun can grab the ש Shin and take the ר Reish hidden within the ב Bet. נשר Eagle. Did you notice that this is on top of the small square with the Atbash נחש Serpent, but in the opposite direction?

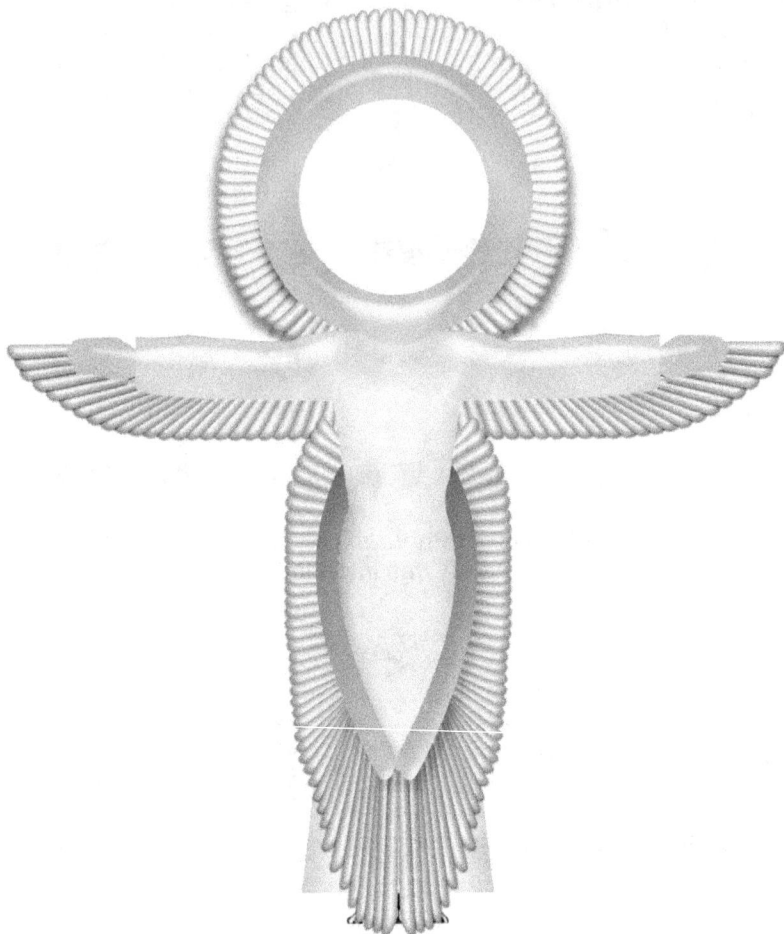

When trying to draw the Seraph, I kept being prompted to make the top two wings covering the face more round, like the Sun. It was during this attempt that I realized what I was drawing, but this version showed me something that I had seen before. Imagine that the garment is made of leather, that these are Eagles feathers, and there are swastikas around the band of the feathered headdress of an Indian Chief. We will look upon the Seraph after examining the code.

Years ago I saw the pipes of the Menorah become wings and it began to fly. It literally looked like a Menorah flying, but I understood it to be a Seraph.

Let's look at Isaiah 6:2, "Seraphim . . . six wings [כנפים wings, skirts, edges, borders, corners, extremities, ends]: with two he covered his face, and with two he covered his feet, and with two he flew."

So what is the connection between the Seraph and the Serpent, because a serpent does not have feet. . . It's time to learn something new.

Creating Words in Hebrew :

In order to reveal this mystery, I need to teach you how the Hebrew letters receive values [meanings] which create words.

We will be back-engineering how words are created. However, there is much that won't be understood about this before more work is done.

I see clues that word values from within letter-overlays may be used, but I wouldn't want to claim this before having more data to confirm this theory.

I am writing this not long after it was revealed to me that the letters within the letters [compound letters] may be deconstructed for use in the code, so I haven't even begun to look at, or attempt to create tool tables which include all of the variables. To be completely honest, if I had to do this by hand, you might not get to read this before the end of the world. So I am hoping to get enough money from this book, or donations, to have a program created that will push out word tables and recognize common themes [within letters which make up words]. Once we fully understand the "why", we will be able to define the rule which dictates "why" certain words are used and not others . . . back-engineering the original language. **The only connection that I can clearly see is a common theme** running between letters, and this may well be all there is to it. *Think of it like words within each of the letters which describe the intent of the word you are creating.*

The good news is that back-engineering word definitions is much easier, because we know what descriptors [words] we are looking for.

let me give you an example :

Without using anything from the Menorah Code, try the word "watcher" ערא using only the descriptors of the letters which anyone can easily find on-line. ע Ayin, the eye + ר Reish, the head + א Aleph, YHWH. Think about it.

Many of you already know the problem associated with using "known" Hebrew letter meanings. There are not enough "known" words to support this theory of constructing words. . . until now.

The Menorah Code, or perhaps I should say, the Trees of Knowledge and Life, literally contains volumes of information. I believe that this code was used by our forefathers as a teaching tool. All they needed to do is memorize the placement of the 22 letters, add the Atbash letters beneath, and flip the center pipe to create the Tree of Life.

I'll stop digressing and we will begin by looking at the word שטן "Satan". Why? Because it is coiled into a loop with the נחש "Serpent" in two small squares which feed each-other.

שטן Satan :

[small square שן tooth,
נחש Serpent, חבש to bind,
חשב woven band] [small
square שרף Seraph,
to burn, burning, fiery
serpent]

The large square (left) also
has an ע Ayin at the top from
the TOK, giving it : פה mouth;
צפע serpent, viper, adder,
cockatrice ; deconstruct the ה
Hei, and I see חרצבה bond,
fetter, pang.

There is alot to take in here. The (בש) pair is literally shame. That
pair can connect directly to the (ט over נ) using a ruler of 2, but
you will see that I have reasons for focusing on this loop.

The ט Tet being targeted by the compass
has the word קן nest, cell, chamber.
ruler of 2 שט = apostate, and ruler of 2
from the ב Bet to the נ Nun gives us בן Son.

Bird of Prey עיט
hits the second
letter, Nun נ/ט Tet pair

There are a lot of descriptors here but I'm going to keep it simple
and say that שטן Satan, defined as "the adversary", is a serpent in the
nest, the apostate son.

It should be noted that there may be more relevant descriptors at these locations,
but I am working backwards. I looked for words known to be associated with the
traditional definitions, and threw in some others that I came across. Digging deeper would require completing word tables for each tool which is assigned to each
letter in question.

[נחש Serpent] ש Shin :

Remember previous words :
שן tooth, נחש Serpent, חבש to bind,
חשב woven band, שרף Seraph,
to burn, burning, fiery serpent,
פה mouth, צפע serpent, viper, adder,
cockatrice, חרצבה bond, fetter, pang

נ Nun :

ruler of 2 לנן to murmur,
טנן to be moist, be damp

ח Chet :

ruler of 2 שח bent, bowed, גח [JAram., - Syr.] = גיח to burst forth,
נחז to remove, displace, נט to shut [the eyes], to besmear,
חח hook, ring; fetters

You can see that I have moved the right side of the cylinder to meet the left. Now the "loop" which connects "Satan" and the נחש "Serpent".

Do you remember the image of the MAN in the Kabbala Tree of Life?
Do you remember the "Sun of Righteousness" rising?
Do you believe that this is the first time that these things have been revealed?

No. Note how the man in the Zoroastrian symbol is grabbing this "loop", the Serpent Satan with his left hand. Those who have read the New Testament will recognize the priests of this religion who were known as the MAGI.

How many of you noticed that the word נחש Nechash appears to be missing the known descriptors, "bronze, sign, and prophecy"? It is because those words do not come from this loop which uses the Atbash letters, and is not linked to that definition. I'll show where this comes from in a minute, but for those of you who are "offended" by seeing the Winged Sun Disk symbol, know that this was used in ancient Israel as well, and I'll get to that as soon as we finish defining the נחש Nechash.

[נחש bronze, sign, and prophecy] NOT Serpent :

The "Serpent" and associated words uses all Atbash letters [black background] while the "Other definitions" come from letters which are 100% opposite.

פנ metal sheet, thin plate
נח [Noah] rest

Your job here is to look at all of the words which belong to the "opposing" נחש letters in white. In my "opinion", this word gained a "serpent" connection by being used for "evil divination". Yet it appears that it was not originally associated with "evil" in the code.

Descriptors for the ש Shin below :
נבואה prophecy ; מופת sign, wonder ;
אות a sign ; {מ}זהב gold or golden color

[נ] עין eye
[נ] בן Son
[נ] דין to judge
[נ] חן favor, grace

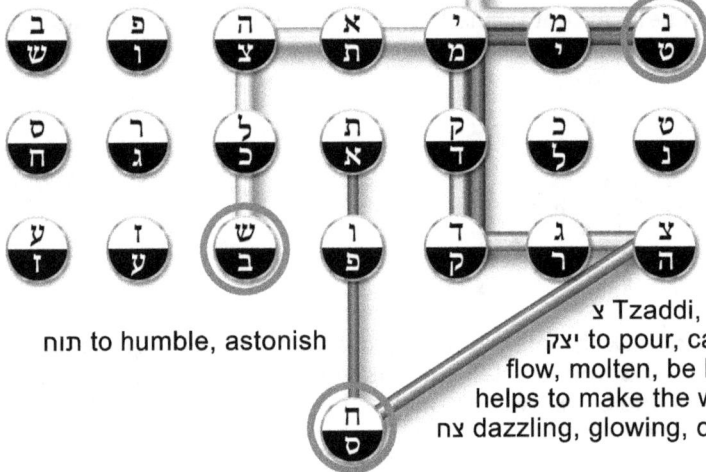

תוח to humble, astonish

צ Tzaddi, owns
יצק to pour, cast, flow, molten, be hard
helps to make the word
צח dazzling, glowing, clear

I am guessing that the various definitions of נחש are defined by the Masoretic vowel points, but the translators completely missed the true definition. It was lost to history when Hezekiah destroyed the "sign", and the code was forgotten.

The Serpents which bit the people, and the Seraph which Moses raised up WERE SYMBOLIC OPPOSITES. One brings death, and the other, life.

We are nearing the end of your lesson on word definitions being based on the letters used to create them. There is still an eye opening reveal that will bring everything which you have learned about the letters together.

I have shown you the "evil" of the נחש Serpent, and the שרף Seraph [burning] associated with the שטן Satan / נחש Serpent loop on the left side of the tree.

Now we are delving into the "opposing" definitions and where they come from.

You have seen some of the definitions given to the ש Shin [circled image left]. This letter which has "sign, wonder, and prophecy", is associated with another שרף Seraph. When this is revealed, you will see how these definitions which land within the various tools aggregate to show you things you could not have otherwise known.

Let me begin by showing you definitions which fall within the same ש Shin used in the Seraph which Isaiah describes.

שרפים Seraphim, שש six, כנפים wings, בשתים with two, פניו his face, ובשתים and with two . . . Does these pieces sound familiar? They are in the same ש square.

Note : Please bear in mind that there are words which I am listing which use a נ Nun riped from the מ Mem, a ר Reish ripped from a ב Bet, ה Hei, or a ת Taw . . . de-constructed letters. It might help to look up Isaiah 6:2.

While there is another Seraph in the פ Peh overlay, I am going to focus on the section around the Temple for reasons that will become obvious on the next page.

Remember our main theme is examining the נחש serpents which bit the people. From descriptions within the code, and being associated with a שרף Seraph [burning], I'm guessing that these were a cobra [wings, borders, extensions], with burning venom which would blind the people [by spitting], and / or may have been red [burning/fiery] in color.

Now we are looking at the נחש = "bronze, sign, and prophecy" as a descriptor of what Moses lifted up, along with another שרף Seraph in another place within the code.

I am literally writing this book as I go from page to page, trying to explain some of the things in my head. . . and last night, I was reviewing the code in my head along with what I would do the next day and I had one of those moments.

Do you remember when I said years ago I saw a vision of a Menorah flying in my head and I was given the impression that it was a Seraph?

מנורה Menorah goes right to left across the center three posts of the Menorah, and gives that value to several locations in the tree.

The Full Matrix : TOK [left column], TOL [right column]

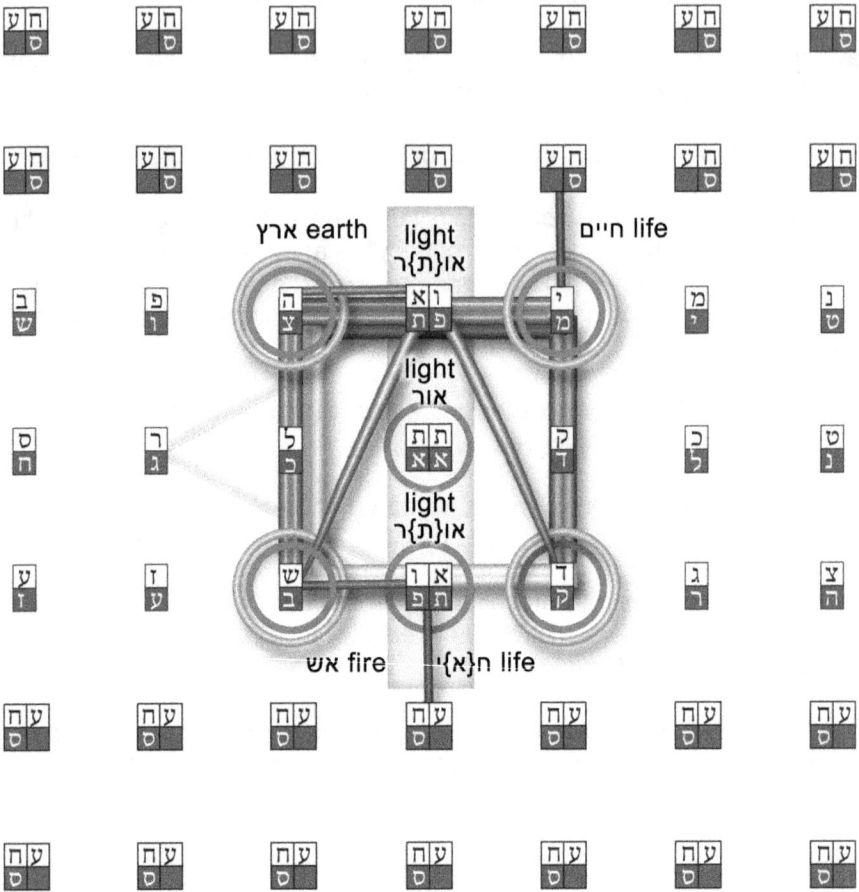

ארץ earth   light   חיים life
אור{ת}ו

light
אור

light
אור{ת}ו

אש fire   ח{א}י life

Let's use the two trees within the Menorah and read them as one. The split columns have what you would see in the Tree of Life on the right, and the Tree of Knowledge on the left.

The smaller circles all have the word שרף Seraph [see the connections to the "burning" "Menorah"]. These are "owned" by the same letters which make יהוה YHWH, the Holy Name . . . and the "good" ש Shin used in these Seraphim.

Note that a ר Reish may be ripped from the ב Bet, or ת Taw to make the word שרף Seraph which we see precisely where it would be expected, in the center pipe of the Menorah.

Do you remember what else is associated with that location? בר Son, ברא Creator, דבר Word . . .

This brings us to the larger circles which hold the word מנורה Menorah.

Do you remember Zechariah? These are the two Menorah [lamp stands] which sit on the right and left hand. . . it may be best if you read it and refresh your memory if you haven't read it in a while.

I have been showing you that words which aggregate into letters used in the tools may be transmitted into the target letters meaning.

If you target the ילי Son [ק] with a compass you also have Seraph, and Menorah. If you target the שו Lamb with a [ל] compass you have Seraph and Menorah. If you examine the compass which you see on the opposite page, you see that it adds Seraph and Menorah to the דבר word, בר son, and ברא creator.

Who is the center pipe of the Menorah with אור "light" landing everywhere on it? Who has a Menorah on his right and another on his left? These are the two witnesses. Each is described as a Seraph [fiery one], and a Menorah [lamp stand]. So, do you see that this is a purely metaphorical description of the two witnesses, and the Son, which come as men upon the earth?

Why then do you not understand that these are NOT "serpents". Why do you suppose that the center post, the "creator", is a serpent?

I am speaking directly to my brethren, the Jews. Why do you believe that Moses lifted up an image of a serpent? Look back at that image on page 32, because Hezekiah, known for eliminating all things pagan, is about to show you the נחשת Bronze, נחש prophecy or sign [not serpent].

The word נחש has a Gematria which is the same as משיח Messiah, but the true image which Moses lifted up was not the נחש-שטן [Serpent-Satan], Hezekiah's play on words in 2 Kings 18: 4, where he calls it the נחשתן Nehushtan.

Don't believe me, let's see what Moses really raised up, and see what it says.

This is Hezekiah's bulla, or signet ring seal.

Note the winged sun disk. The three vertical lines going up and down tell me it is placed between the Tree of Life [in the heavens] and the Tree of Knowledge [on earth] (see page 19).

Now look at that Ankh. Could this possibly be the bronze sign and prophecy lifted up by Moses in the desert? Let's use Isaiah's Seraph description and see.

Isaiah 6: 2 "Seraphim . . . six wings [כנפים]: with two he covered his face [these two extensions overlap and share the same point as the ע "eye" which they cover], and with two he covered his feet [sharing the same point as the feet], and with two he flew."

כנף, the root word, means: wing; skirt; edge, border; corner; extremity; end.

נחש (prophecy, sign, bronze) does have the same Gematria as משיח Messiah [358], & it is relevant [to this image]. Clockwise : take the נ in point 1, a ש from 2, pull a י Yud [hand] out of the פ in 3, and end with a ח Chet on 4. משיח MESSIAH. Now do you understand that it is a Prophecy of the Messiah in Bronze?

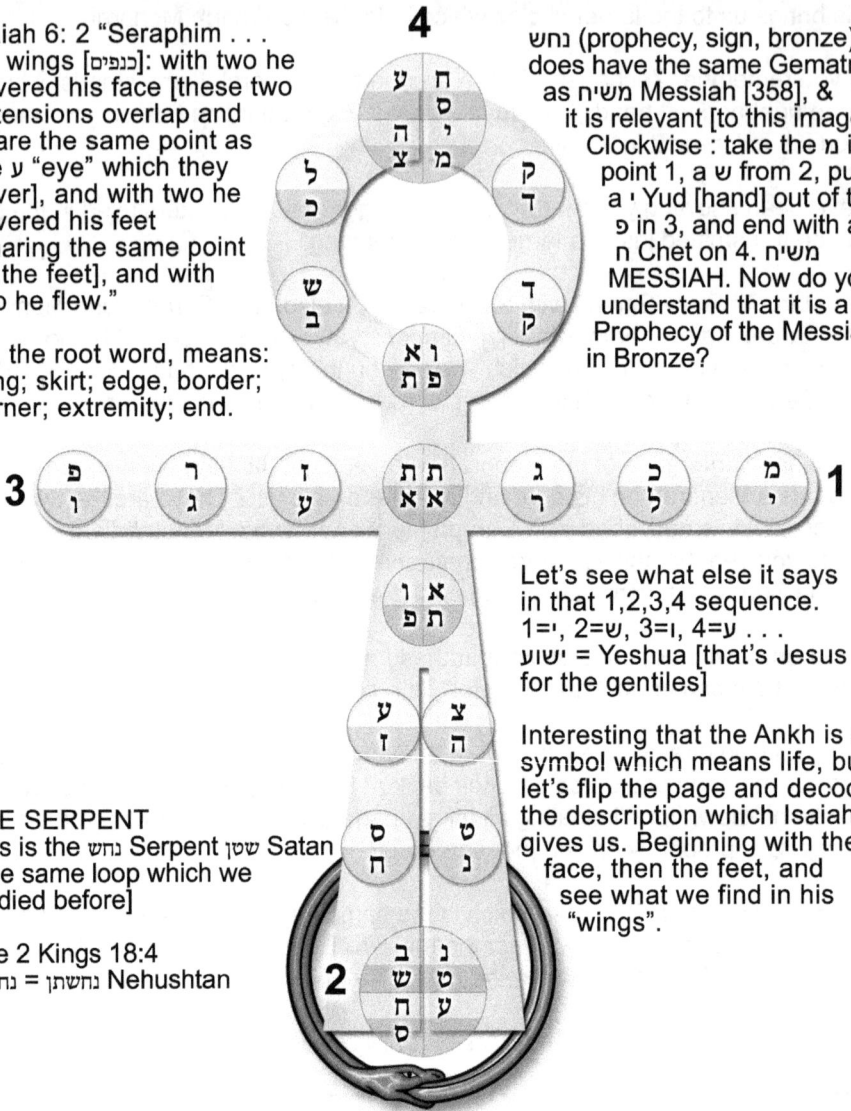

3 ... ... **1**

Let's see what else it says in that 1,2,3,4 sequence. 1=י, 2=ש, 3=ו, 4=ע . . . ישוע = Yeshua [that's Jesus for the gentiles]

Interesting that the Ankh is a symbol which means life, but let's flip the page and decode the description which Isaiah gives us. Beginning with the face, then the feet, and see what we find in his "wings".

THE SERPENT
This is the נחש Serpent שטן Satan [The same loop which we studied before]

See 2 Kings 18:4
נחשתן = נחשטן Nehushtan

2

If you remember the story of the Jews bowing down before and burning incense to the image which Moses lifted up in the desert, you know that King Hezekiah destroyed it saying that they had turned it into the Nehushtan. No, they treated it as an idol, and turned it into the Serpent Satan. Say it fast [in Hebrew] and see if you can tell if it is one word or two, because I see why he said that written in the Serpent at the Messiah's feet. It makes perfect sense.

Recall as well that Isaiah was a contemporary of Hezekiah, and Isaiah knew the Menorah Code. He, as well as Hezekiah, understood the letters.

So, let's go face, feet, and wings . . . let's see the prophecy Isaiah sent us.

Isaiah 6: 2 "Seraphim . . . six wings [כנפים]: with two he covered his face [these two extensions overlap and share the same point as the ע "eye" which they cover], and with two he covered his feet [sharing the same point as the feet], and with two he flew."

כנף, the root word, means: wing; skirt; edge, border; corner; extremity; end.

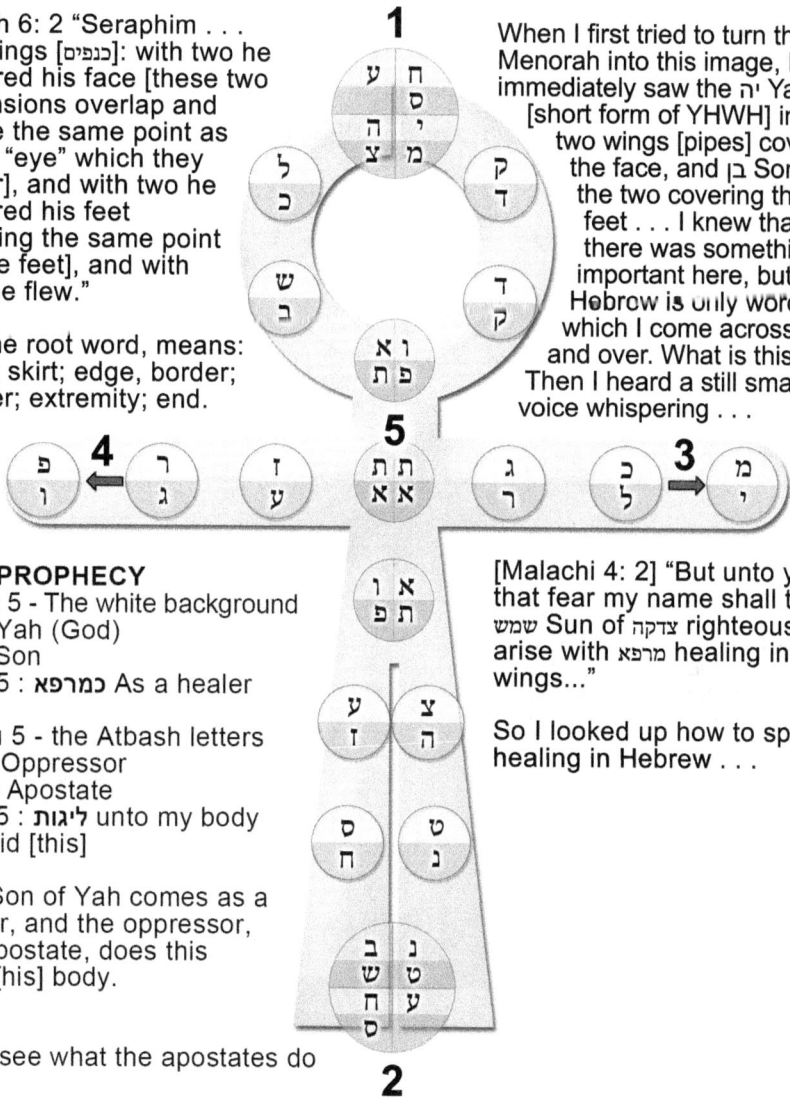

When I first tried to turn the Menorah into this image, I immediately saw the יה Yah [short form of YHWH] in the two wings [pipes] covering the face, and בן Son in the two covering the feet . . . I knew that there was something important here, but my Hebrew is only words which I come across over and over. What is this? Then I heard a still small voice whispering . . .

THE PROPHECY
1 thru 5 - The white background
1. יה Yah (God)
2. בן Son
3, 4, 5 : כמרפא As a healer

1 thru 5 - the Atbash letters
1. מץ Oppressor
2. שט Apostate
3, 4, 5 : ליגות unto my body you did [this]

The Son of Yah comes as a healer, and the oppressor, the apostate, does this unto [his] body.

Let's see what the apostates do

[Malachi 4: 2] "But unto you that fear my name shall the שמש Sun of צדקה righteousness arise with מרפא healing in his wings..."

So I looked up how to spell healing in Hebrew . . .

Recapping . . . "The Sign" :
The א [Aleph; the **first** letter] ו [Waw; prefix which may mean "**and**"] ת [Taw; the **last** letter] : אות A SIGN. The center of the Menorah is filled with this word.

עץ "Tree" and "Life" חיים are sitting right there in #1. The Ankh is a symbol, which tradition holds, means "life". Noah gave this knowledge & symbol to Ham . . .

Do you remember the section on "The Sun of Righteousness"? That "Sun" is sitting in the circle of the Ankh.

You know the story that it was telling us. This symbol is part of the same story.

Going down the left side :

עץ : tree, beam / על : Yoke
צלב : to hang, impale, crucify
* Atbash pair rules apply *
של : to put off, loose; error,
offense, crime that
belongs to / בך : in you
[Atbash of של]
עו{ז}{ש}י{ל} Yeshua
שלה : draw forth
from the water

Going down the right side :

יקד : to kindle to burn
מדקרה : piercing, stabbing
קד : he tore, cut away
דק : thin curtain [the veil]

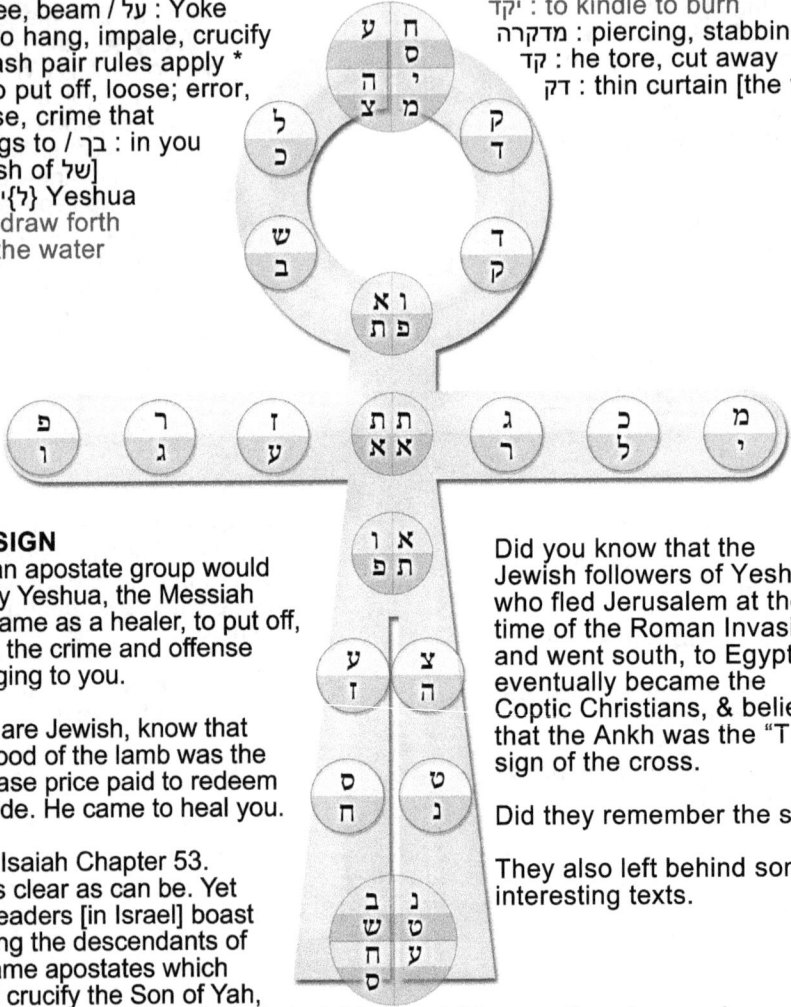

THE SIGN

That an apostate group would
Crucify Yeshua, the Messiah
who came as a healer, to put off,
loose, the crime and offense
belonging to you.

If you are Jewish, know that
the blood of the lamb was the
purchase price paid to redeem
his bride. He came to heal you.

Read Isaiah Chapter 53.
It is as clear as can be. Yet
your leaders [in Israel] boast
of being the descendants of
the same apostates which
would crucify the Son of Yah,
then justify it with lies which their children's children continue to preach.
שט Apostates, serpents in the nest.

Did you know that the
Jewish followers of Yeshua,
who fled Jerusalem at the
time of the Roman Invasion
and went south, to Egypt,
eventually became the
Coptic Christians, & believed
that the Ankh was the "True"
sign of the cross.

Did they remember the sign?

They also left behind some
interesting texts.

My brethren . . . know that as the sign was a prophecy, this thing was part of the
plan since the foundations of the world were laid. It was necessary.

Let's take a step back and look at Numbers 21 :

4. Then they set out from Mount Hor along the route to the Red Sea, in order to
bypass the land of Edom. But the people grew impatient on the journey
5. and spoke against God and against Moses: "Why have you led us up out of
Egypt to die in the wilderness? There is no bread or water, and we detest this
wretched food!"
6. So YHWH sent venomous snakes among the people, and many of the Israelites
were bitten and died.

7. Then the people came to Moses and said, "We have sinned by speaking against YHWH and against you. Intercede with YHWH so He will take the snakes away from us." So Moses interceded for the people.

8. Then YHWH said to Moses, "Make a SERAPH and mount it on a pole. When anyone who is bitten looks at it, he will live."

9. So Moses made a A SIGN OR PROPHECY IN BRONZE and mounted it on a pole. If anyone who was bitten looked at the bronze SIGN, he would live.

Look at the prophecy we were meant to see. We have the rebellious, intermingled with YHWH's faithful people. יהי Apostates, serponto in the nest. Blessed with manna from heaven, they complain against YHWH and rebel against his ANOINTED [same word as MESSIAH]. So the anointed one above, THE Messiah, sent them a prophecy, a sign in bronze, promising to make intercession for them. . . and that all they had to do, was look to the Messiah, Yeshua, and live. Yet the venom which the serpent injects them with goes beyond the blinding or death of the flesh. The true healing in the wings of the Messiah, is spiritual.

ISAIAH 53 :

1. Who hath believed our report? and to whom is the arm of the YHWH revealed?

2. For he shall grow up before him as a tender plant, and as a root out of a dry ground: he hath no form nor comeliness; and when we shall see him, there is no beauty that we should desire him.

3. *He is despised and rejected of men*; a man of sorrows, and acquainted with grief: and we hid as it were our faces from him; *he was despised, and we esteemed him not.*

4. Surely he hath borne our griefs, and carried our sorrows: yet we did esteem him stricken, smitten of God, and afflicted.

5. But *he was wounded for our transgressions, he was bruised for our iniquities*: the chastisement of our peace was upon him; and *with his stripes we are* **healed**.

6. All *we like sheep have gone astray*; we have turned every one to his own way; and **the YHWH hath laid on him the iniquity of us all**.

7. He was oppressed, and he was afflicted, yet he opened not his mouth: he is brought *as a lamb to the slaughter*, and as a sheep before her shearers is dumb, so he openeth not his mouth.

8. He was taken from prison and from judgment: and who shall declare his generation? for **he was cut off out of the land of the living: for the transgression of my people was he stricken**.

9. And he made his grave with the wicked, and with the rich in his death; because he had done no violence, neither was any deceit in his mouth.

10. Yet it pleased the YHWH to bruise him; he hath put him to grief: when **thou shalt make his soul an offering for sin**, he shall see his seed, he shall prolong his days, and the pleasure of the YHWH shall prosper in his hand.

11. He shall see of the travail of his soul, and shall be satisfied: by his knowledge shall my righteous servant justify many; for **he shall bear their iniquities**.

12. Therefore will I divide him a portion with the great, and he shall divide the spoil with the strong; because he hath poured out his soul unto death: and he was numbered with the transgressors; and **he bare the sin of many, and made intercession for the transgressors**.

Can you see a type or image in the Serpent injecting its venom into the people and what is happening today? OPEN YOUR EYES & LOOK TO THE SIGN!

Know that there will come a day of reckoning, and most of your religious leaders will be exposed as blind dupes, or servants of the Serpent. שט Apostates, serpents in the nest. How many of your "so called" leaders have made secret deals, joining hands with The Vati-Can [Latin : Mouth of the Serpent]? How many Rabbi's stand in open rebellion against YHWH and HIS ANOINTED [MESSIAH - YESH-UA]?

Do not place your faith or trust in any MAN. The children of the Most High have a birthright which allows them to inquire of YHWH for themselves. If indeed, he is your Father, he will hear your cry; and if you are counted among his Sheep [children], you will hear his voice.

I therefore call upon the children of Adam to call upon YHWH, in the name of Yeshua, and ask HIM all things which you should do. Call upon the name of YHWH, praise and extol the name of YHWH, and do it as our fathers did... OUT LOUD! **Words have meanings, and names have power**.

Your first step is repentance . . . and then . . . to pray with real intent, and humbly ask.

Father, I call upon the Holy Name of יהוה YHWH, as my fathers before me. . .
I pray Father, that you will forgive my trespasses, as I forgive those who have trespassed against me. Open my eyes father, shed forth your light upon me that I may understand the truth of all things. Show me if Yeshua was truly your son. Circumcise my heart that I might know these things with every fiber of my being. Send forth רוח הקדוש the Holy Ghost to speak to my heart and soul. Hear the cry of your child, Father. I come before you with a righteous offering of a broken heart, and a contrite spirit. If ישוע Yeshua is truly the son who brings Salvation, I pray that you will answer my humble prayer.

Once you KNOW the truth, you should end each prayer in the name of our Salvation, Yeshua the Messiah, Amen.

Know that just reading the words above will do you no good whatsoever. You must FEEL the words. It is the **EMOTION**, the **CRY**, the **LAMENTATION of the HEART**.

Before seeking YHWH on any matter of importance, I will often say a prayer of protection first. Ask that YHWH will send his servants into your midst to protect you. That you might have his spirit to be with you as you pray.

Make no mistake, we are at war with the powers of darkness. As long as you do nothing, you feel safe, and all is well in the world. However, when moving towards the gate, expect to feel continuous attacks. The enemy is mad, and constant prayer is often needed to break away from the enemy's grasp. If the evil one cannot get to you directly, he will try to do so through those closest to you.

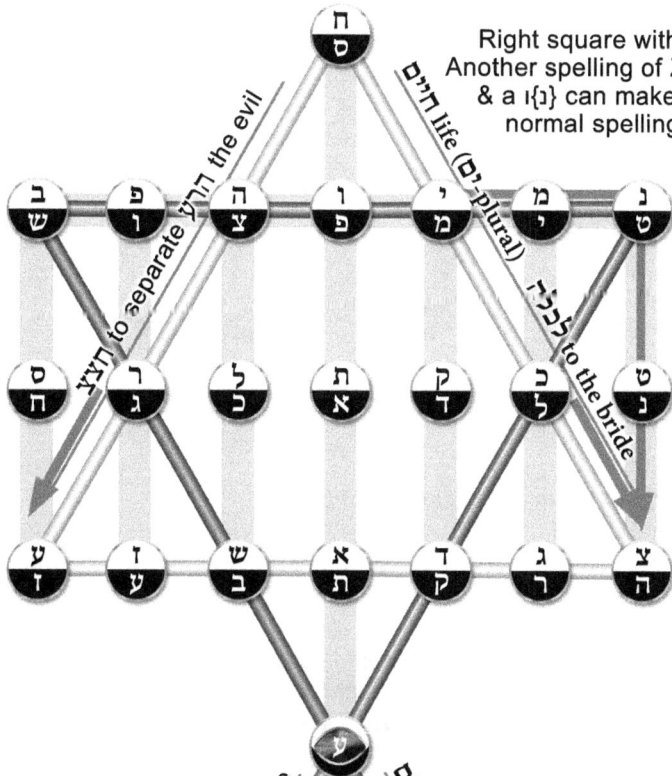

Right square with צין,
Another spelling of Zion
& a ו{נ} can make the
normal spelling ציון

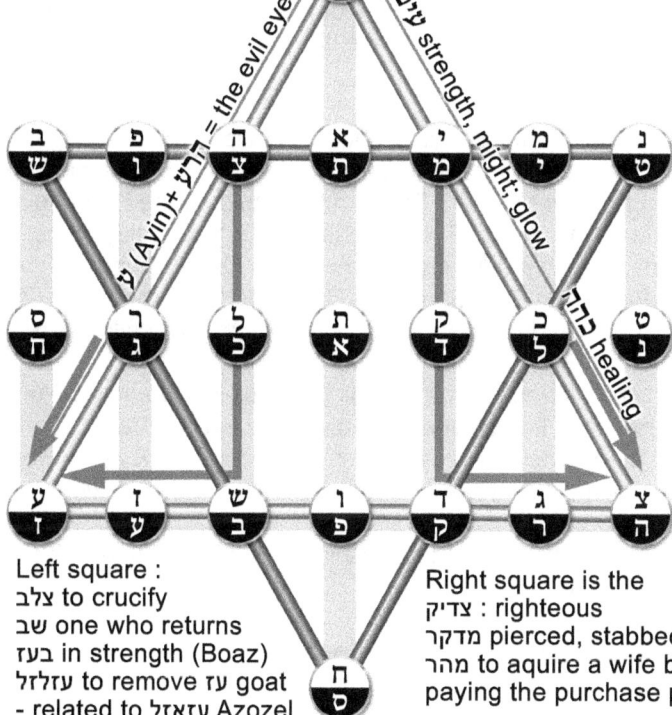

הרע to separate the evil

חיים life (ם' plural)

לכלה to the bride

הרע = the evil eye

ע (Ayin)+(ן)ר = ע

עז strength, might, glow

כהה healing

Left square :
צלב to crucify
שב one who returns
בעז in strength (Boaz)
עזלזל to remove עז goat
- related to עזאזל Azozel

Right square is the
צדיק : righteous
מדקר pierced, stabbed
מהר to aquire a wife by
paying the purchase price

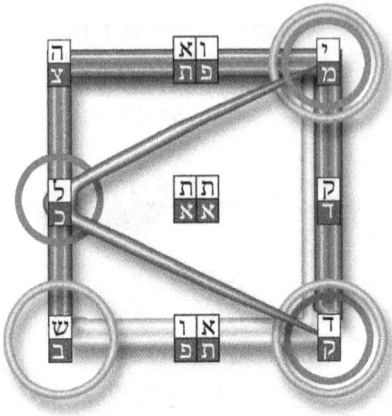

A lot of meat left on the bones of that last graphic.

This one, will give you hours of fun.

As I said before, there is layer upon layer in the code, and the only real "rule" I am able to find is one of context.

Let's take a look at

THE PASSOVER

Your main focus will remain the large squares.

Begin with the square running across the bottom and ending on your top-right. The word משקוף for "lintel" [of a door] is deposited on the top-right corner.

Now look at the two squares with end-points on the bottom-right, and bottom-left. Both of these run across מזוזה, "mezuzah", or doorpost. [Note: the ז{מ} // the Zayin is being pulled from the מ Mem, as well as a ו Waw. Corner hits are a higher value]

I put the compass into this mix because of what is connected at these points. We see the large circles on the bottom have the word for doorposts, while the large circle on top has the lintel.

Look for the דם blood [lands on top-right], שה the lamb [from compass landing on the ל Lamed - left center], and part of the compass shown contains דל, or door targeting the ק Kuf [right center]. Blood of the Lamb on the Door. I also see קתל to slay [landing on the ל Lamed] + שה lamb + אל El . . . to slay the lamb of Elohim. The ק Kuf compass, by the way, spells ילד a son. Can you find the א{ה}רי, א{ת}רי Lion of יהודה Judah, the ב{מ}ן Son of דוד David, ב{מ}ן Son of יהוה YHWH? Play with which tools you can find it in and note the targets the words land on.

This puzzle is one for you to practice using the full Menorah grid. You will find such details that it will amaze you. Start by going to Biblehub.com and looking up the passover, then switch the view to Hebrew and see how many words from the Passover you can find. Then determine where they fall using which tool.

NOTE : Each letter has specific tools assigned to it. See the Aleph-Bet section before attempting this.

PS. Don't forget to look for the "unleavened bread" landing on "my body", or the blood and the יין wine.

It's time to take you a little deeper into the anomaly surrounding the Temple. I call it that because there are two places where two squares feed into each-other. The one with the Serpent Satan is fairly straight forward. Look at the places that begin and end each of the two squares and you will see that it is going in a smooth counter-clockwise direction. The Temple, however, contains 4 large squares which overlap. Two going clockwise, and two counter-clockwise.

As there is nothing quite like this [especially after adding the swastikas] in the rest of the code, I thought it necessary to spend some time explaining this while showing you examples.

Pause and consider the fact that "the blood of the lamb on the door" is a compass receiving words from other tools which just happen to land on the compass corners. Now realize that everything landing in the squares surrounding the Temple is pushed into the letter('s) owning the square which the word landed on.

Example : the word שב "Lamb" is part of a compass landing on the ל Lamed, but it lands on a square belonging to the ש Shin, as well as being a natural word in the ש Shin square. Now consider that it also lands on a square belonging to the ה Hei, as well as being a natural word of the ה Hei square. Regardless of how it ended up in that spot, it would have become part of two squares. If a word landed on a corner, it would effectively be deposited into three squares and three corners.

As a rule, I look at sayings like, "I am in the Father, and the Father is in me". I see that the Father is the י Yud / מ Mem in the upper right hand corner of the Temple. I also see that the Son is in the מ Mem / י Yud sitting on its right. How about, out of the mouth of two or more witnesses should every word be established. Is there something to this in creating words within the code? . . . or establishing the truth of a matter within the code? Time will tell.

In this lesson, you will take what you have learned and apply it to the Seraph [small circles], the Menorah [large circles], and the light או{ת}ר.

Now let's de-construct the מ Mem נ{מ} and take the ע Ayin [above י / מ] (עין=Eye), and introduce it to the mix. Are you beginning to understand our ancestors placing the "Sun Disk" in the place where the ע Ayin (eye) rests between the two trees when they are separated?

Take that same נ{מ} and use the corners which contain the word שמש Sun. What do we see? We see the בן Son. Do you see the light of the Sun/Son, the burning [seraph] Menorah, filling every corner of the בית מקדוש Temple?

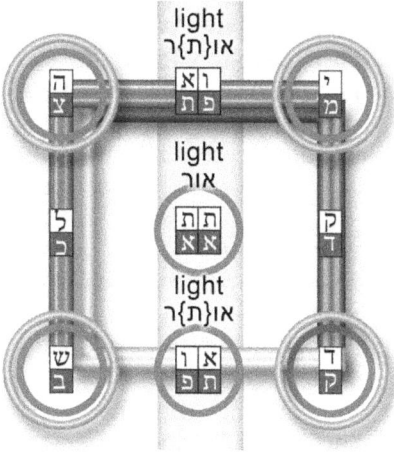

THE TWO WITNESSES

Let's begin with Deut. 33:16 where we see Moses blessing Joseph, the prince of his brothers. In vs. 17, he speaks of Joseph's horns, like those of a ראם wild ox. They push together the ten thousands of אפרים Ephraim, and the thousands of מנשה Manasseh.

I see a reflection in Isaiah 51:19 "these two" are come unto thee . . . vs. 20... כתוא as a "wild bull, wild ox, or antelope" depending on the translation. These are full of the fury of YHWH.

זית Olive Tree   light אור   שנים two

light אור

light אור

שקד Almond Tree   עד witness

This should be read in context to understand that of all the "sons" Jerusalem has brought up, there is no one to guide her. Yet these two [sons - not brought up in or by Jerusalem] bear the symbols of Joseph, Ephraim, and Manasseh when we look at what Moses said [Deut. 33:16, 17]. You should really read all of the quotes here in context. It shows that the Jews are drunken, but not with wine, with the cup of trembling & famine, sword, and destruction. Why? שט Serpents in the nest, apostates among them.

Those who lead Israel's Synagogues today boldly claim that the Sanhedrin which crucified Yeshua, the Messiah, were their ancestors. It is through this apostate lineage that they claim their power and authority. However, it should be noted, that **according to the Torah**, *if they have no genealogy connecting them to Aaron,* **they have no right to the priesthood.** These are just **men claiming authority**.

Yet what can you do if you live under the power and authority which these apostates have given to themselves? Look to the sign which Moses lifted up and live.

The two anointed sons of Joseph appear to take the cup of judgments from Jerusalem, and give it to their enemies. This tells me that the Jews appear to have repented, at least to an extent acceptable to YHWH, and the two witnesses full of the fury of YHWH, do their thing.

I have seen the day in the future when one of them will use the Urim and Thumim to declare the lineage of the sons of Levi and the sons of Aaron. It was a beautiful sight. Have hope, for I tell you in the name of יהוה YHWH, the Almighty Elohim of heaven and earth, that day will come.

Before moving on... Note that the word for Olive Tree זַ{מ}{פ}יִת & מ}זִית [ruler of 2], and Almond Tree שקד [compass], are assigned to the center pipe as well.

Let us continue...

Zechariah 4: 14 calls these the two היצה anointed בני "sons" [בָ{מ}{נִ}]. Rip the נ Nun from the מ Mem and see that they fall on the same ends of the squares with the word שנים two [שׁ{מ}נִים]. Now note what tool('s) all of these words fall on, and you will see them propagated into the points which stand on the right and the left of the word מנורה [ת{הר}ה or מ{מ}נ{מ}הר}ה] Menorah.

Note the word עד witness on the bottom right corner, and know that there is a שהד, "to bear witness" belonging to the ה Hei in the upper left corner.

I'm not sure how much more I should reveal on this subject at this time. If I feel moved to do so, I will reveal it to you with the helmet of salvation in the ז Zayin.

While we have this graphic up, and the בני "sons" are before you, consider the אור light which extends to every corner of the Temple. The sons of light. There will come a point when I will reveal the curse of the ל Lamed. When I do, I would like you to remember that the word חשׁך [Atbash rules] "darkness" is there, sons of darkness, and the punishment is severe.

Now I know I have mentioned "Atbash rules" several times. There is more in the "rules" section, but for now, just think of it as a coin. One side is heads, and the other is tails. With the word Menorah, I can walk from the מ,י, drawing letters out of that combination, then move on to the center פ,ת,ו,א and draw letters from that combination, and then move on to the צ,ה, and end the word (ה)+(ו}{ר}ת)+(נ}{מ}מ) מנורה Menorah.

If you use the "Atbash rules", you must remember that if you go from a letter on top of the pair (heads) to a letter on the bottom (tails), the meaning derived will belong to the Atbash "pair" (entire coin) being targeted. The entire coin [both sides] may also be used before moving on to the next (coin).

Easy example : Think of the word used for crucifixion צלב [down the left side of the Temple]. You begin on צ tails, the next coin is ל heads, and the last is ב tails.

On the next page we are going to build upon some of the things which you have learned so far. This time, we will be looking at the letters AND the letters which may be drawn from them.

{ע: ו,י} {ח: ו,י} {o: ו}

{ר,י: ה}
{צ: ו,י}

{י: }
{מ: י,ו,ז,נ}

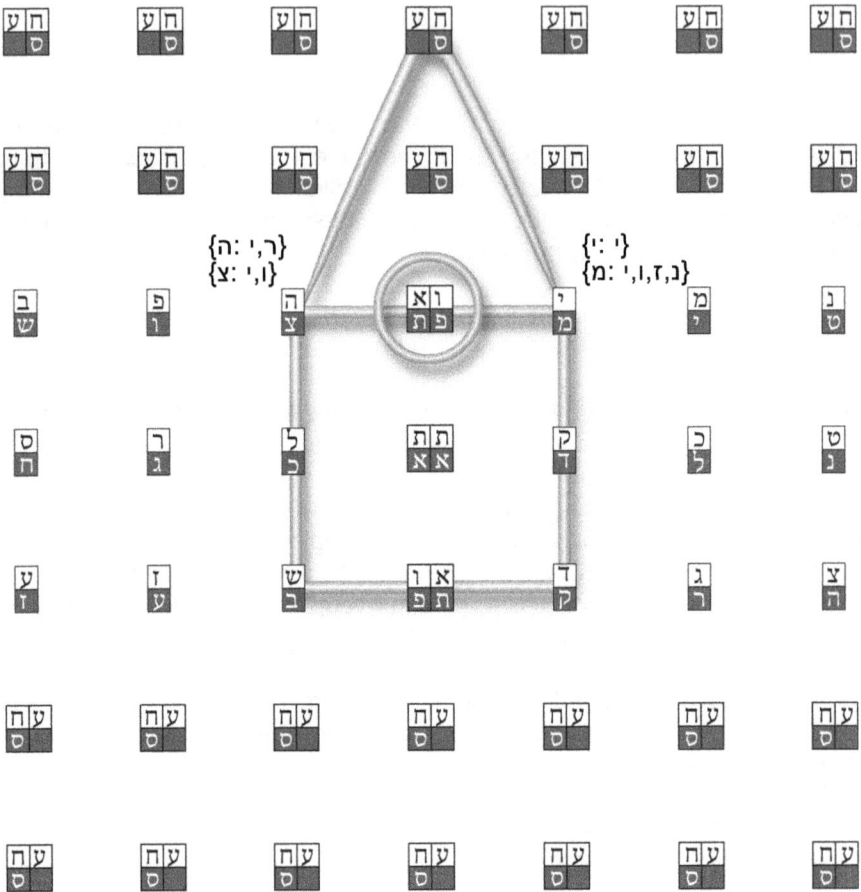

Note that this is a breakdown of the letters which may be drawn from the letters, not the repeats.

Example : The מ Mem, if completely broken down would have a ו Waw with a י Yud [hand] on top of its head on the left side. This is a ז Zayin. The נ Nun on its right is made up of two י Yuds and a ו Waw.

I don't want to get into the letters before the section on each letter, so this will have to suffice for now.

Do you remember when we were going around the Temple and spelling קדוש ליהוה Holiness to YHWH? (p.24) I'll bet that a lot of you thought that יהוה YHWH was a bit forced since the rest streamed clockwise very nicely around the Temple.

Tell me, can you see the מחסה refuge [top compass + Atbash rules] of כבוד glory [square coming up on left side belonging to the Atbash rules ה/צ pair]?

So this word for refuge in the compass has "glory" in one of its three corners. The compass is the actual "top" of the "Temple".

Look again at that compass יה{ע}ו{וה} YHWH. THIS is not using both sides of the pair [No Atbash rules], and targets both the א Aleph and the ו Waw. So קדוש ליהוה Holiness to YHWH does wrap clockwise around the Temple using all letters with white background. You just need to read the top like the compass that it is.

Now look into the compass and see if you can find the מנורה Menorah.

Look at the פה mouth [open end of the compass]. Watch it swallow מות death in נצח victory [also eminence and perpetuity].

Can you see the light and life of the earth? If not, you will need to review the words I have given you so far. There is a lot left to cover, so it is time to begin the rules section.

I need to move from beginner to intermediate explanations, and know that those who seek something more will be able to find it.

Before we begin with the "The Rules of the Tools", I want to touch on statistical probabilities.

For example; did you know that you could find the first three verses in the book of Genesis within the one large square which ends on the ש/ב? If I had to guess, I would say that it appears to have a lot of the most commonly used letters. That means that you would find a lot of words, and you need to use methods which will help you to discern relevance.

My number one guide in this is looking for the statistical probabilities least likely to be random. These come from reading the letters on top, while ignoring the Atbash letters [or vice-versa]. We will see exceptions like the word מקדוש "Temple", which is obviously following a sequence. That sequence, in my opinion, is the least likely to be random, and most likely to be a theme which the underlying letters will talk about.

Then we come to meanings in the corners [compass or square] which tend to corroborate the testimony of what is found naturally, within that tool.

This brings me to my number two rule, "two or more witnesses". Time after time, I find words which verify target definitions or known stories found in the Bible.

Rule number three : remember that a Hebrew word could have many definitions defined by Masoretic vowel points which never existed in the original language. So, you should always **look up all definitions for that letter sequence**. Then, consider the possibility that some, or all of the definitions may be valid at the same time. The only way to know, is to tear it down as we did for נחש, sign or serpent.

Chapter 2 : Rules of the Tools

As you have decided to "read" the Menorah [Tree of Knowledge/Life], I should throw out a helpful hint or two for English speakers who, like me, do not speak Hebrew.

Most people have access to the Internet, digital music players & etc., so let me tell you how I learned the Aleph-Bet. Go to YouTube, and find a little song called "Aleph Bass". It is much better than the Alphabet song that most of us grew up listening to.

Now that you have learned the Aleph-Bet, you need to be sure to recognize the "final form letters". *These are letters which have a* **leg** *that changes position when it lands at the end of a word.* Amazingly, this is actually relevant in definitions found in the "letter overlays".

Here is the Aleph-Bet with the final form letters in [ ] square brackets. Don't forget that Hebrew is read from right to left.

א ב ג ד ה ו ז ח ט י כ[ך] ל מ[ם] נ[ן] ס ע פ[ף] צ[ץ] ק ר ש ת

You are now ready to look up Hebrew words.

Ruler of 2 :

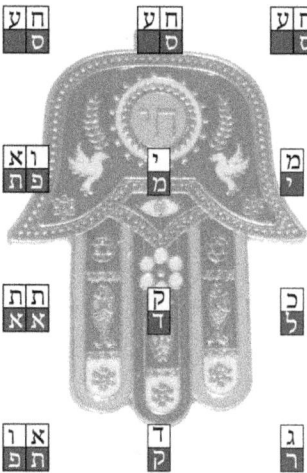

The **Hamsa** [hand with the eye in the middle]. This was going to be an entire lesson, but we are just going to use the symbol as part of an example.

חי "life" is a ruler of 2 belonging to the י Yud.

The letter or pair [mixed] the word ends on, "owns" it.

Break up the מ Mem [below the י Yud] into its component parts {מ: י,ו,ז,ן}. As יד "Yud" means "hand" [see in Aleph-Bet]. Come down from the top center and find the word עין "eye". This conjunction is now mixed because the "eye" uses both the regular and Atbash letters. So, "technically", it belongs to the י/מ Atbash "PAIR". However, a string in sequence may receive a little extra power based on intent [to attach to a theme or story].

"Reflected" ruler of 2 : מת "Death", from string חיים life (מ), די{מ}ן Judgment (י/מ) or ד{מ}י{מ}ן (מ), to מאז{מ}ר{מ}ן the scale owned by the א/ת [small (י/מ)(א/ת)(ת/א) square].

מת a dead person, judged, on a scale or balance, returns to life (מ) [מתם "whole, sound, people, men"]. Do you see the reflected sequence in the ruler of 2?

Large Squares :

What you saw on the previous page is the basic layout of the large squares. However, as some of the squares depicted overlap underlying squares, the direction indicated by the chevrons is lacking full disclosure.

The **large squares** are the main pipes or branches, and **may not extend to the other side of the cylinder**.

When you get to the "Aleph-Bet", each letter will have a graphic of tools assigned to it.

The large squares may contain a large number of words. Think of it like an aircraft carrier [native words], with water and air craft [tools] attached. That makes things chaotic, so take a perspective from the tower.

Look for strings of words where the letters appear in sequence. That is a high value word. Next, pay attention to word combinations made by letters in the three corners. Then *contextually relevant* words from other tools landing on the square.

Look for patterns. Generate word lists using only regular, or only Atbash letters.

Are there two or more words with the same definition? Where do they land?

You will see examples as we go, but in the end, I still try to "feel" connections. The Holy Ghost will teach you, unless your disbelief grieves her. Just ask, and listen, setting aside your ego, and preconceptions. Feel the answer in your heart.

A simple example would be a theme guided by the native words. Yet the reality requires eyes to see.
... I'll show you an example in a bit.

Small Squares :

This is how the drawing of the small squares began. That's right, I just drew it trying to "feel" the right pattern. It wasn't until after I began trying to separate the squares into the two trees that I noticed the two swastikas in the center.

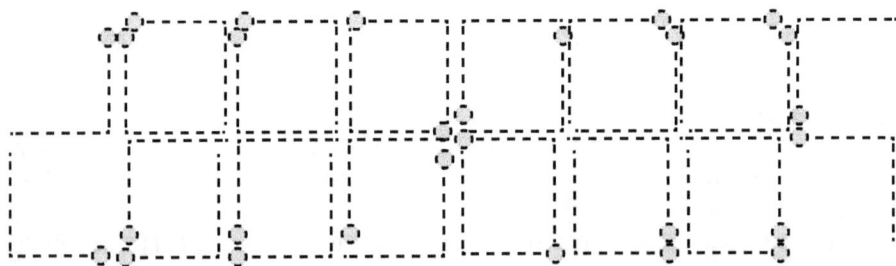

The small squares are easy. It is three corners with regular letters, Atbash letters, and mix of both. Words with regular letters are assigned to the regular letter in the target. Words with Atbash letters are assigned to the Atbash letter in the target. Mixed [regular and Atbash] words are assigned to the ATBASH PAIR in the target.

Compass :

The rules are the same as the small squares, but the target lies in the mouth of the open end. My only reservation is in crossing between tree borders [right & left sides] on the cylinder. I haven't actually confirmed it. So, I have to say, unknown.

This being said, the נ Nun compass crossing between trees has so many connections that I can recognize with my limited Hebrew, I believe that the pattern crossing between trees may be correct. While I haven't done the work to prove it, I see the נ Nun saying look! So a compass crossing between trees will be outlined.

Atbash Pairs :

The best example I can think of comes from the all Atbash [bottom letter] loop which has the "Serpent Satan" (p.35).

Use the full tree and find : [square on top] עיט bird of prey [mixed] belongs to ט/נ Atbash pair. On its right you will see a ב Bet which has a ר Reish in it allowing a ruler of 2 נשר Eagle [mixed] belongs to the ש/ב Atbash pair. Now take a small square, set it on top of the ע,פ,ב [target is the ש/ב]... rip a י Yud from the פ Peh, and spell ישוע Yeshua [mixed].

In this case the Atbash pairs are grabbing the Serpent Satan from above. This is the origin of the Eagle grabbing the Serpent. The Eagle, in this case shares the Atbash Pair with Yeshua.

Before you turn the page, I am going to tell you not to freak out. I have a limited amount of time to explain these things to you, so I needed to find a way to allow the non Hebrew speaking people to follow along.

So, I created a limited map of tools which focuses on the center, or Temple section of the Tree. I say limited because it is not showing the directions of all of the tools. Why? Because it is just too crowded. So much so, that I omitted the small squares simply because it is already divided into sections which contain their shapes.

We are going to jump right in, beginning with examples of each of the tools, and then, we will begin looking at it a little differently...like a series of combination locks or a puzzle box. Think of it as a flow chart of information where repeating or similar words begin to form a word cloud with the most repeated words and themes becoming the strongest identifiers.

Two Trees in One
TOK in Left column / TOL in Right column

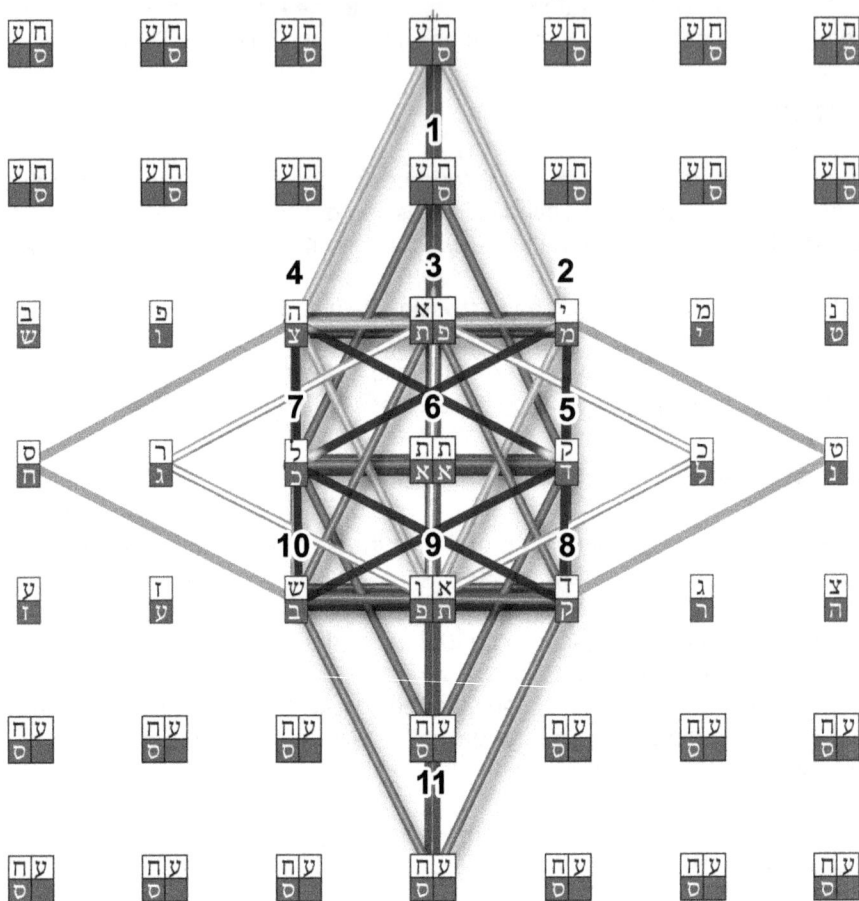

The Great Rule : I have said it over and over. You must NOT use Hebrew words which are non-Biblical. By this, I mean NO MODERN HEBREW. When I go through my ETYMOLOGICAL DICTIONARY OF THE HEBREW LANGUAGE FOR READERS OF ENGLISH, by Ernest Klein, and I find a single "Biblical" Hebrew word on a page, I understand **Zephaniah 3: 9, 10**. The Hebrew which is spoken today, is a far cry from the "pure" language which this code is based on.

The Ruler of 2 : 6, 10 : אב = father [remember that Hebrew is read right to left]. The letter that the word ends on owns it. In this case, it is the Atbash ב Bet.
6, 2 : אם = mother. The Atbash מ Mem on 2 owns it.
6, 10 : אש = fire. This word mixes a letter assigned to the almond bud & one from the almond flower [knops bowels of the Menorah]. So, the word belongs to the ב/ש ATBASH PAIR on 10. This is 100% true, yet the 9, 10 אש targets the ש Shin alone.
10, 7, 10 : שלש = Three. This is a "reflected" ruler of 2, and belongs to the ש Shin. Rulers may cross the cylinder which joins the left and right side of the tree.

The Ruler of 3 : 10, 7, 4 : שלה = to draw forth from the water. This belongs to the ה Hei (4).

4, 7, 10 : צלב = To hang, impale, or crucify. This mixes regular and Atbash letters and is therefore owned by the ש/ב ATBASH PAIR on 10.

Let's get a little more complex and decompile the מ Mem and the ה Hei in 2, 3, 4. If you haven't read the very beginning of the book yet, you need to see the Abbreviations (p.8). מ{מ}נ{נו}{ה}ר{ה = מנורה Menorah. This can also be made with a 1, 2, 4 target (3) Compass.

The Compass : 2, 4, 9 targets the (3). As there are sets of both the Tree of Life, and the Tree of Knowledge on 9 and 3, it is important to realize that while combined, the meaning is true . . . Yet the word יהוה YHWH, specifically targets the א Aleph in the TOK [Tree of Knowledge].

Your next example is the word אהיה I AM. Another 2, 4, 9 which targets the (3), but uses the TOL [Tree of Life] and targets the ו Waw. So you now have I AM & YHWH on a אות "sign" (3), with או{ת}ר Light, and 1, 2, 4 (3) ר{ה}{ו}{ע}נ{מ}מ a Menorah.

Take another look at 1, 2, 4 (3) : We are going to decompile the composite letter ע Ayin, which contains a ו Waw. יהוה YHWH. . . another witness targeting the א Aleph on the 3 spot.

Using what we have learned so far, take a look at the 4, 5, 10 (7) compass and see the 10, 4 שה lamb, all regular letters, so it targets the ל Lamed. The same letter which has a 3, 7 Ruler of 2 giving it the word אל EL. Remember the Lamb of EL [short for Elohim] while we look at a . . .

Large Square : In the temple section we have 4 large carpenters squares overlapping. So I'll call them out by number ending on the target. 2, 4, 10 contains that same שה lamb ending on 10. 8, 10, 4 also contains שה lamb. So now we have positions 4, 7, and 10 with the word lamb. . . And we have 3 rulers of 2 going 3, 7; 6, 7; 9, 7 which make אל EL. . . Three lambs of god, and the lamb runs down the same 4, 7, 10 as צלב, To hang, impale, or crucify.

Now I'm going to rip a י Yud from the א Aleph on 9 and show you a **small square** which goes 11, 9, 10. {א}ישוע Yeshua. Compass 8, 10, 11 (9) = וי{ד}ישי{ע} Yeshua [same target as creator, son, and word].

2, 4, 10 contains ב{מ}ן son and יהוה YHWH. And how can I cease to repeat the 10, 7 sets של "to put off, loose, error, offense, crime that belongs to" בך "in you" [which also belong to the 2, 4, 10 square].

Running down meanings which overlap the 4, 7, 10 square, lamb, lamb, lamb. . . I AM, son, YHWH, עץ tree, or wooden beam, to crucify, lamb, El, Yeshua, to put off the crime which belongs to you.

Yes, the "I AM" אהיה is a name which specifically targets the ו Waw, the son, in the TOL 9, 2, 4 (3) compass. It is shown to be the son & creator ב{ת}רא in the 10, 3, 8 (9) TOK compass, but now we are moving on to the words for son ילד, בן, בר which begin to show up in the same way as lamb, sign, light, Yeshua, and lion.

Two Trees in One
TOK in Left column / TOL in Right column

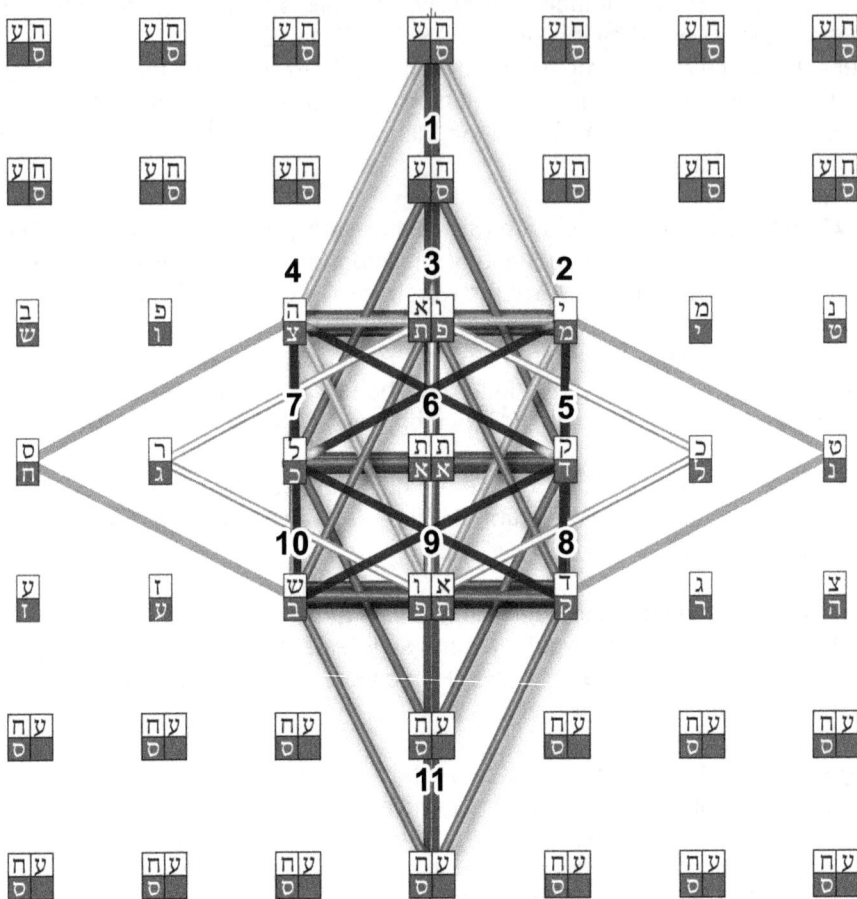

Words owned by a target may be elements in word definitions, or sayings in the tools, or overlays, but not necessarily all of these.

Let's show a basic example in the 10, 8, 2 square. שדי Almighty. This taps the corners in sequence and is owned by the י Yud.

Now I'll tap the י Yud with a 3, 8, מ [just right of 2] compass and give the י Yud the word אדם Adam, or man. Then I add the קדוש, a native string in the 10, 8, 2 square, and another name for the Almighty appears as אדם קדוש Man of Holiness.

How about a known saying within this square [remember that we want to see words with repeating names or meanings]. We see a nice string in the מקדוש Temple. Now add these words falling in the square. שחת destroy, שדד destroy, שלש three, יום day, ימים days, בנ{מ}ה to build, תקו to become straight, קום to arise, stand up, תקום will rise up.
"Destroy this temple, and in three days I will raise it up again" (see John 2:19).

REALITY of sifting through themes in a square. Looking at the מ Mem square(s).

The מ Mem which we examined early on was defined as the son of man, a traveler or sojourner, sitting on the right hand of power (see p.18).

There is a lot more here than I am going to go into now, but מיכל, a spelling of Michael which = 100, same as the ק Kuf which the 2, 7, 8 (5) compass identified as ילד a son. A compass which also contained the same spelling of Michael. There is an א Aleph available within the large square to produce the traditional spelling of מיכאל Michael, but the way this lines up is striking

The מיכל string ends on the ל Lamed, which has a ruler of 2 דל door, and a compass which has ארי Lion. A small square; (ק/ד) = Son+Michael + a (ל/כ) Lion+Michael+door that merges with the (מ/י) Michael square with traditional spelling, and אל El, מלך king, יד hand, יתד nail, וו nail, דק veil, תא inner room [of the Temple], אות sign. . . I know I lost a lot of you, but take it slow, and try to follow along.

This is just a quick overview of looking at a large square. There is a lot here, so I use the things which I know are related and see a panorama showing a progression of events which appear to be related to judgment day.

ruler of 3 down
י{ע}עמד shall stand up

חיים life
פ{ה}רץ r2- to break through
ה{ה}רס break, tear down
ב{ה}רד lg. square hail
ס{ת}ה{ה}ר sm. sq. hiding place,
secrecy, covering
ב{מ}ן son
אדם of man
מתם wholeness
מקדוש Temple
יום day
קולי my voice
כ{מ}זרם like
a flood
מים water
גפרית brimstone
יקים will rise up
תקום stand up
מיכל Michael
מיכאל Michael
גר sojourner
קד to rend
דק veil
תא inner room
ילד son
אדם man
כל the whole, all
גדל great
מלך king
מלכים kings
מלאך angel
נקם/נקמה vengeance
מהומה confusion
צי{מ}ן zion
מק{ה}רק{ה} break down
קי{ה}/ק{ה}ר/ wall
דם blood
קד to rend
דק veil

כלה destruction
א{ה}רץ earth
תפל foolish things, untempered
מת death
ילד son
מיכל Michael
ארי lion
דל door
ג{ד}ר wall

ruler 2
שר{ת} to minister
ש{ת}ר prince
ב{ת}ר son
שופ{ת}ר shophar
שבת sabbath
ב{ת}ר son
ב{ת}רא creator
ד{ב}{ת}ר word
ב{ת}רד hail
גדר wall

lg. square
צלב crucify
יהוה YHWH
צבאות of hosts
פ{מ}נת corner
אב{מ}ז stone
sm. square
belonging to (ב/ש)
{א}ישוע Yeshua
שביעי seventh
שע{ת}ר storm, horror

יום day
ח{א} life
יהוה YHWH

בקע V breach

When you have completed the book, return and try to see how many repeat words [witnesses] are found in connecting tools, or only listed once. Isaiah has shown me that prophecy and skill in the tree combine to allow position a place in determining hidden meanings.

Note the צלב crucifixion on the left in which שה lamb [belongs to each position that the word passed through].

Then look at the ארי "lion". A compass gives שה lamb to the כ/ל target, then another gives ארי lion to the כ/ל target.

The צלב crucifixion is owned by the same ב/ש target as Yeshua, corner, stone . . . Take a good long look at that graphic. . .

ruler of 3 down
ע}יעמד} shall stand up
חיים life

r2- פ{ה}רץ to break through
סר{ה}ה break, tear down
lg. square ב{ה}רד hail
sm. sq. ר{ה}תחo hiding place,
secrecy,covering

ב{מ}ן son
אדם of man
מתם wholeness יום day
מקדוש Temple

קולי my voice
כ{מ}זרם like
a flood
מים water
גפרית brimstone
יקים will rise up
תקום stand up
מיכל Michael
מיכאל Michael
גר sojourner
קד to rend

כלה destruction
א{ה}רץ earth
תפל foolish things,
untempered
מת death
ילד son
מיכל Michael ארי lion

דק veil
תא inner room
ילד son
אדם man
כל the whole, all
גדל great
מלך king
מלכים kings
מלאך angel

ruler 2
ש{ת}רת to minister
ר{ת}ש prince
ב{ת}ר son
שופ{ת}ר shophar
שבת sabbath

ב{ת}ר son
ב{ת}רא creator
ד{ת}בר word
ב{ת}רד hail
גדר wall

דל door

lg. square
צלב crucify
יהוה YHWH
צבאות of hosts
פ{מ}נת corner
אב{מ}ז stone
sm. square
belonging to (ב/ש)

יום day
ח{א}י life יהוה YHWH
נקם/נקמה vengeance
מהומה confusion
צי{מ}ו{ן} zion
מק{ה}ר{ק}{ה}ר break down
קי{ה}ר/ק{ה}ר wall
דם blood
קד to rend
דק veil

א{א}ישוע} Yeshua
שביעי seventh
שע{ת}ר storm, horror

The identity of the son, creator, and word is connected with a compass to Yeshua on one side of the דק Veil, and Michael on the other.

His first coming is as a lamb, but the second [related to Judgment day], he comes as a lion.

One should remember that "Judgment day", as far as our earthly existence is concerned, is the time of Jacob's trouble. It is also the reason that I have a deadline to release this book. A period of tribulation [Judgment], which precedes the Judgment of the quickened and the dead [Second Coming / Resurrection].

I included a lot of the words around the Temple, because I know that he will begin cleaning in his own house first, and the target square begins there. . . That part, I will wait until later to expand upon.

STEP 1
I look at the obvious who. Michael running down the right side, with a connecting prince at the other.

I see the (אים) terrible day of YHWH with tons of descriptors attached to the large square. Some of these will have multiple witnesses giving them more value. Other words, known from association with Michael or Judgment day in scripture, receive additional witnesses from that.

STEP 2
I see that the strongest word is the string מיכל Michael. That this is going to be a mixed [Atbash] theme. It must therefore be condensed into what we know from scripture. Then, recognize that there are many scriptures on this subject speaking of different events which take place during this period.

In other words, you can read this square very simply and say Michael the prince, the sojourner will rend the veil as a sign. Or, you can go beyond what you see on the surface and look at . . .

STEP 3
The connections : Begin with the fact that all of *the large circles are places where the large squares intersect.* That's right, the two large squares closest to the right target the מ/י pair. So everything you have or will learn about the center pipe of the Menorah has a direct connection to the Michael we have been looking at.
All of the small circles are places where the word son is connected.

So what have you learned from the large square with the string Michael? That he is Yeshua. That he came the first time as a lamb [a sacrifice], and in the great and terrible day of YHWH, he will come as a LION. . . There is obviously more here, but that would need to be broken down scripture by scripture to examine those connections.

I didn't want to slam you with the chaos of a large square overview, but it you want to break down the code for yourself, you will need to understand the reality of how it begins.

Find a theme or word that stands out in the large square, and see if you can use words found in scriptures which line up with that theme.

The Overlay :

I haven't done too many letter overlays, but what I have seen from the result is pretty awesome.

The concept is to expand the letter so that it sits in the grid. So, think of the underlying square as the Hebrew letter מ Mem or final Mem ם.

In this case, we are using the מ Mem in the top center, and looking only at the regulars letters with the white background.

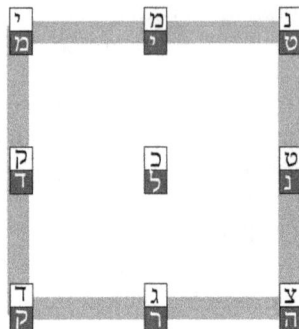

STEP 1
Make a list of letters here - ג,ד,ט,י,מ,נ,צ,ק

STEP 2
Pretend that it is a puzzle, and see how many words you can make from these letters.

Overlay Words :
(מם) Mem [name of letter]
(מן) Manna ; out of [Ruler of 2 belongs to Nun, final Nun invokes favor, grace]
(ימין) f.n. the right hand, right side, the right ; the South (i.e. the right side if one faces east).
(מגן) Protector
(טנן) to be moist, be damp. [final Nun invokes favor, grace]
        I think this is related to (תאן) weep, lament, wail
(יצג) To set in place [I think the י Yud may be able to connect with any of these letter combinations]
(דג) fish [connection to Gimmel, the follower in final Mem]
(גצץ) to flash, to glitter [is this NEW HEBREW?]
(יגדד) to cut off [belongs to Dalet, door in the final Mem]
(יגדד״) to gather in troops or bands [belongs to Dalet, door in the final Mem]
(דד) breast, teat, nipple
(דק) Veil [ruler of 2 belongs to Kuf kingdom of YHWH on earth - Temple]
(יקד) to be kindled, burn [ruler of 3 - Dalet]
(יד) hand [not in sequence, but thin line may be making Yud available?]
(ידד) to be friends, become friends.
(ידיד) friend, beloved
(יגן) to be grieved, be sorrowful [final Nun invokes favor, grace]
(יגן) garden + (י) my = (יגן) My Garden? [final Nun invokes favor, grace]
(גן) garden [final Nun invokes favor, grace
(גי) valley, vale
(נגן) to play an instrument
(ני) wailing, lament
(גנן) to defend, protect, guard, shelter; to garden

STEP 3

Putting it all together. You must let the spirit guide you.

I actually did this one years ago, but each time that I came across it again, I kept feeling like it was supposed to begin with a "Thus saith YHWH". So I looked up how to spell that in Hebrew and found that the large square belonging to the ד/ק drops those words in that spot.

The lesson was telling me that tools can actually drop words onto the overlay. However, I prefer it to be as clean as possible. So I will add the words I felt in-spired to, and leave it alone.

Thus saith YHWH, Being grieved for my garden, in the terrible day of the Lord, the hand [of] your protector, shall burn your enemies and raise up the sea, to cut off and pull down the nations. I shall gather in my followers and feed them manna [food from heaven] and nourish them [breast - possible Holy Ghost reference]. I will set them in place and establish the veil of my Temple among them; for they are my friends and my beloved in whom I am well pleased.

I was just a baby in learning the code when I first wrote that, and I see so many things which I missed before. . . The day may come that I search this out more, but the feeling of inspiration while teaching me and writing it the first time, let me know that it is delivering the intended message.

This being said, there is an Atbash Mem in the upper left corner just waiting for someone to try . . .

Before leaving the tools section, I think it is time to go back to the beginning and take a closer look at a huge key used to decrypt the Menorah.

The hand sign of the Aaronic Blessing done with both hands, the right way. We have seen how "tradition", especially when dealing with "symbols", is the first thing to become corrupted when the TRUE meanings behind the symbols are lost.

I look at the sign in bronze which Moses raised up, and how it so quickly became a misunderstood lie, which then became tradition. . . We now know that the word נחש was used because of a typology [an anti-thesis], and the ability to use a word which meant "a sign", as well as a numerological [Gematria] equivalent of "Messi-ah". Yet today, you have those who worship the serpent. TRADITION.

"Symbols", without the true interpretation, are just begging for someone to fill that void with "opinion". Symbols from the Almighty have a meaning, and throughout history HE has revealed the mysteries of the Tree of Life to those who sought the truth at HIS hands.

Imagine Isaiah using his hand over the Menorah code and seeing the מים Waters in the well of the [י Yud] hand, and the שמים Heavens stretched between the [short] span [tip of thumb [ש] to tip of the index finger [מים] of the hand = שמים.

Isaiah 40: 12 "Who hath measured the waters in the hollow of his hand, and meted out heaven with the span"

A "short span" is the length between the thumb and index finger.

HAND
מ

The letter and word "Yud" means "hand"

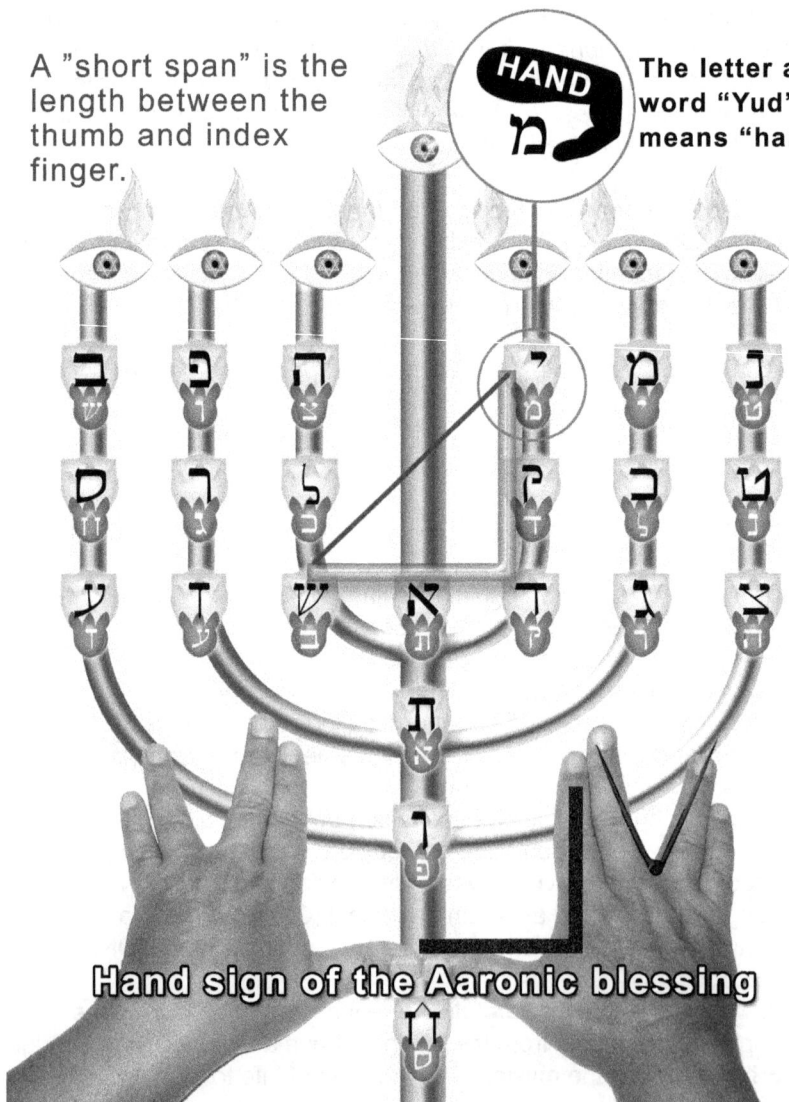

Hand sign of the Aaronic blessing

My soul loves to feast on the words of Isaiah. He shows me over and over that he not only understood the Menorah Code, he was a master of using it.

I included a little piece of one of Isaiah's sayings in hopes that it is simple enough for those just learning to understand.

Going beyond Isaiah's example, I would like the reader to take note of something which you do not currently have the instruction to see.

There are three upward targeting large squares on the right side of the Menorah, ending on the tip of the index finger, just as there are three upward branches. . .
These have *reflected* squares in the center allowing meanings in the thumb and finger to duplicate on both ends. Yet once that square made with the right hand crosses over to the left side of the tree, the target moves from the finger to the thumb.
Take the left hand, for example, cross to the other side of the tree and put your thumb on the צ Tzaddi while your index finger is on the י Yud. That square belongs to the צדי Tzaddi.
Now imagine that the tree of life, with branches pointing down is merged with it, and vertically mirror those tools and their targets.

Note : in the standard matrix, or grid, you would see the "תר{ת}ר{מ}" = "span" in the center (ת/א, also owned by sm. sq. י/מ), between the index finger and בהן "thumb" [owned by LG (ש/ב) sq.].

Note : the compass made by dividing the middle and ring finger. . .

There is so much to explain, and so little time to try to bring you up to a level of understanding. I'm not sure how much detail I will be able to give in the Aleph-Bet section, but there you will be given the tools to understand each individual letter. Then, perhaps, you will fully appreciate the importance of the tools and the awesome secrets held within the letters. . . I will try to show you as much as I can in the Aleph section, but most of what I have in my notes does not include the compound letters or merged trees.

END OF TOOLS SECTION . . .

Chapter 3 : Garments & Gammadia

It is becoming more and more difficult to relate the full truth of the gospel to an audience of babes entrenched in the traditions of men. Most "so called" Christians fail to recognize two very important truths.

1. Early followers of Yeshua were seen as a sect of Judaism. The Elohim of Abraham, Israel, and Moses is the same truth which Yeshua taught. He was simply trying to bring the sheep to a **new covenant** (see Jeremiah 31:31-34).
2. By the time Rome became involved, the "church" had already splintered into many different factions with many different beliefs. So Rome did as the Romans do. They labeled every "Christian" nation or sect which would not bow down to the false "bridge", or "mediator" between god and man (1 Timothy 2:5), as pagan or heretic. Then they went on a thousand plus year killing spree, torturing, murdering, and making war to eradicate the resistance.

If you will allow me to have a personal belief, this is what I see.

I see a group of Mitre wearing fish heads which worshiped Enki & Enlil [the Serpent & Satan] under Nimrod in Babylon. The same Nimrod which I believe came out to the people with garments dyed red and says, "worship me", claiming to be the "Sun god" [a perverted understanding of the Menorah code prophecy which I believe existed]. The same Nimrod which was known in Asia Minor as "Santa" [Langer's Encyclopedia of World History].The same Mitre wearing cult which was kicked out of Babylon by Cyrus [my guess is because of their secret combinations]. The same Mitre wearing pontiffs with a Pontifex maximus which showed up in Pergamon [the seat of Satan] and were imported into Rome during the Carthaginian war [around 200 BC because Rome needed a Mother/Moon goddess due to what sounds like an exoplanet]. The same cult which sits on Vatican Hill. The same hill which worshiped Vatika. The same hill which has an alter to Lucifer [still under the Vatican]. The same Vatican which sings songs to Lucifer and his son the Christos which will never be defeated. The same Christos which was the title of Apollo [Sun god] under the Greeks. The same Vatican which literally means Vati [mouth] & Can [serpent]. The same Pontifex maximus which still has a Santa/Nimrod outfit. The same church which is responsible for killing more people than any entity in the History of the world. "Anti"-Christos [in Greek] = "Vicar" of Christ [in Latin], and don't get me started on the names of blasphemy [Holy Father, His Holiness the Pope "Father" - see Matthew 23: 9] . . . and I could go on and on. Yet their origins, as shown by the sects fish head Mitre, Sun god worship, Moon/Mother goddess worship, and Serpent worship, are Babylon. . . .

Oh, wait, that's not true! We changed their names and made them "Christian". Well, knowing the origin [Apollo->Christos->Christian] of that word doesn't inspire a lot of confidence in your [Nimrod->Santa->Saints]. Study the etymological word origins of Lord, Christos, Angels, and god.

Don't be such a little NIMROD. Words have meanings, and names have power.

So if the Catholic [Universal] Church is in fact, the whore of Babylon, wolves in sheep's clothing [search Romulus and Remus story], the feet of Daniels prophecy, and I believe this 100%, . . . who, pray tell, are the harlots spawned by this whore?

They are called harlots because their mother taught them her traditions. Don't believe it? Do you **remember the sabbath day** to keep it Holy? No, because your **whore** of a **mother** took it upon herself to declare that the **new Sabbath** would be on **Sunday, in honor of Sol Invictus** [same as the Greek **Apollo**], the "**SUN GOD**". So you worship on the day which that whore of a mother taught you. You reject the 10 commandments, written in stone by the hand of YHWH, to endure forever; and you think that the followers of Yeshua worshiped on "YHWH's day" [translated as "the Lord's day" in Revelations], but YHWH's day was SATURDAY", Sabado, on the Sabbath, for hundreds of years before the whore took over.

Yes, you are a harlot. One of the deaf, dumb, and blind ‎עם apostate children. Even if you don't bow down to your "Saint" [from Santa/Nimrod] graven image and ask them to be your bridge or mediator between you and your god like your whore of a Mother. She has taken more from you than you know.

You believe that you understand what the early [pre-Rome] church believed, yet you ignore the fact that Rome destroyed anything from other sects which it declared Heretic. You only know what the whore allowed you to know.

Believe what you will, but the truth of YHWH is in the Tree of Life, and I see fragments in ancient sayings of the Nag Hammadi, hidden behind a wall in a Synagogue in Egypt around the time Rome decided to cleanse the Heretical teachings [and people]. I'm not saying that these texts are 100% pure, but I see truth in many of their sayings which I recognize as remnants of the Tree of Life.

I see fragments in the ancient gammadia. Symbols which decrypt sacred covenants encrypted within the Tree of Life. Symbols which I recognize. Symbols of my clan which reveal the law and covenants of YHWH burning upon my heart. Yet the symbols, without the key to decipher it [the Menorah Code], diminishes the "sacred" in the symbols. When you wear these sacred symbols in the Menorah, the light of YHWH burns within you, and we become sons [and daughters] of light.

Jeremiah 31:31-34

31. Behold, the days come, saith the LORD, that I will make **a new covenant** with the house of Israel, and with the house of Judah:

32. *Not according to the covenant that I made with their fathers in the day that I took them by the hand to bring them out of the land of Egypt; which my covenant they brake, although I was an husband unto them*, saith the LORD:

33. But this shall be the covenant that I will make with the house of Israel; After those days, saith the LORD, **I will put my law in their inward parts, and write it [‎על on, upon, above, over] their hearts**; and will be their God, and they shall be my people.

34. And they shall teach no more every man his neighbour, and every man his brother, saying, Know the LORD: for they shall all know me, from the least of them unto the greatest of them, saith the LORD: for I will forgive their iniquity, and I will remember their sin no more.

Perhaps if we move on to the markings found on early Christian burial garments found in Fayum Egypt, you will begin to understand.

This is the Image which you saw on page 27. The first thing I want you to do is compare it to the image on the opposing page and note that they are mirror opposites.

This is the Image which you saw on page 27.

IMAGINE THE WEARER OF THE GARMENT PRESSING THEMSELVES INTO THE TREE OF LIFE
THE PLACEMENT OF THE "TOOLS" DEFINES EACH ORDINANCE

LEFT SIDE   RIGHT SIDE

compare with
Early Christian Textile Markings
found in Fayum Egypt

PERSPECTIVE :

Imagine that the Tree in the image above is a brand. Now put on the garment (opposite page), and press your chest into the tree. Just think of the garment as a veil, with a perspective from the other side.

You should have learned enough about what is in the tree to understand Paul, in Galatians 6: 17, saying, **"... I bear on my body the marks of Jesus [Yeshua]."**

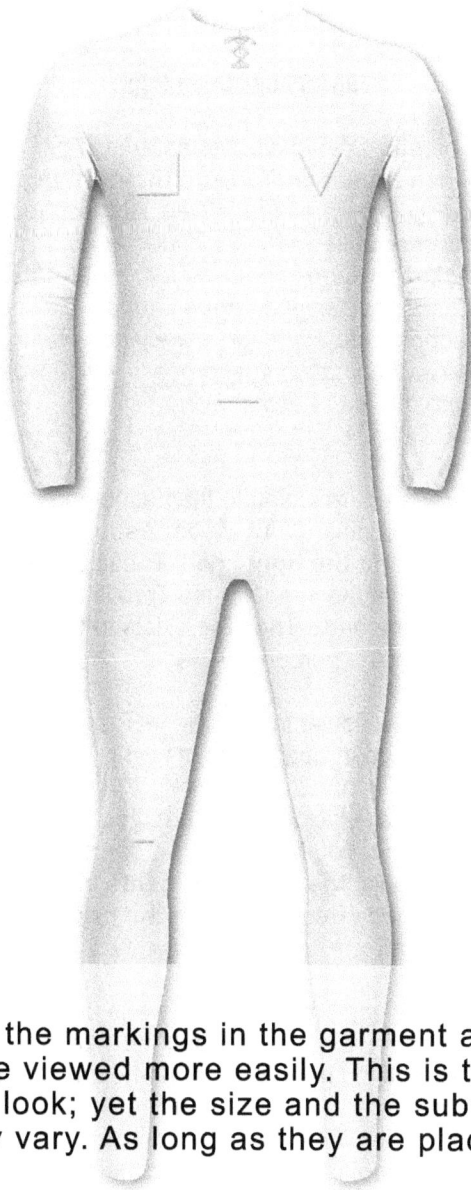

I have made the markings in the garment a little darker in order to be viewed more easily. This is the way it is supposed to look; yet the size and the subtlety of the symbols may vary. As long as they are placed correctly.

I don't want to mislead the reader as to precisely what was found in the early Christian burials in Fayum Egypt, but you must see the full pattern to recognize the pieces of the puzzle.

The following information is from . . .

"Evidences of a Christian Population in the Egyptian Fayum and Genetic and Textile Studies of the Akhmim Noble Mummies Genetic and Textile Studies of the Akhmim Noble Mummies"
https://scholarsarchive.byu.edu/cgi/viewcontent.cgi?article=2848&context=byusq

"...small rosettes have been woven into the material in particular locations. There is **one rosette over each breast and one on the right leg near the knee,** *but there is no corresponding rosette on the left leg. Across the lower abdomen, the material also has* **a hemmed slit** *about six inches long.*
Considered all together, the various items of clothing all previously unused and many containing symbols and designs, argue strongly for belief not only in an afterlife, but also for appropriate attire, most likely accompanied by or represen-tative of a multifaceted and complex ritual process which would assure safe and successful passage into the realm of the divine."

On the exterior of the garment reaching to the palms and the ankles [previous page], we see five basic symbols. What we don't see in that garment, are the **rosettes on each breast and the right knee**. These are hidden on the inside of the garment. Remember that the image of the Tree is a mirror opposite because you are looking at it from the back. The Tree exists in the garment, and its flowers bloom towards its front and the person wearing it.

These are created by the ץיצ flower in the letter צ Tzade attaching itself to specific places in the Tree. We will go through these as we go through each symbol.

For now, I would like the reader to consider that there are a total of 8 visible sym-bols [a ninth in the double knot of the neck] on a garment reaching to the palms and ankles. Of these symbols, **the burial garments hit on all three rosettes, and the line across the belly button. Half of the original markings are pres-ent in VERY specific locations.**

So this is where I went to sleep last night, and woke up with an understanding of what happened to these people buried at Fayum Egypt. The understanding which I was given was that something happened to the holders of the keys to bind and seal in heaven and earth.

The people in Fayum were doing the best they could without one with the sealing powers among them. This is more than being a Melchizedek priesthood holder. The powers to seal were given by Yeshua to the original Apostles, and passed down by them to specific individuals charged with overseeing the ordinances.

The type of garment which we are speaking about has actually been a subject with many opinions based on the word which describes it . . .

What's the Truth about . . . Joseph's "Amazing Technicolor Dreamcoat"? https://jewishaction.com/religion/jewish-thought/whats-truth-josephs-amazing-technicolor-dreamcoat/

"Rashi understands "passim" as referring to the material from which the coat was made, describing the fabric as "kli milat"; based on other statements of Rashi (Shabbat 54a, s.v. l'milat; Yechezkel 27:18, s.v. v'tzemer tzachar; and Chullin 50b, s.v. makom she'ein), "milat" is understood as clean, white wool (Maharsha, Megillah 16b, s.v. milat; Rashash, Bava Metzia 78b, s.v. batlei). Others translate pas or passim as a silk garment (Rav Saadia Gaon; Ibn Ezra to Esther 1:6 in conjunction with Megillah 12a; Rabbi Yosef Chaim miBaghdad [the Ben Ish Chai], Od Yosef Chai, 25a). Thus, one possibility is that the ketonet passim was special because of its fibers, either fine wool or silk. Such material might have been reserved for clothing worn by upper-class citizens on special occasions.

Another possibility is that the adjective "passim" is describing the garment's particular style. The singular "pas" appears in Aramaic in Daniel 5:5 (pas y'da) describing the hand King Belshazzar saw writing on the wall. In that context, pas is understood to mean the palm of the hand. Based on this, some interpret ketonet passim as **a long-sleeved garment (i.e., reaching the palm) or one reaching to the ankle**..."

"A third possibility is that "passim" means a unique pattern. Ibn Ezra (Bereishit 37:3), Ramban (Shemot 28:2), and Metzudat Tzion (II Shmuel 13:18) understand that the garment was "m'rukemet"—**embroidered with designs**, checkered or plaid. Targum Neofiti and Targum Pseudo-Jonathan say the garment had designs or pictures on it."

What's the proper translation of what Joseph's coat looks like? https://hermeneutics.stackexchange.com/questions/31354/whats-the-proper-translation-of-what-josephs-coat-looks-like

The word in question is כתנת פסים (ketonet passim). The word פסים (passim) is unclear, and only appears in the Bible in connection to the coats of Joseph and Tamar (the sister of Amnon, not the daughter-in-law of Judah) in II Samuel 13:18,19. The corresponding Aramaic word (פס) has two meanings: strip and palm. Daniel 5:5 (written in Aramaic) is an instance of the meaning "palm." Both of these meanings actually appear in Mishnaic Hebrew (עושין פסין = strips, Eruvin 2:2; פס ידו = the palm of his hand, Menachot 1:2).

The meaning "a striped coat" derives from the an interpretation of the word as "strip." The "variegated"/"many-colored coat" translation of the Septuagint (χιτῶνα ποικίλον) is apparently an interpretation of what these "stripes" were. On the other hand, the Septuagint to Samuel translates χιτῶνα τὸν καρπωτὸν, "**tunic to the wrists**," apparently understanding it to be derived from the other meaning, "palm." The explicit statement in II Samuel 13:18 that the virgin daughters of the king wore כתנת פסים, which also makes the fact that Tamar tore her "coat" after being raped more understandable. Based on Middle Assyrian laws that discuss which women are eligible to wear a veil (paṣanu, the Assyrian form of the Akkadian pasāmu, from the root psm), Heath Dewrell ("How Tamar's Veil Became Joseph's Coat," Biblica 97 pp. 161-174) proposes translating the word as "veil," which was worn by virgin daughters of the king. This translation fits the context of the story with Tamar very well, but it doesn't explain why Joseph would be wearing it..."

Some say that Joseph was given the garment of Adam. Whether it belonged to Adam or not, I think that If it was a garment of the High Priesthood after the order of Melchizedek, it would explain why Joseph's brothers were jealous. The birth-right, and the right to rule on a religious level, clearly places Joseph above his brothers, on every level... Then Joseph had to tell them about his dream.

As we go through the symbols, I'm going to throw in some quotes from the Gospels of Thomas and Phillip found in the Nag Hammadi Library. Discovered in 1945, their importance goes beyond a witness of the ordinances found in the Tree of Life. It contains sayings which move the followers of the Father to become one, in more ways than one.

"When you make the two into one, and when you make the inner like the outer and the outer like the inner, and the upper like the lower, and when you make male and female into a single one, so that the male will not be male nor the female be female, when you make eyes in place of an eye, a hand in place of a hand, a foot in place of a foot, an image in place of an image, then you will enter [the king-dom]" ... Gospel of Thomas, The Nag Hammadi Scriptures, Meyer, p. 142, 143.

We are going to begin with an overview of the n Chet, and the words belonging to that place in the tree. Then we will go just a little deeper before getting to the flower (ɣ) and its attachment to the knee position.

For now, I'd like you to note the font difference between the standard n Chet, and the one you see as an overlay ⌠⌠ on the next page.

The older letter looks like the "eye of the needle", a low covered passage through a narrow gate which a camel would have to get on its knees to go through. This is the older form of the Aramaic block letter Hebrew, so it is the one we will be using.

There is just so much here I won't have the time to get to . . . I need to keep it as simple and straightforward as possible, and move on . . .

Note that it is the n Chet [gate] on the bottom which leads to the n Chet [gate] on top.

The ח Chet is on the knee : The original letter = חֿ
This is the eye of the needle, or the gate

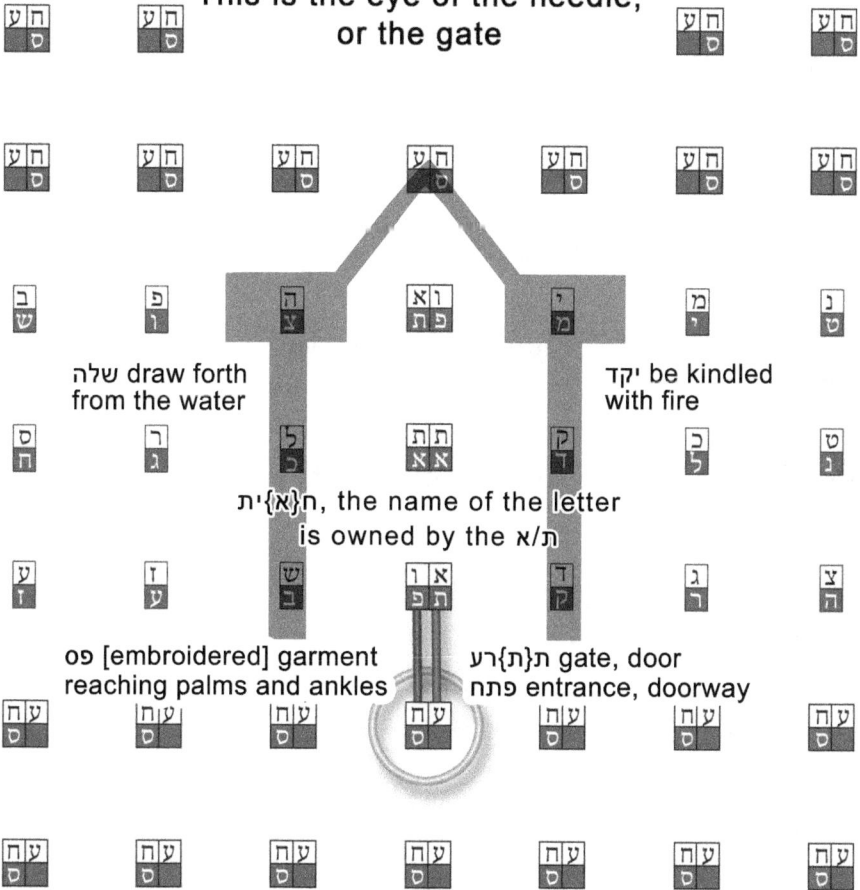

שלה draw forth from the water

יקד be kindled with fire

ח{א}ית, the name of the letter is owned by the ת/א

פס [embroidered] garment reaching palms and ankles

ערּ{ת}ע gate, door פתח entrance, doorway

Note that the name of the letter, ח{א}ית Chet, belongs to the ת/א.

The same position which has :
סף (פ) [gate, threshold, basin]
חדש (ת/א,פ,ו) new [upward compass]
ב{ב}ר{א}ית (ת/א) covenant
שו (ו) equality

Then we have a simple string going up the left side, and down the right.
שלה to draw forth from the water.
יקד to be kindled with fire. Ending on a ד Dalet whose Square is connected to the Holy Ghost.

In words which are within the letters overlay, or land on it, I see: every knee to bow and every tongue repent & confess, that Yeshua is the Messiah.

OVERLAY WORDS

כל every

בּ{בּ}רך knee

שוח bow down, bend; to walk [sm square landing on שׁ]

אבּ{בּ}רך to kneel, bow the knee [lg square landing on שׁ]

כל every

לשׁו{מ}ן tongue; language, speech [lg square landing on שׁ]

שׁ{שׁ}וב to return, to repent

ידה confess, give thanks [lg square landing on ד]

{א}ישׁוע Yeshua [sm square landing on בּ/שׁ]

המשׁיח the Messiah

מזוזה doorpost [ז,ו are in מ ; mezuzah - belongs to ב/שׁ, א/ת, ד/ק, & ח Chet overlay]

דם blood [right doorpost]

שה lamb [left doorpost]

דל door [compass ק]

משׁקוף lintel [lg square landing on מ/י - just above the ק door]

בּ{ה}ן son

אל El

צלב crucified

עץ tree, wood beam

על yoke

{ה}יתד nail ‖,

יד hand [compass ק]

רגל foot [ruler 2 ל/כ]

שׁל to put off, loose, error, offense, crime, which belongs

בך in you

מ{מ}ז{ה}רח sunrise, east [compass on top]

יקים will rise up

תקום will rise up [lg square landing on י]

ק{ק}ום will rise up

מתם wholeness, soundness; people, men [reflected ruler of 2 מ]

עולם eternity, eternal

נ{מ}ח rest

אוצ{ה}ר treasury, storehouse [ruler of 2 צ/ה]

שלה (ה,שׁ,י) draw forth from the water

מים (מ/י) water

אשׁ (ו,שׁ,י,ה) fire, foundation

יקד (ד,י,ה) be kindled with fire

שׁער (בּ/שׁ) a gate

סור (בּ/שׁ) "a turning aside", a gate of the temple

תוה (תּ/א) ד, שׁ, ה,) to make or set a mark, confession, sacrifice, giving thanks

I think we get the message... Sorry, I need to move on...

74   The Menorah Code

WORDS ENDING ON KNEE POSITION

(ח/ס) פס passover, the feast of sparing, lame [connects to gate below and above]

(ח) שׁ{ח}וֹ bow down, bend; to walk

(ח) שחח bowed down, be humbled

(ח) שׁ meditation, talk; bent, bowed

(ח/ס) כבס to wash

(ח/ס) סח to have pity, spare

(ע) כ{ב}רע to bow down

(ח) קח take

(ח/ס) פתח entrance, doorway, opening

(ע) ת{ר}ע gate, door

(ע) דע to know, knowledge

(ס) פס [embroidered] garment reaching to palms and ankles

THE FLOWER IS THE צ TZADDI ץ

(צ/ה) ציצה flower

(צ/ה) רחץ to wash, wash off or away, bathe

(צ/ה) כלה bride, to be completed

(צ) צדיק righteous

(צ) צוץ to blossom, shine

(צ) ציץ to blossom, flower, wing

(צ) ציון zion

(צ/ה) צעה to stoop, bend, incline

(צ/ה) טה{ה}ר to be clean and pure

The צ Tzaddi contains a ו Waw, and a י Yud, and can make the word צוץ blossom/shine, or ציץ flower/blossom all by itself.

When we פסח attach the צ Tzaddi [flower] to the knee [the ח Chet is on the knee], we get צח dazzling, glowing, bright, clear, pure.

Looking a little deeper, this is not just a "normal" flower. The ח Chet contains a י Yud, and can make חי "life", by itself. The צ Tzaddi also receives עץ tree, and ח{צ}י life [Rulers of 2]. This is the "Flower of Life" from the "Tree of Life".

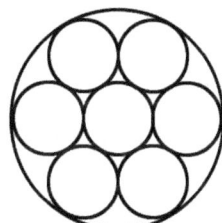

The Flower of Life symbol is symbolized as a rosette, or small flower with 6 petals.

In spite of the awesome meaning behind the צ Tzaddi being joined to the ח Chet, we should remember that the flower is the righteous bride being conducted through the gate, and *everything which that entails.*

This means repentance, baptism, and receiving the gift of the Holy Ghost. . . The bride must be made clean through the sacrifice of the Lamb of El as HIS blood stands as a witness on the lintel and door-posts of the gate. Only then can the bride take shelter in his house while our betrothed stands in the gate as our shield and protector. Only then will the destroyer pass you by, for then, you have Life in HIS death. The purchase price HE paid for his bride. This is the love which he has for those who hear his voice, repent, and come unto ישוע Yeshua [the son who is Salvation].

This symbol on the knee of the garment in question represents the gate where every knee must bow, and every tongue repent and confess that Yeshua IS the anointed son which brings salvation. It represents the gate of the Celestial Kingdom which the bride enters pure and bright. Her beauty is then as a flower which does not fade, for she has humbly received the gift of HIS life.

The "Gate", is what separates the sheep [domesticated animals] from the undomesticated animals. . . So which side of the gate are you on?

Do you understand that it is a gate, door, or entrance to something that has been hidden behind a veil?

Do you think that you can truly make the outside like the inside without allowing the spirit to conquer the flesh?

Pray always, for when your spirit follows the spirit of YHWH, your spirit becomes one with HIS. Then one day, you will realize that it is the connection between your spirit, and the spirit of the Almighty which has allowed your spirit to subdue the flesh. This is the goal.

The flesh is an animal disconnected from its spirit. The new man, or woman, born of the water and the spirit, must have a spirit at peace with the flesh. Then the outside may become as the inside, and the real you will begin to shine through. Only then can you truly embark on the path to know yourself, and remember who you really are.

When you begin your journey in contrite prayer . . . your emotions . . . your feelings . . . and that which you know to be true in your heart will become magnified. Your heart will swell and burn with the fire of the Holy Ghost as your mind is led to answers and you are compelled to utter words which are not your own. This is the beginning of the path. Let the Spirit guide you toward the light, and you will know the truth with every fiber of your being.

I am just a messenger. You must become the ג Gimmel, the follower of the Father who takes his hand. You must find your answers in contrite prayer. HIS Sheep will hear his voice guiding them to Salvation. No MAN can do this for you. Hearing his voice speaking to your heart is not an option, it is a requirement.

Why haven't you heard about any of this? . . .

"The multitude professing Christianity were therefore divided by them into the "profane," or those who were not yet admitted to the mysteries, and the "initiated," or faithful and perfect. . . and as none were permitted to be present at these "mysteries," as they were termed, save those whose admission into the fellowship of the church was perfect and complete, so likewise was it expected that, as a matter of duty, the most sacred silence should be observed in regard to everything connected with the celebration of them, and nothing whatever relating thereto to be committed to the ears of the profane." Johann L Moshrim, Historical Commentaries on the State of Christianity, Vol 1, (New York; S. Converse, 1854), p390-391.

Did you know that "Esoteric" ordinances were discontinued before 350 AD and books with these teachings were burned prior to 367? [The powers of "Rome" didn't like "Christians", whom they claimed to embrace, practicing things in secret]. Cyril of Jerusalem (350 AD) began writing down parts of these practices, such as the anointing segment of the endowment. "As soon, then, as ye entered, ye put off your tunic; and this was an image of putting off the old man with his deeds. Then, ye were anointed with exorcised oil from the very hairs of your head to your feet, and were made partakers of the good olive-tree, Jesus Christ."; "The ointment is symbolically applied to thy forehead and thy other senses, and while thy body is anointed with the visible ointment, thy soul is sanctified by the Holy and life-giving Spirit. And ye were first anointed on the forehead . . . Then on your ears: that ye might receive the ears which are quick to hear the Divine Mysteries. . . Then on the nostrils. . . Afterwards on your breast: that having put on the breast-plate of righteousness, ye may stand against the wiles of the devil . . ." The initiate was given a new name after receiving inner clothing. [Note: It is the anointing from which the word "Christian" applied to the members, not just that they were followers of "Christ"="Messiah"="Anointed"]

Then you have the Christians in upper Egypt hiding their "Esoteric" scriptures behind the wall in a synagogue [Nag Hammadi]. If not for the fact that they remained hidden until 1945, they would have been destroyed as well.

Did you know that early Orthodox Christians and Coptic Christians practiced Baptism for the Dead? [Else what shall they do which are baptized for the dead, if the dead rise not at all? why are they then baptized for the dead? 1 Cor. 15:29]

Did you know that Theosis and Divinization was held to be a valid "Christian" belief until the 5th Century? [Rom. 8:17; 1 John 3:2; Revelation 3:21; etc.].

Did you know that a pre-mortal existence was doctrine until 543?

Why haven't you heard about any of this? Because your Mother was a Whore, and the Mouth of the Serpent has blinded you. The eradication of the fullness of the gospel, and those who practiced it, had to be as thorough as possible to establish her alleged orthodoxy.

Square / Flower on Right Breast

TOK TOL

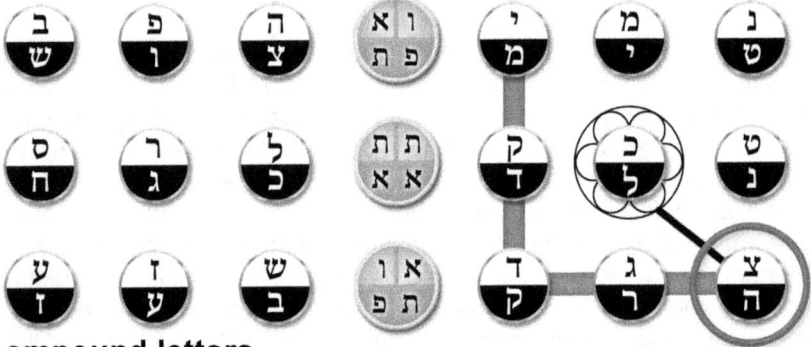

compound letters

[(א)= ו,י][(ב)= ו,ר][(ג)= ו,י,(ז?)*][(ד)= ו][(ה)= ו,י,ר][(ז)= ו,י]
[(ח)= ו,י,(ז?)*][(ט)= ו,י][(כ)= ו,י,ר][(ל)= ו,י][(מ)= ז,ג,ו,י][(נ)= ו,י]
[(ס)= ו][(ע)= ו,י][(פ)= ו,י,(כ,ר?)*][(צ)= ו,י][(ק)= ו,י][(ר)= ו]
[(ש)= ו][(ת)= ו,ר]

I'm now entering an area which I have no intention of going into more detail. I'm sorry, but I recognize these things because I am what would have been referred to as "initiated". Those who have been through the ordinances in an LDS Temple will recognize many of these words and be able to figure out what goes where, and what other words to look up. There is, however, an oath taken here, and I am not comfortable going beyond what you will see here.

As a little added bonus, I added words which appear in Isaiah 28. It is regarding those who have been weaned from their mother's breast. The full import of this must be taken as part of the ג Gimmel, the follower, being weaned from his mother's breast and taking the Father's hand. . . a comment on the growth experienced in going from an infant to a toddler.

It should be noted that many of these words will not show letters taken from compound letters listed. Also, that this square, belonging to the צ Tzaddi is listing naturally occurring words within that square, AND relevant words landing on it.

"The tree of life, however, is in the middle of the garden. It is an olive tree, and from it comes chrism, and from chrism comes resurrection." . . . "Chrism is superior to baptism. We are called Christians from the word 'chrism', not from the word 'baptism'. Christ also has his name from chrism, for the Father anointed the Son, the Son anointed the apostles, and the apostles anointed us. Whoever is anointed has everything: resurrection, light, cross, Holy Spirit. The Father gave all this to the person in the bridal chamber, and the person accepted it. The Father was in the Son and the Son was in the Father. This is heaven's kingdom."
Gospel of Thomas, The Nag Hammadi Scriptures, Meyer, p. 178.

THE SQUARE

(מ/י) חיים [lands on LG (ה/צ) sq.] life

(מ/י) חדש [lands on LG (מ/י) sq.] new

(מ/י) שם name [in LG (מ/י) sq.]

(מ/י) זבד endowment, gift [in LG (מ/י) sq.]

(מ/י) מאד power [(מ/י) compass]

(מ/י) שמן oil, anointing [in LG (מ/י) sq.]

(מ/י) ראש [in LG sq.] head

(מ, ה/צ) שד [in LG sq.] breast

(מ/י) דדי [in LG sq.] breast, teat, nipple

(מ/י) שפה [lands on LG sq.] lip, speech, edge

(מ/י) ימני right hand

(מ/י) אזן an ear [R2]

(מ/י) בהן thumb, big toe [lands on large (מ/י) square]

(מ/י) פז refined, pure gold [R2]

(מ/י) לבש [lands on LG sq.] to put on, wear, clothe, be clothed

(מ/י) לבוש [lands on LG sq.] a garment

(מ/י) שית [in LG sq.] a garment

(ק) דל door

(ק) דק veil

(ק) יד hand

(ק) ילד son

(ק/ד) חק covenant, statute, decreed, commandment [R2]

(ק/ד) קדקד head, crown of the head

(ק/ד) מדה garment

(ק/ד) דמה to cause to cease, cut off, destroy

(ד) מד measure, garment

(ד) גדד to penetrate, cut

(ד) קד to rend

(ד) חד one

(ד) דוח to rinse, cleanse, wash, cast out, purge [in small sq.]

(ר/ג) גן garden [LG sq.]

(ר/ג) מגן shield, protector [LG sq.]

(ר/ג) גזר to cut, divide

(ר/ג) מצדד follower [compass]

(ר/ג) עדה congregation [compass]

(ה/צ) מצדד follower

צדיק (ה/צ) righteous
מדקרה (ה/צ) piercing
גרון (ק/ד, ה/צ) neck, throat
רחץ (ה/צ) to wash, wash off or away, bathe
נזר (ת/א, ה/צ) consecration, crown, Naziriteship
נזור (ת/א, ה/צ) one consecrated, devoted
גמל (ר/ג) to wean [camel, name of letter - ג Gimmel] [LG sq.]
אם (מ/י) mother [R2]
שד (צ/ה, מ/י) [in LG sq.] breast

I am only revealing words which those who have been initiated will recognize. They will be able to look up missing words, which they know go there, and stitch the square together.

The point of this exercise is to show that these ordinances belonged to these symbols since the time before time. They are eternal.

THE FLOWER
צל (ל/כ) shadow, shade, shelter, defense, protection
מיכל (ל/כ) Michael
כלל (ל/כ) to complete, perfect
סוך (ל/כ) to pour - in anointing, anoint // 123 down
הלך (ל/כ) to go, come, walk
יצהר (ה/צ) anointed oil

The righteous follower of the Father receives the golden oil of the Tree of Life as a golden crown of life on their head. The Flower of Life, becomes a Crown.

TOK   TOL

compound letters

[(א)= י,ו][(ב)= ו,ר][(ג)=י,י,(ז?)*][(ד)= ו][(ה)= ר,י,ו][(ז)= י,ו]
[(ח)= י,י,(ז?)*][(ט)= י,ו][(כ)= ר,י,ו][(ל)= ו,י][(מ)= י,ו,ג,ז][(נ)= י,ו]
[(ס)= ו][(ע)= י,ו][(פ)= ו,י,י,(ר,כ.?)*][(צ)= י,ו][(ק)= י,ו][(ר)= ו,ו]
[(ש)= ו][(ת)= ו,ר]

I have been searching for words which I know are supposed to go in these places. In this case, we can recognize the story with very little information, yet only the women will recognize this drama in the Temple.

THE COMPASS

(ה) פה mouth, speech, saying, command
(ה) יהוה YHWH
(ה) פה mouth, speech, saying, command
(ה/צ) צר enemy, adversary, distress, trouble
(ש) נחש serpent
(ה) חוה Eve
(ה) ערה to be naked
(ז/ע) זוע, עז to tremble, quake

There is far more here than I have listed. I just don't have the time to break down more than this . . . Those who know will recognize it.

THE FLOWER

צר (א/ת, ה/צ, ג/ר) enemy, adversary, distress, trouble, rock, flint, Syr. he bound, tied, he constrained, restricted

צרר (א/ת, ה/צ, ג/ר) to bind, tie up, be restricted; to be sharp, flint knife

שר (א/ת, ה/צ, ג/ר) umbilical cord

שרר (א/ת, ה/צ, ג/ר) navel

The Flower : Only those old enough to remember the LDS garment, before it was changed, will understand it.

For those who are only interested in the connection between the symbols in the tree, and the symbols found on the burial garments in Egypt. . . I'm sorry, but they are definitely connected to the sacred garment.

To the many people who have not completed the ordinances in the tree, I'm sorry again. I can relay enough information for those who recognize the ordinances, and the associated symbols, but these ordinances are sacred, and belong to the Temple.

Line Across the Navel

TOK TOL

compound letters

[(א)= ו,י][(ב)= ו,ר,י][(ג)= ו,י,(ז?)*][(ד)= ו][(ה)= ו,י,ר][(ז)= ו,י]

[(ח)= ו,י,(ז?)*][(ט)= ו,י][(כ)= ו,ר,י][(ל)= ו,י][(מ)= י,ו,ג,ז][(נ)= ו,י]

[(ס)= ו][(ע)= ו,י][(פ)= ו,י,(כ,ר?)*][(צ)= ו,י][(ק)= ו,י][(ר)= ו]

[(ש)= ו][(ת)= ו,ר]

The line across the navel appears to belong to the scale in the center. Yet I could be wrong, it could actually belong to the ק Kuf, the דק veil. Why do I say this? because a circle with a line going through it is also an ancient Paleo-Hebrew symbol for the letter ק Kuf. Yet this could just be an indicator of an oath to cross the veil.

The שת{ת}ר{ת}ר "navel", however, is where the מאזנים scales [sm sq. also in the hand (מ/י) of the שדי Almighty] reside. Those who go towards the "right hand" are blessed, while those who go towards the "left" are cursed.

This is an oath. We see the Aramaic Hebrew word קתל "to slay" in a string for those going from right to left.

I can easily see the יד hand of the ילד "son" at the דק veil on the right, and the "sons of darkness" in words attached to the ל Lamed on the left.

This line, however, appears to have a clue hidden in the description, "**a hemmed slit**". It seems that they took a cutting instrument, made a slit, and sewed it up. . . and that's the only additional clue that you will get from me at this time. Not that the content should be hidden, but something you will find in the sign.

Lace (compass) facing Right

TOK TOL

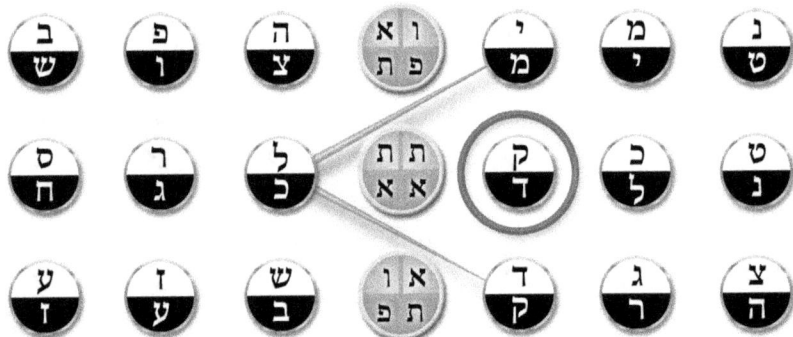

compound letters

[(א)= י,י] [(ב)= ר,ו] [(ג)= י,י,(ז?)*] [(ד)= ו] [(ה)= ר,י,י] [(ז)= י,י]

[(ח)= י,י,(ז?)*] [(ט)= י,ר] [(כ)= ר,י,י] [(ל)= ו,י] [(מ)= י,ו,ג,ז] [(נ)= י,ו]

[(ס)= ו] [(ע)= י,ו] [(פ)= כ,ר,(ר,כ)?*] [(צ)= י,ו] [(ק)= י,ו] [(ר)= ו]

[(ש)= ו] [(ת)= ו,ר]

Here the target is definitely the ק Kuf. The theme overlaps the Line Across the Navel and belongs to the veil.

So many things which I have mentioned so far belong to this tool: The blood of the lamb on the door [that which allows our return], the son of David, son of man, lion of Judah, lamb of El, the hand and the nail in the תו Taw, sign [Paleo-Hebrew cross].

אות (מ/י) sign [in small (מ/י) sq.]

אחז (מ/י) [sm. sq. top] to grasp, take hold, take possession

יד (ה/צ, ק/ד, מ/י) hand

בן (מ/י) son

דק (ה/צ, ק/ד, מ/י) veil

ברית (מ/י) a covenant [in LG (מ/י) sq.]

יתד (ד) tent peg, nail [R3]

אחד (ד) to make, create, or become one, to unite [in small sq.]

אל (ל) EL [short form Elohim]

מיכל (ד/ק) Michael [compass]

Lace (compass) facing Left

TOK TOL

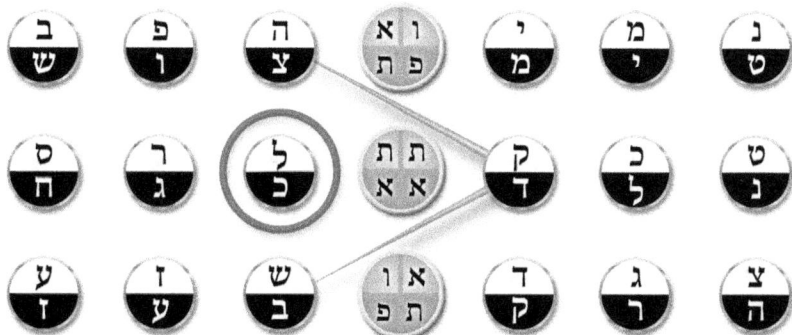

compound letters

[(א)= י,ו][(ב)= ו,ר][(ג)= י,ו,(ז?)*][(ד)= ו][(ה)= ר,י,ו][(ז)= י,ו]
[(ח)= י,ו,(ז?)*][(ט)= י,ו][(כ)= ר,י,ו][(ל)= י,ו][(מ)= י,ו,ג,ז][(נ)= י,ו]
[(ס)= ו][(ע)= י,ו][(פ)= ו,י,(כ,ר?)*][(צ)= י,ו][(ק)= י,ו][(ר)= ו]
[(ש)= ו][(ת)= ו,ר]

This theme also overlaps the Line Across the Navel, but it belongs to those who go to the left after coming to the veil. This is the covenant penalty of מות "death" and שאול "hell" [LG sq. ending on (ב/ש)] which Isaiah speaks of in chapter 28. חשך darkness belongs to the (כ/ל) [3up], but I believe that בני "sons" [LG sq. ending on (ב/ש)] are added to that by the compass (sons of darkness).

(כ/ל) שקר deception, liar, falsehood, disappointment
(כ/ל) קשה hard, severe
(כ/ל) קש chaff, stubble [עור, ששש חשם = chaff x3 on left]
(כ/ל) קצץ cut off
(כ/ל) קצה to cut off
(י,ה,ו) שדד **destroy**, deal violently with, devastate, ruin
(ש) שחת **destroy**, go to ruin
(ב/ש) כרת to cut off, cut down

TOK   TOL

compound letters

[י,ו =(ז)][י,ו =(ו)][ר,י,י =(ה)][(ד)= ו][*(?ז),ו,י =(ג)][ר,ו =(ב)][י,ו =(א)]

[י,ו =(נ)][י,נ,ג,ז =(מ)][י,ו =(ל)][ר,י,י =(כ)][י,ו =(י) *(?ז),י,י =(ט)][י,ו =(ח)]

[י,ו =(ס)][י,ו =(ע)][י,י,ו =(פ)][*(?ר,כ),ו,י =(צ)][י,ו =(ק)][ו =(ר)]

[ר,ו =(ת)][ו =(ש)]

THE DOUBLE אגדה KNOT אחד אחד [TARGET = ∧ א ALEPH POSITION TOP]

חפף (פ) to surround, cover [under the cover]

חפה (צ/ה) to cover, bridal chamber [of the chuppah (bridal chamber)]

מקדוש (מ/י) temple

קדוש קדושים (מ/י) Holy of Holies

קדש (פ/ו, מ/י, צ/ה) set apart, consecrated, clean, holy

חף (פ) to be pure, innocent [standing in the center (א/ת)]

כתר (ת/א) a crown [R2]

אשה (ב/ש, צ/ה) wife

כלה (צ/ה) bride

קדם (מ/י) to come or be in front, meet

חתן (מ/י) bridegroom

איש (ב/ש, מ/י, צ/ה) husband

אחד (ד, מ/י, צ/ה) to become one, to unite

בשר (ב/ש, מ/י, צ/ה) flesh

שלב (ב/ש, צ/ה) to be bound or joined

ודבק (מ/י, צ/ה) and be joined

ראי (מ/י) mirror [in front of you]

מראה (צ/ה) a mirror, a vision [and a mirror behind you reflects the eternal iteration of lives together - place yourself in א Aleph position]

חיים (מ/י) the plural of חי life [eternal lives]

עד (ד, מ/י, צ/ה) eternity, everlasting, world[s] without end

ברית (מ/י) a covenant [in LG (מ/י) sq.]

עונה (ת/א) marital duty, cohabitation

קבל (צ/ה) to receive

כבוד (צ/וו) splendor, glory

נזר (ת/א) crown, consecration, set apart, hair

מנזר (ת/א) consecrated ones, princes, crowned

נזיר (ת/א) one set apart, consecrated - as a prince, Nazarite

כתר (ת/א) crown, circlet, diadem

תפארה (צ/ה) beauty, glory

"And when the king came in to see the guests, he saw there a man which had not on a wedding garment: And saith unto him, Friend, how camest thou in hither not having a wedding garment? And he was speechless. Then said the king to the servants, Bind him hand and foot, and take him away, and cast him into outer darkness; there shall be seeping and gnashing of teeth. For many are called, but few are chosen." Matthew 22: 11-14

Now we move down to verses 23-30 where the Sadducees ask a question about a woman married seven times, and which husband she would be married to in the resurrection. Yeshua tells them none, for "**in the resurrection** they neither marry, nor are given in marriage."

So how does this square with the gospel of Philip which speaks of this mirrored bridal chamber saying, "A woman is united with her husband in the bridal chamber, and those united in the bridal chamber will not be separated again." . . . The gospel of Philip explains it towards the end. "If someone becomes an attendant of the bridal chamber, that person will receive the light. **If one does not receive it while here in this place, one cannot receive it in the other place.**"
   The question regarding the woman under the Mosaic Law was answered correctly. This covenant REQUIRES that the man be a Melchizedek Priesthood holder. A higher Priesthood and law, with a higher reward had among a people who would be priests and kings of the Most High. That is something that YHWH has wanted for the house of Israel for a very long time.

In the mirrored bridal chamber you have a mirror before you, and a mirror behind you. Look into the iterations in your reflections, and ponder which one you are in.

It has been more than 25 years since I went through the Temple. I'm undoubtedly forgetting things, along with the things which had been removed before I went through. Yet I understand, from the symbols in the tree, what has been removed.

NOTE TO THE READER :

Beyond this point, you enter the realm of the foundation which the code sits on.

I hope that in the near future I will be able to have a computer program written which will put together all of the pieces which belong to each tool. Completing this foundation is required before truly finishing off the things uncovered in this book.

Check themenorahcode.com website for the latest information.

Chapter 4 : The Aleph-Bet

This section will show you which tools belong to each location in the Matrix.

While I will be pointing out some of the things found in the letter overlays, I only have a few overlays in a satisfactory state of decryption. Most of this is a work in progress. I showed you what I had for the נ Mem overlay in the rules section, but other than that, you will be left with a great puzzle to work on.

What has not been noted in the "Rules" section is that if you do a letter overlay from a letter with an extension [ל, ק and final form letters ך, ן, ף, ץ], the extension touches letters in the [n/o/ע] section. These connections are added to letters beneath the overlay, while other letters, no longer covered by the overlay, will be excluded. This being the case, I would look for differences between the two sets of letters to see if the overlays are to be read together, or separately.
Sorry, the vast majority of my time has been spent back-engineering the code, and sifting through the dictionary to test it. If you have no other resources, I include these things so *you can search words in this text* [e-book available online].

Extension letters may also contribute to that letter's "Tool" values as a ruler of 2. words connected to the [n/o/ע] and ending on that extension letter should be examined.

For example, if the final ן Nun is being used in a word, I would look at the set of [n/o/ע] letters which the final ן Nun touches, and is not present when using a regular נ Nun. I would also suggest examining the meaning in the overlay.

Why? Because the Menorah Trees of Knowledge and Life give letters their meanings, and the letters define the words which are made from them. This will be important for those who wish to back-engineer the ORIGINAL Language, or settle a debate over the true meaning of a word. For most people trying to work the code, it is only important to understand the concept.
The coding comes from an intelligence far beyond my comprehension. Even with all of the "hints", HE made me work the code to understand how it worked.
How is it possible? I have looked into what it might take for a complete break-down and can only conclude that the information encoded in the Menorah's 22 letters, would literally take volumes of books to completely lay it all out.

If you decide you would like to give it a try, but you don't have a good Biblical Hebrew Dictionary, try this. Go to biblehub.com and switch to the HEBREW search. You can type in Hebrew Letters; or type in English, and if that English word appears in a Hebrew word definition, it will pop up.

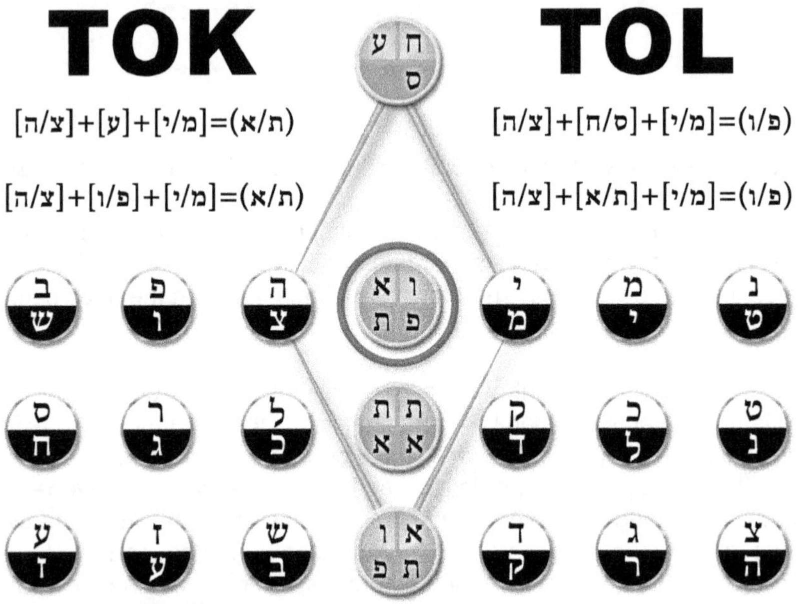
TOK
TOL
[צ/ה]+[ע]+[מ/י]=(ת/א)
[צ/ה]+[ס/ח]+[מ/י]=(פ/ו)
[צ/ה]+[פ/ו]+[מ/י]=(ת/א)
[צ/ה]+[ת/א]+[מ/י]=(פ/ו)

compound letters

[(א)= י,ו][(ב)= ר,ו][(ג)= י,ו,(ז?)*][(ד)= ו][(ה)= ר,י,ו][(ז)= י,ו]
[(ח)= י,ו,(ז?)*][(ט)= י,ו][(כ)= ר,י,ו][(ל)= י,ו][(מ)= י,ו,נ,ז][(נ)= י,ו]
[(ס)= ו][(ע)= י,ו][(פ)= י,ו,(ר,כ?)*][(צ)= י,ו][(ק)= י,ו][(ר)= ו]
[(ש)= ו][(ת)= ר,ו]

To get you started, I'm going to cut and paste some old work. This means that most of it won't have any de-constructed compound letters. What you see next was only for the א Aleph.

Remember, these are unfinished sections with notes inserted to myself.

Note : I have done so much work in notes on paper, and looked so deeply into the Aleph, most of that is not written. . . and sections which I did write Aleph comments on will be omitted. I have not brought you along far enough to grasp these things. This is something which you need to search out for yourself.

אלף **א** Aleph

Dictionary : oxen, bullocks, cows, cattle (notice it is in the plural); domesticated animals; part of a tribe; אחד ONE; 1000

Made from : the (י) Yud, the (ו) Waw, and the "foreleg" of the (ה) Hei in the upwards facing compass which defines the letter. An interesting note is that the Jews say that the Aleph is made from the (ו) Waw and two (י) Yuds. This is also true as the (י) Yud is defined as : hand, forearm, or "foreleg".

However, the intrinsic meaning within the (א) Aleph is a representation of (יהוה) YHWH. This being said, the (י) Yud, without the (ה) Hei, cannot be (יה) Yah, and the (י) Yud and (ו) Waw without the (ה) Hei would not be (יהוה) YHWH.

We must therefore conclude that while it may technically be two (י) Yuds, the (י) Yud, the (ו) Waw, and the (ה) Hei, from the compass which defines the letter, must be the definition used in order to reference YHWH who was, and is, and is to come.

Confirmation is found within the (א) Aleph used as a prefix meaning, **"I will"**; this comes from the main set of letters within the V compass (ו,ה,י) plus the target being defined, the "א" Aleph. Simply put, I see (אהיה) **"I AM"** with a (ו) Waw on the end. The (ו) Waw being a suffix which changes the tense [to future in this case]. (אהיהו) = **"I will"**.

Later we will see that the name (אלף) Aleph is found within the crossing (ו) Waw, in the Tree of Life Aleph overlay, which appears to tell a story of Adam and Eve.

The Aleph's Definitions are actually pretty simple in this section. However, we will also be looking at the Alephs as they appear in other configurations.

Note : We are only using the letters with the white background, the bowls, or flower petals of the Almond tree.

Tool Tables :

I am going to begin with the downward facing compass from the Tree of Knowledge in order to make a few comments before proceeding with the rest of the tools.

∧ Compass :
- The first 4 are in the ∧ Compass as well as the V Compass.

(הה) alas!

(היה) to be, exist, happen, become, was, existed, became, it came to pass

(יהי) will be

(יה) Yah [short form of YHWH]

-

(יע) shovel [for cleaning the altar]

(יעה) to sweep together and carry away; shovel

(עי) heap of stones [associated with ruins, or rubble]

Full mix צ,ע,מ,י,ה

1(הה) alas! [also Hei]

1(היה) to be, exist, happen, become, was, existed, became, it came to pass [also Waw]

3(הם) they [also Dalet] [A/T]

3(המה) to murmur, growl, roar [Arab. it went astray - said of camels without herdsmen] [also Dalet] [A/T]

3(המיה) sound, noise [also Dalet] [A/T]

3(המם) to make a noise, confuse [also Dalet] [A/T]

1(יה) Yah [short form of YHWH] [also Dalet]

3(ים) sea; lake; large basin, reservoir; west [also Yud]

3(ימים) days, year [also Yud]

1(יע) shovel [for cleaning the altar] [also Ayin]

1(יעה) to sweep together and carry away; shovel [A]

3(יעץ) to advise, give counsel [A/T]

3(יצע) to lay, spread, Aram. he laid, he expounded [A/T]

3(מהה) to linger, tarry; to be worn out, be shabby, be tattered [A/T]

3(מהם) what are they?; from them [A/T]

3(מי) who?; whoever; someone, anyone [also Yud]

3(מים) water; to mix with water, to hydrate [also Yud/Mem]

3(מימים) long since [also Yud/Mem]

3(מיץ) squeezing, pressing [A/T]

3(מעה) grain [A/T]

3(מעי) bowels, intestines; heap of stones, ruin [also Yud, Taw]

3(מעים) bowels, intestines [also Yud]

2(מעם) from [away from being together with] [also Yud, Taw]

2(מץ) oppressor; chaff [also Atbash Taw, Atbash Kuf]

3(מצה) unleavened bread; strife, contention [A/T]

2(מצמץ) to suck, lick; to blink, wink [also Atbash Taw, Atbash Kuf]

2(מצע) couch, bed; to be in the middle; to spread on a couch [also Taw]

2(מצץ) to suck [also Taw, Kuf]
1(עי) ruin, heap of ruins [also Yud]
3(עים) strength; glow [also Yud/Mem] [A/T]
2(עם) people; kinsman, relative; together with, with; close to, beside; as long as, while [also Mem, Taw]
3(עמה) to be dark, to be dim, to be weak; joining, connection [A/T]
2(עמם) to darken, to dim; to join, connect [also Mem]
2(עמעם) to dim, darken, obscure [also Mem]
2(עמץ) to close [the eyes] [also Taw, Kuf]
2(עץ) tree; timber, wood; handle [also Tzaddi]
3(עצה) to close the eyes; to convert into wood, lignify; wood; spine, backbone; counsel, advice; plan [A/T]
2(עצם) to be strong, be mighty, be powerful, to be numerous; to close the eyes; to break a bone; bone; force, might, power; bones [also Taw]
3(עצמה) force, might, power [A/T]
3(צי) ship, boat [pl. ציים]; wild animal(s) [living in deserts] [A/T?]
3(ציה) dryness, drought; dry country, desert [A/T]
3(ציץ) to bloom, blossom, flower; to look at, glance; to twitter, chirp; to furnish with fringes; blossom, flower; a shining plate of gold; ornament; wing [A/T]
3(ציצה) blossom, flower [A/T]
2(צם) he fasted [also Taw, Kuf]
3(צמה) lock, plait; woman's veil [A/T]
3(צמים) snare, trap [A/T]
2(צמם) to press, draw together [also Taw, Kuf]
2(צמצם) to press, reduce, contract [also Taw, Kuf]
3(צעה) to stoop, bend, incline [also Hei] [A/T]
2(צעצע) to adorn, ornament [also Ayin]

Make a mental note of the "(עי) heap of stones" [adding the ה, a prefix for "the"] = העי 'The' heap of stones, in the shape of a pyramid [the compass]. The letters in that compass are the [(ע) Ayin] "Eye" of (יה) "Yah". This is where the symbol of the eye in the pyramid came from.

That's right, a symbol which was originally part of the Holy Tree of Eternal Life is currently being used by a group which most would agree is evil at its core. Well guess what? We will find that **many symbols** within the Tree of Eternal Life are used by groups which had lost the knowledge of the meanings within the tree long ago, and become "apostate".

Usurpation by deception is the "Modus Operandi" of the father of all lies and his minions.

"The rulers wanted to fool people, since they say that people have a kinship with what is truly good. They took the names of the good and assigned them to what is not good, to fool people with names and link the names to what is not good. So, as if they are doing people a favor, they take names from what is not good and transfer them to the good, in their own way of thinking. For they wished to take free people and enslave them forever."
The Gospel of Philip, The Archons 54, 18-31

יהוה YHWH is the fountain of Truth, Knowledge, and Eternal Life. The Menorah is a coded gift with the fullness of the gospel. A gift of LIGHT preserved for us in these last days of darkness and confusion. For the House of my Father is NOT a house divided against itself. It is NOT a house of a thousand doctrines. It is NOT a house of the blind groping in the dark. It is a house of light and perfection.

If you are following a man claiming to be a Shepherd or Prophet, you are follow-ing because you are blind. Ask the Father of All to guide you. Ask in the name of the true mediator between the Father and mortal men, the name of Salvation = ישוע = Yeshua. For you will soon come to understand why David proclaimed that YHWH has become my Salvation. He is my strength and my song!

Pray to know all things that you should do, that you might feel HIS fire in your heart bearing witness of HIS truth. Fill your lamps and ask to see the light, until that light catches fire in your eyes and shines as the light of his Menorah in the darkness. Become that people made up of Priests and Kings of the Most High. Follow your Father which is in Heaven, the true "Holy Father", and LIVE, לחיים !

Ruler of 2 :
(לא) no, not
(קא) vomit
(הא) lo!, behold! [This link, with the letter "הא" Hei named, is "part of the Aleph"]
(תא) Room, compartment (especially in the temple)

NOTE : LOOK AT THE Taw / Aleph after finishing the lists.

V Compass :
(הוי) alas!, woe!
(הה) alas!
(הו) alas!
(וו) Waw : nail (associated with a son, and creator - also holds up the veil.)
(יהיו) was
(הוה) that you may be; become; to fall; to be; ruin; disaster
(היה) to be, exist, happen, become, was, existed, became, it came to pass
(היהו) will be, will exist, will happen, will become, it will come to pass
(יהיה) it shall be, will be, will become, will have
(יהי) will be, let there be, let, become, is as
(יה) Yah [short form of YHWH]
(יהוה) YHWH

SAVE THESE NOTES FOR OVERLAY DECRYPTION :
Additional Definitions : (from Aleph overlay words, and use in Biblical Hebrew)
1. create, creator, creates
2. a son, son of Yah (from the same diagonal ו Waw that describes the creator)

Note : both of these definitions appear to be used in the (ו) Waw because of this. Remember, this comes from the (ו) Waw tilted to the left in the Aleph Overlay with relevant selections from the word lists of those three letters.

(ה) the mouth, [of] the lamb, to declare, life -

(ת) to decree, light, -

(ד) the offspring, [of] Yah, door, my glory, the hand, [of] power.

RE-CHECK AFTER RE-DOING ALL LETTERS!!

Examining the overlay :

Let's begin by explaining what I see, according to the rules, with words beneath the overlay of the Aleph. This is like a puzzle where you try to find all of the words which are made from the letters beneath the giant Aleph over the grid. [LETTERS WITH WHITE BACKGROUND ONLY]

You will see how these overlay words become a piece of text as we divide them up into relevant categories. This makes the story come together much easier than just looking at a long list.

Overlay words [See large א in graphic over grid] : א ד ה ו י ל ק ש ת

(אד) mist, vapor, gas

(אדה) to bring about, to cause; to evaporate

0(אדוק) attached to, fastened to; pious, devout, religious, observant

(אדק) to attach, fasten, connect

(אדש) to be indifferent; Aram. he was silent

(אהה) woe! alas! ah!

(אהי) where

(אהיה) I AM - [name of the (ו) Waw in Tree of Life]

(אהל) to pitch a tent, to dwell in a tent; tent, shelter; tabernacle; dwelling, habitation

0(או) or

0(אוד) to bend; to oppress; brand, firebrand

0(אדות, אודות) cause (?), inducement (?)

0(אוה) to desire, long for

0(אוי) woe!, alas!

0(אויה) woe!, alas!

0(אויל) foolish, silly, stupid; a fool

0(אוילי) foolish, silly, stupid

0(אול) to be in front; to be strong; health, sound; to be foolish

0(אולי) perhaps, maybe

0(אוש) to make a noise; Aram. he made a noise, shouted

0(אושש) to rustle

0(אות) sign, signal, symbol, token; miracle; to consent, agree; to signal

(אי) coast, region; island; not; where?; jackal, goblin; woe!, alas!

(איד) to vaporize, to steam

(איה) hawk, falcon, kite; where?

(איל) ram; head, chief, leader; projecting pillar; hart, stag, deer; power, strength; help

(אילה) hind, doe

0(אילות) power, strength

(איש) man; husband; masculine; hero; everyone, each one, anyone, anybody

(אית) to spell a word

(אל) EL (Elohim); not; nothing; power; to, unto, toward, into, at, by

(אלה) an oath, to swear, curse; an oak; these; God, god; to wail, lament; obligation by oath

0(אלהות) divinity

0(אלה, אלוה) Elohim, diety

(אלי) my God; to, into, towards

(אליה) fat tail (of sheep); lobe (of ear)

(אליל) idol, false god; no value, worthless

(אלל) to be weak; to spy out

(אללי) woe! alas!

0(אקו) wild goat, ibex

(אש) fire: [Strongs 787] foundation

(אשד) to pour; Syr. he poured out; waterfall, cascade

(אשדה) slope of a mountain; waterfall

(אשה) woman, wife; offering made by fire

(אשיה) pillar; foundation, base

(אשישה) raisin-cakes

(אשל) tamarisk

(אשש) to strengthen; take courage

(את) untranslatable mark of the accusative; you, thou; with; plowshare

(אתה) to come; to address a person familiarly; you, thou

(אתת) to signal; sign, signs

(דא) this

(דאה) to fly, to glide (in the air); a bird of prey

(דד) breast, teat, nipple

(דדה) to move slowly; walk

(דהה) to fade, become dim; JAram. אדיה he made weak or faint

0(דוד) David; beloved; uncle; kettle; a large basket

0(דודי, דודא) mandragora, mandrake

0(דודה) aunt

0(דוה) to be ill, unwell, sick, faint

0(דוי) illness, sickness; very ill, very sick

0(דוק) to consider, be exact

0(דוש) to tread, thresh; to pedal, treadle

0(דות) pit, cistern

(די) sufficiency, enough; who, which, that; of; about

(דיה) a bird of prey, the kite

0(דיו) ink

0(דיק) bulwark, siege wall [related to Syr. דוקא lookouts, watchtowers]; to be exact, be precise

(דיש) threshing

(דית) to sweat, to exude; to ink

(דל) door: poor; thin, lean; powerless, low, weak

(דלדל) to weaken, loosen, impoverish; to hang down, dangle

(דלה) to draw (water); the poor; thrum (warp threads on a loom); unbound hair

(דלי) bucket

(דליה) branch, bough ; Yah has drawn

(דלל) to become poor, to become weak, to become thin; to hang down loosely

(דלק) to burn; to chase, pursue

(דלקת) inflammation

(דלת) door; column of a book

(דק) the veil; a thin curtain (used as "the veil" in Menorah-trees, and Isaiah 40: 22)

(דקדק) to examine minutely, to be strict

(דקק) to crush, pulverize

(דשא) to sprout, shoot, grow; green grass, green herbage

(דשש, דשדש) to tread, trample

(דת) decree, law, usage; religion

(הא) lo, behold

(הד) joyous shout; thunder clap; echo

(הדא) this, that, that is what is written

0(הדק) to press together

(הדהד, הדד) to reverberate

(הדה) to stretch out (the hand)

0(הו) ah! alas! woe!

0(הוא) he; it

0(הוד) beauty, splendor, glory, majesty; to resonate, reverberate

0(הוה) to fall; destruction, ruin, disaster; desire

0(הווה) present, actual

0(הוי) ah! alas! woe!

0(הולל) mad, foolish

0(הוללות) madness, foolishness

0(הות) to rely on; to rush upon, fall upon

(היא) she

(הודד) joyous shout, cheer

0(הידות) songs of praise

(היה) to be, exist, happen, become; was, existed; came into being, became; he remained; it came to pass, happened

(הילל) star; morning star; howl, wail

(הלא) to be removed far away; do I not?, do you not?, is it not so?

(הלאה) farther, further, beyond

(הולדת, הלדת) birth

(הלה) that

0(הלול) praise

(הלל) to boast, praise; to shine; to be foolish (to receive derision, scorn)

0(הללו) these, those

0(הללויה) hallelujah, praise the Yah

0(הקהלות) being gathered together, gathering, assembly

(השתה) putting, placing, setting

(התל) to deceive, mock

(התת) to rush upon

0(ודה) to confess

0(וו) nail, hook, peg; Waw - name of 6th letter

0(ולא) and if not, or else

0(ולד) child

0(ותק) to praise; to become veteran

(יאה) to befit, to become
(יאל) to be foolish; to be willing, consent; to be in front
(יאש) to despair
(יד) hand, arm; foreleg
(ידד) to be friends, become friends
(ידה) to confess, give thanks; to throw, hurl, cast
(ידיד) friend, beloved
0(ידידות) friendship
(יה) Yah (יהוה)
(יהד) to become a Jew
(ילד) to bear, bring forth, beget; child, son, boy, youth
0(יהודאי) Jew
0(יהודי) Judean; Jew
0(יהודית) the Hebrew language
0(יהוה) the proper name of THE Elohim of Elohim, YHWH
0(יוקש) fowler, snarer; entrapped
(ילד) to bear, bring forth, beget; child, offspring, boy, son, young man
(ילדה) girl, female child
0(ילדות) childhood
0(ילוד) baby, child; newborn, born
(יליד) son
(ילל) to howl, wail; howling, wailing, lament
(יללה) wailing, howling, lament
0(ילק) a kind of locust; the first creeping phase of the locust
(יקד) to be kindled, burn
(יקהה) obedience
0(יקוד) hearth; that which is kindled; burning
0(יקוש) fowler, hunter, trapper
(יקש) to lay bait, lay snares
(יש) possession, property, there is, there are
(ישיש) old man, elderly, very old
(יתד) peg, pin, tent pin, nail; to peg, wedge up
(יתוש) mosquito, gnat

ת ש ק ל י ו ה ד א :

2(לא) no, not
*2(לאה) Leah: to be weary, tired
(לדה) birth, childbirth
2(להה) to languish, to faint, to be tired
2(להלה) to confuse; to drive crazy
(לי) to me, my
*13(ליד) beside, near, close to
2(ליל) and (לילה) night, at night
*23(לשד) at destruction; juice, juicy or dainty bit, a dainty
3(ללת) (near) to be delivered; about to give birth
*3(לתת) to give, to marry, to fasten, to execute (do), to deliver (give)
(שאה) to make a din or crash, crash into ruins; to ruin, to lay waste; to wonder, to be astonished, amazed
2(שאיה) desolation

(שאל) to ask, to inquire; to beg, to borrow, to entreat

(שאלה) request, petition; a thing asked for

(שאת) took, to bear, to carry, to accept, to show partiality; exaltation, dignity, swelling, uprising; he lifted, lifted up; elevation; strength; majesty, dignity; swelling, eruption; an elevated place

3(שד) female breast; violence, havoc, devastation, ruin

(שדד) to plow, to harrow; to overpower, destroy violently, to rob, devastate, ruin; to despoil, to ravage

(שדה) field, land; a beautiful woman [we need to point out the שדד, to plow - open the field to prepare for seed]

(שדי) the Almighty; a field, my field; breasts, my breast

(שה) (young) sheep; lamb; small cattle (goats, sheep)

(שהד) witness

-(שהה) to tarry, to linger; to stay; to delay, to be late in coming

(שי) a gift (offered as homage); gift, present

(שיא) height; loftiness, pride

(שיד) lime, whitewash, plaster

(שידא) demon, evil spirit

(שילה) perhaps "he whose it is", Shiloh, a Messianic title; a city in Ephraim

(שיש) to rejoice; white marble, alabaster

(שית) to set, put, place, lay; a garment; a thorn bush

(של) To purposely let fall ; to loose, put off, remove; error, offense, crime; prep. belonging to, of

(שלה) to draw out (of the water) - base of שליה = afterbirth; insolence, rebellion; at ease, at rest ; another spelling of שילה Shiloh, a Messianic title; a city in Ephraim

(שלי) my, mine; quietness, tranquility

(שליה) afterbirth, placenta

2(שליש) officer, captain; a dry measure (possibly a third part of an ephah); a three stringed instrument; third

2(שלישי) third

1(שלישיה) a group of three, trio, triplet

1(שלישית) one third

(שלל) a prey, spoil, plunder, booty; to draw out (sheaves); to remove, to refuse, to negate, deny; to tie with loops; he stitched loosely; he chained, fettered

(שלש) three; to multiply by three ; to divide by three ; was of the third; pertaining to the third

1(שלשל) to let down, lower; to chain down; to couple

(שש) six; white marble; Egyptian linen

1(ששה) six; to divide by six; to multiply by six

1(ששי) sixth

1(ששית) sixth; one sixth, sixth part

(שת) Sheth - a son of Adam; posteriors; buttocks; foundation, basis, stay; he put, he placed; six

*12(שתה) to drink; to warp on a loom, to weave

2(שתי) drinking; warp on a loom

(שתיא) Aram. - Syr. - Arab, Satan (thread, warp)

1(שתיה) drinking

(שתיל) transplanted shoot, slip

(שתל) to transplant, plant
(שתת) to set, put, place, lay; to lay the foundation of, to found, establish
(תא) cell, room, compartment (esp. in the temple)
2(תאה) to mark out a boundary
1-(תהד) to resound
1-(תהה) to be astonished, amazed, dumbfounded; to meditate; to repent; to smell; to examine
13(תהלה) praise, glory; fame, renown; song of praise; folly, error, profanation, sin
1(תי) suff. my
3(תל) mound, hill; heap of ruins
(תלא) to hang
*3(תלאה) will you become impatient? will you become grieved?
(תלה) to hang
(תלי) quiver with its arrows
(תלל) to deceive, laugh at, mock, deride
(תלש) Aram.-Syr. to tear off; to pluck
(תלתל) lock of hair, curl; date-cluster
*3(תשיש) it shall exult, it shall rejoice
1-(תשש) to be weak, feeble

[שלש three]

Below you will see word definitions from this list in brackets. I do this in order to keep the context of the word or its definitions in mind.

[ישיש old man] [שדי the Almighty] [שתל to plant, transplant] [שתיל transplanted shoot] [דשא to sprout, shoot] [ילד to beget; boy, offspring, young man] [לדה birth] [אהיה I AM] [שלה to draw out (from water)] [שליה afterbirth, placenta] [אשה woman, wife] [לי my] [יליד son] [אתה to come; you, thou] [- to tarry] [אהל to tabernacle; dwelling, habitation] [איש man, husband]

[הא lo, behold] [שה lamb] [of] [יה Yah] [שלל to draw out sheaves; to remove, to negate] [error, folly, sin] [של to purposely let fall ; to loose, put off, remove; error, offense, crime; prep. belonging to, of] [ידיד friend, beloved].

[שידא evil spirit] [תלי quiver with its arrows] [to persuade, entice] [התל to deceive, mock] [תלל to deceive, to laugh at, mock, deride] [התת to rush upon] [תלש to tear off, to pluck] [hair] [תלתל lock of hair]
[יתד a nail, to wedge up] [תלה, תלא to hang] [את] THE [איל chief] [שאת lifted up; strength, majesty; took, to bear, to carry, to accept] [-to sweat, to exude] [דל door: poor; thin, lean; powerless, low, weak] [juice, sap; vigor] [-to fade, to become dim] [די enough; who, which, of, about] [-to bring about, to cause; to evaporate] [דלל to become poor, to become weak, to become thin; to hang down loosely]

[דת decree, law] [אל EL] [אלה an oath, to swear, curse; an oak; these; God, god; to wail]
[שת Sheth - a son of Adam; posteriors; buttocks; foundation, basis, stay; he put, he placed; six] [אשש to strengthen; take courage] [-to be weak] [ידה to confess,

give thanks; to throw, hurl, cast] [to repent] [שיד lime, whitewash, plaster]   / [שאל
to ask, to inquire; to beg, to borrow, to entreat] [שהד witness] [(שלי) my, mine;
quietness, tranquility] [שיש to rejoice; white marble, alabaster]

[שילה Shiloh] [הדה to stretch out (the hand)] [יד a hand] [דאה to fly, to glide (in the
air); a bird of prey] [שתת to set, put, place, lay; to lay the foundation of, to found,
establish] [דלת door] [תא a room in the temple] [שי a gift] [יאה to befit, to become;
proper] [שדה field, land; a beautiful woman] [שש Egyptian linen] [שית to set, put,
place, lay; a garment; a thorn bush] [(אש) fire; foundation] [דד breast] [to wonder,
to be astonished, amazed] שאלה request, petition] [הד joyous shout, thunder clap]

[אי woe!] [this, that] [אליל idol, false god; no value, worthless] [(שתיא) Aram. - Syr. -
Arab, Satan] [ילל to howl, wail; wailing, howling, lament] [שיא loftiness, pride]. [this]
[door] the [woman] [to fly, to glide in the air] [toward] [to me] [praise, shine] as [דיה
a bird of prey, the kite] [שאה to make a din or crash, crash into ruins; to ruin, to lay
waste; to wonder, to be astonished, amazed] [to resound] [to reverberate] [tread,
trample] [אדש thresh] [שדד to plow, to harrow; to overpower, destroy violently, to
rob, devastate, ruin; to despoil, to ravage]
[putting, placing, setting] [to be removed far away] [to mark a boundary] [to chain
down] [to languish] [that] [desolation] [night] [where] [there is, there are] [wailing,
howling, lament]

Note : The overlays are basically complete. They require only two things.
1. An expert in Biblical Hebrew who can find additional words which I missed.
2. A vetting of each words usage. This should be done in Hebrew, then translated.
For now, I will clean it up according to the best of my understanding.

The Aleph overlay theme :
   The Almighty, shall plant a shoot to beget a son. אהיה [I AM] shall be drawn forth
from a woman. My Son shall come to tarry, to tabernacle with man.
   Behold, the Lamb of Yah shall purposely fall [for the] offense of his beloved.
   The evil spirit with his quiver and arrows shall persuade, entice, and deceive, to
mock, laugh at, and deride. "Rush upon and tear off, pluck the hair!"
   The hand and a nail to wedge up, to lift up, he was hung up and suspended to
hang down and dangle. The Chief [of] strength and majesty to become weak, [his]
vigor to fade and become dim. . . Enough! . . . [He] hangs down loosely.
   The decree of EL, sworn with an oath; he placed a foundation to strengthen the
weak. Confess, and give thanks. Repent, and be made white, to become beautiful.
Draw out sheaves to remove and negate the error and folly of sin. Ask and inquire,
entreat [for] the witness of my tranquility and rejoice.
   My Son shall establish a door. A room in the Temple [with] a gift for a beautiful
woman. He has laid out a white garment, a hedge of protection with fire in the
bosom to astonish and amaze. Request [your] petition with a joyous shout!
   Woe! To that false god Satan. Howl and lament your loftiness and pride! This
door [is for] the woman to fly toward me. [Their] praise and glory [shall be as] the
bird of prey, to resound and reverberate, to tread, to trample, and to thresh; to
overpower and destroy violently. [You shall be] removed and placed far away with

a boundary. Chained down to languish in that desolation of night where there is wailing, howling, and lamentation.

Remember, all of the prophecies in the Menorah had to have existed, or been encoded into the Aleph-Bet at the time the Language was created. . .

Individual letters beneath the overlay : [The ultimate sacrifice]
(א) I AM, will become
(י) man.
(ש) Born of a woman to become a gift of white linen.
(ה) The lamb, to draw out [blood and water], to forgive and lift up a beautiful woman.
(ת) He paid a ransom, took a yoke, lifted up & thrust in. Accused falsely
(ל) The lamb of אל [EL], slain, to intervene, to remove the offense of the weak.
(ד) to whitewash my offspring and gather the nations to the door of my glory.
!!!!!!RE-CHECK AFTER ALEPH_BET HAS BEEN RE-DONE!!!!!!!!!!!!!!!!!!!!!!!!!!!!!!!!!!

His arms stretched out, as the Seraph, on a cross. A sacrifice made by the Son of Yah. The Sun of Righteousness has risen with healing in his wings.

Next : Combine the tools, overlay & letter-by-letter.

The message of the Aleph :
Behold YHWH, the Son of Yah, which was and is and is to come.
The Almighty, shall plant a shoot to beget a son. אהיה [I AM] shall be drawn forth from a woman. My Son shall come to tarry, to tabernacle with man.
I AM, will become man, born of a woman, to become a gift of white linen. The Lamb, to draw out [blood and water], to forgive and lift up a beautiful woman.
Behold, the Lamb of Yah shall draw out sheaves to remove and negate the error and folly of sin. [He shall] purposely fall [for the] offense of his beloved.
He paid a ransom, took a yoke, lifted up & thrust in. Accused falsely. The lamb of אל [EL], slain, to intervene, to remove the offense of the weak, to whitewash my offspring, and gather the nations to the door of my glory.
The evil spirit with his quiver and arrows shall persuade, entice, and deceive, to mock, laugh at, and deride [the Son]. "Rush upon and tear off, pluck the hair!"
The hand and a nail; to wedge up, to lift up. He was hung up and suspended to hang down and dangle. The Chief [of] strength and majesty to become weak, [his] vigor to fade and become dim. Enough! . . . [He] hangs down loosely.
The decree of EL, sworn with an oath; he placed a foundation to strengthen the weak. Confess, and give thanks. Repent, and be made white, to become beautiful. Ask and inquire, entreat [for] the witness of my tranquility and rejoice.
My Son shall establish a door. A room in the Temple [with] a gift for a beautiful woman. He has laid out a white garment, a hedge of protection with fire in the bosom to astonish and amaze. Request [your] petition with a joyous shout!
Woe! To that false god Satan. Howl and lament your loftiness and pride! This door [is for] the woman to fly toward me. [Their] praise and glory [shall be as] the

bird of prey, to resound and reverberate, to tread, to trample, and to thresh; to overpower and destroy violently. [You shall be] removed and placed far away with a boundary. Chained down to languish in that desolation of night where there is wailing, howling, and lamentation.

The Aleph Symbol distilled into a basic meaning :
(א) Aleph = יהו Yahoo "he/she creates", יהוה "YHWH" [translated as "LORD"]

Note : Remember how YHWH is translated, I will no longer be using this pagan sun-god title [LORD] in brackets.

Note : I woke up this morning with a message in my mind. I could continue trying to clean up, or perfect these messages as much as I want. However, I already know that this could take a VERY long time. Get the message out! Yet, I am afraid of people taking any of this as word for word scripture. The root, or message, being understood, is a witness. The witness was designed into the Aleph-Bet. Regardless of the eloquence or perfection of the wording, the message is clear.

Take some time to put one of these together yourself. Let YHWH guide you. From the beginning of this book, I know the reader will have questions in their mind about why I didn't just fix each section before moving on. You have no idea of the endless hours spent doing all of this alone.

When back-engineering code, I need to begin with first identifying how it was intended to work. This requires doing enough to test it. This is the phase you see in front of you.

I know that what I have done so far is valid, however, I have seen issues which need to be resolved. Rules which need to be refined. Is there a mechanical rule to help with "by their fruits you shall know them"? A way to more easily identify and separate the good from the evil? Other patterns which I see within the code. Atbash pairs which have word translations in the dictionary while other's appear to be words or meanings which I will need to identify, to make words for them.

Every change in the word lists will require going through anything which touches that letter. It is like re-working every line of code from scratch. No, the symbols, rules, and word lists must be completed first.

To that end, and to avoid the need to print something as thick as several dictionaries, I hope to be able to somehow obtain enough money to have a programmer create a special Biblical Hebrew search which will allow you to put in x letters, and have it output every word those letters will make.

NOTE :
Remember, all of the prophecies in the Menorah had to have existed, or been encoded into the Aleph-Bet at the time the Language was created. . .

Atbash ת Taw :

Tools :

Ruler of 2 :
(עת) time; season; appointed time
(מת) dead; a dead person, corpse
(דת) decree, law, usage; religion
(את) with, you; cutting instrument (usually rendered plowshare); את
(כת) party, faction, sect, class; group; herd
(צתת) to kindle

∧ Compass :
(עם) kinsman, relative
(עמם) to darken, dim; to join, connect
(עץ) tree; timber, wood; handle
(עצם) to be strong, be mighty, be powerful, to be numerous; force, might, power, to close the eyes; bone, to break a bone
(מץ) oppressor
(מעץ) couch, bed; to spread on a couch; to be in the middle
(צם) he fasted
(צמם) to press, reduce, contract

V Compass :
(פפפ) to stuff, to gorge oneself
(פץ) was dispersed, was scattered
(פצץ) to break, break asunder
(פצם) to split open; Aram. he cut out; Arab. he caused to crack, cracked
(צף) it floated, flowed; float, buoy
(מפץ) shattering; hammer

Atbash Taw Overlay Words :

Atbash Taw letter-by-letter :

Distilled definition : Sign or mark, light, instruction ; portion of his spirit which guides us ; balance, scales ; sacred things to be had with reverence and Holiness to YHWH in the Temple. Note the (ו) Waw within the letter (ת) Taw. The אלף Aleph, the ת Taw, and the ו Waw are ALL related to YHWH and a (ו) covenant.

The ש/ב

TOK   TOL

$(ש/ב)=[ש/ב]+[ו/פ]+[צ/ה]+[ע]$ $(ש/ב)=[ש/ב]+[ו/פ]+[צ/ה]+[ס/ח]$

$(ש/ב)=[ש/ב]+[פ/ו]+[ע]$ $(ש/ב)=[ש/ב]+[ו/פ]+[ס/ח]$

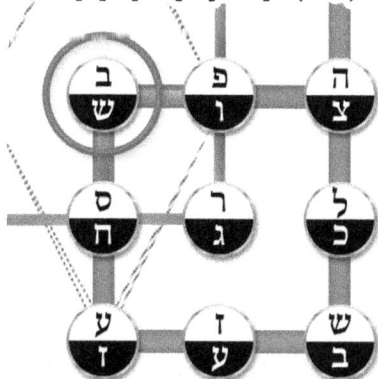

compound letters

$[(א)= י,ו][(ב)= ר,ו][(ג)= (ז?),י,ו]^{*}[(ד)= ו][(ה)= ר,י,ו][(ז)= י,ו]$
$[(ח)= (ז?),י,ו]^{*}[(ט)= י,ו][(כ)= ר,י,ו][(ל)= י,ו][(מ)= י,ו,נ,ז][(נ)= י,ו]$
$[(ס)= ו][(ע)= י,ו][(פ)= (ר,כ),י,ו]^{*}[(צ)= י,ו][(ק)= י,ו][(ר)= ו]$
$[(ש)= ו][(ת)= ר,ו]$

NEW NOTE : The good/evil connections here could be due to that "Serpent Satan" loop, and a more detailed explanation may be buried in this location. I don't want to label anything here as certain until there is enough information to see what is really going on.

ב Bet   בית

בית Bet = 412

Dictionary : house, home, family; Temple

Made from : the (ר) Resh, the (ו) Waw.

The (ב) Bet is used as a prefix meaning, "in, within, with, by, on". I believe that this comes from a large square, from the Tree of Life which contains **(שב) dwell, settle, stay, tarry**; gray, old; an old man; one who returns & **(בה) in her, in it**.

The name of the letter is found within the main large square of the Atbash (ב) Bet, but what if there are cases when the letters are meant to be de-constructed? I'll try to keep an open mind.

בו = in him, in it, therein

בור = cistern, pit; dungeon; grave; to choose, examine; to lie fallow, to be uncultivated

בר = son; pure, clean; cleanness, purity; lye, alkali, potash; threshed grain or corn; open field

ברור = chosen; clear, distinct, evident, certain; sharpened

ברר = to purify, select, set apart, separate; to sharpen

וו = nail; 6th letter

רב = much, many; large, great; mighty; abounding, abundant; honored, important; enough; lord, chief; bowman, archer; multitude; great quantity, abundance; majority; [P.B.H. Rabbi, master, teacher - see רברב "to aggrandize"]

רבב = to be or become many or much, to be or become great; to shoot; to make rain; to grease, to soil, to stain

רבו = ten thousand

רברב = to aggrandize

רר = it flowed, dripped (saliva or issue)

Note : I see that my ancestors use a mix of regular and Atbash combinations within the tools. However, I try to avoid this simply because I don't feel I have a firm enough grasp on the rules for doing so without spending a lot of time doing it, and I am not an expert on Biblical Hebrew. This means that I need to research every word created by the letter combinations (very time intensive). I also focus on the letters in the three corners of the squares even though I see many examples which show me that my ancestors used the entire square. I'm sorry, but in trying to relay the basics of everything in my head, I need to cut corners to get it out there. So, if you have the time and resources to do the research yourself, you can find gold if you care to dig in.

TOOLS :

Ruler of 2 :

(עב) cloud; thick; thicket; beam, rafter; to cover with clouds [connects with Ayin in heaven]

(עבב) to cover with clouds

(רב) much, many ; large, great ; mighty ; abundant ; honored, important ; lord, chief ; bowman

(רבב) many, to become many or much ; shoot [as in arrow]; to make rain; to grease, soil, stain

(סבב) to turn about, go round, surround.

(טב) Aram. good

(נבב) to make hollow, hollow out

Ruler of 3 :

(שרב) To glow, to be parched, burning heat, parched ground; to get sun stroke; mirage

(שרבב) to stretch out, prolong, let hang down, let down

NEW V/\ Compass : NOT ADDED TO READINGS IN THIS EDITION

(נע) moving, mobile

(נענע) to shake, to stir up

(נפע) to blow

(ענף) branch, bough; to branch off; branches, full of branches

(עף) to fly

(עפעף) to flutter, fly about; eyelid

(פן) lest, in order not to; perhaps

(פנן) to turn; to lend luster like a pearl

(פעפע) to bubble; to pierce; to penetrate

NEW Tree of Life Squares on top :

(בה) in her, in it

(בהה) to be astonished, amazed

(הב) give

(הבה) give; let us

(הבהב) to singe; to hesitate; burnt offerings

(חב) bosom

(חבב) to love

(חבה) to hide

(חח) hook, ring; buckle

(חף) pure, innocent

(חפה) to cover

(חפף) to surround, cover; to rub, cleanse the head by rubbing

The Square(s) :

(שבע) to be sated, satisfied, full

(שבע) base of שבע = seven, and of words there referred to; to swear, and prob. meaning lit.: 'to bind oneself by seven things, or oaths; to do something seven times

(עשב) to cover with grass, to weed out; herb, herbage, grass

(עשש) to waste away, decay

(עש) moth; prob. great bear constellation

(בעבע) to bubble (water bubble)

(עבש) to shrivel, to grow moldy [leaven? corruption?]

(עבב) to cover with clouds.

(עב) cloud; thick; thicket; beam, rafter

(בבה) apple of the eye, pupil of the eye; may be related to Aram. בבא gateway, entrance [or does it refer to one standing in the door looking at you?]

(שבה) to capture, to take prisoner

(בשה) with a lamb

(בש) ashamed, put to shame

(בשש) delayed

(בה) inflected pers. pron. 'in her', 'in it' ; [explains the Bet as a prefix for "in"]

(בהה) related - (בהו) emptiness, chaos. From base בהה ; Arab, bahw = hollow

(הב) give

(הבה) give ; let us ; come or go to

(השב) that was returned, therefore restore, again, render, repay, carry back

(הבהב) singed, scorched ; my burnt offerings; to hesitate

(שב) dwell, settle, stay, tarry; gray, old; an old man; one who returns

(שבב) splinter, fragment ; surrounded, to turn about, go around, surround; to chip, chisel.

(שבש) to entangle, confound, confuse

(שה) (young) sheep, lamb ; small cattle (goat, sheep).

(שהה) to tarry, linger; to stay, to delay, be late in coming

(בעה) to bubble; to seek; to ask questions

(עבה) to be thick

(בר) son; threshed grain or corn; pure, clean; open field; cleanness, purity; lye, alkali, potash

(ברבר) to babble, to prattle

(ברר) to purify, select, set apart, separate; to sharpen

(פר) bull, bullock, steer

(פרך) to clasp, fasten

(פרפר) to brake, to crumble, to crush; to shake, shatter

(פרר) to crush, crumb, crumble, break into crumbs; to brake, violate, annul, frustrate; to shake, shatter

(רב) much, many; large, great; mighty; abounding, abundant; honored, important; enough; lord, chief; bowman, archer; multitude; great quantity, abundance; majority

(רבב) to be or become many or much, to be or become great; to shoot; to make rain; to grease, to soil, to stain

(רברב) to aggrandize

(רפף) to move gently; to waver, vacillate; to loosen, weaken

(רפרף) to flutter, to move

(בסס) to trample, to tread; to base, to establish

(בסר) to be half-ripe; to despise, spurn; unripe fruit; sour grapes

(בר) son; threshed grain or corn; pure, clean; open field; cleanness, purity; lye, alkali, potash

(ברבר) to babble, to prattle

(ברר) to purify, select, set apart, separate; to sharpen

(סבב) to turn about, go around, surround

(סבר) to think, be of opinion

(סס) moth

(סר) sullen, ill-humored

(סרב) to recline, refuse; to rebel; to urge, press; obstinate, rebellious

(סוו) to be stubborn, be rebellious

(רב) much, many; large, great; mighty; abounding, abundant; honored, important; enough; lord, chief; bowman, archer; multitude; great quantity, abundance; majority

(רבב) to be or become many or much, to be or become great; to shoot; to make rain; to grease, to soil, to stain

(רברב) to aggrandize

(רסס) to brake into small pieces, crush; to spray, sprinkle, moisten

(עף) to fly; it flew

(פעפע) to bubble; to pierce, penetrate

(בטבט) to swell, to protrude

(בסס) to trample, tread; to base, establish

(טב) good

(טו) deviation; deviation from the right path; also spelled (שט) = Apostate

(סס) moth

(בחן) to examine, to test; watchtower; examination, trial, test

(בן) son; offspring; branch, shoot; inhabitant of; worthy of, deserving

(בעבע) to bubble

(חב) bosom

(חבב) to love

(חן) favor, grace, charm

(חנן) to show favor, be gracious

(נבב) to make hollow, hollow out

(נבח) to bark

(נבע) to flow, bubble up, gush out

(נחח) to spray scent

(נע) moving, mobile

(נענע) to shake, to stir up

(עב) cloud; thick; thicket; beam, rafter

(עבב) to cover with clouds

(ענב) to make a loop, tie; grape

(ענן) he brought clouds, covered with clouds; to practice soothsaying; cloud

The Tools Theme :

[The] lamb to come dwell, taken prisoner and put to shame. Pierced, a thicket [of thorns], [and] a beam to cover with clouds. The mighty chief to waste away [die].

Therefore restore again the seven oaths to cover with clouds the parched ground. Make rain to cover with grass and surround the apple of the eye. The sheep to be sated, satisfied and full.

Overlay Words :

(בבה) apple of the eye; pupil of the eye

(בה) in her, in it

(בהה) to be astonished, amazed

(בהל) to abhor, to loath; to ripen

(בפה) (ב) "in it" or "in her" + (פה) Mouth ; in the mouth

(בל) not

(בלבל) to confuse

(בלה) to be worn out, to become old; to be frightened, to be terrified

(בלל) to confuse

(בלע) to swallow; confusion, corruption

(בלש) to search, examine, investigate, detect

(בעבע) to bubble

(בעה) to bubble; to seek, to ask questions

(בעל) to rule over, own, possess, marry, to cohabit with; owner, master, husband; Baal

(בשל) it ripened, it boiled, it cooked; for the sake of, because of

(פה) mouth; speech, saying; command; opening, orifice; here

(פהה) to idle, to loaf, to tarry

(פז) pure gold

(פזז) to move quickly, to be agile, be supple; to be gilded, be purified

(פזל) to squint

(פלה) to be separated, be distinct; to search for vermin, delouse

(פלל) to pray; to judge, to arbitrate

(פלפל) to discuss, argue, debate; to pepper

(פלש) to roll; to open through; to penetrate, invade

(פעה) to groan

(פעל) to do, to make, work; deed, action; reward, wage

(פעפע) to bubble; to pierce, to penetrate

(פש) haughtiness, folly

(פשה) to spread, extend

(פשל) to leave behind; throw back, to roll back

(פשע) to step, march; to rebel, to transgress; transgression, trespass; guilt of transgression

(פשפש) to examine, to search

(הב) give

(הבה) give; let us

(הבהב) to singe; to hesitate; burnt offering; sacrificial gift

(הבל) breath; to become vain

(הלה) that

(הלל) to boast, praise; shine; to be foolish

(הפלה) he made separate, set apart

(לב) heart, mind, will; the inner part; the middle

(לבב) heart; to be understanding, to be likable; to make cakes; to blaze up

(לבה) flame, to set ablaze, inflame; heart

(לעז) to speak a foreign language; to speak ill of

(לעע) to swallow, sip; to talk wildly

(לפף) to wrap up, to envelop, to clasp, embrace

(שב) gray, old, an old man; one who returns

(שבב) chip, chisel; splinter, fragment

(שרה) to take captive, take prisoner

(שבל) to hang down, stretch along, draw along; to be pulled along, dangle; flowing skirt, train of a robe

(שבע) to be sated, satisfied, to be replete, full; seven, to swear; to do something seven times; to bind ones self by seven things or seven oaths

(שבעה) seven

(שבש) to entangle, confound, confuse

(שה) (young) sheep, lamb; small cattle (sheep, goats)

(שהה) to tarry, linger, stay, delay; be late in coming

(שזב) to save, to rescue

(שזף) to catch sight of, to look on; to blacken, to brown, to tarnish; to become sunburnt

(של) error, offense, or crime; that which is (or belongs) to

(שלה) To draw out [from water - related to שליה afterbirth] ; also, to be quiet, at ease, tranquil [the comforter?]

(שלל) spoil, booty, plunder ; fall; to deprive; to draw out (sheaves); to remove; to refuse, to negate, deny; to stitch loosely, join together loosely, to chain, fetter [binding of sheaves?]

(שלף) to draw out, take out, unsheathe

(שלש) to multiply by three ; to divide by three ; was of the third

(שעה) to gaze, to look about; to care for

(שעע) to smooth, to besmear, to blind; to take delight, be delighted

(שעף) disquieting thoughts

(שפה) lip; language, tongue; edge, margin, rim; border, shore; to sweep bare; to be at ease; to incline, to make slanting; to put over the fire

(שפל) to become or be low; low, deep, lowly, humiliated, meek, modest, mean; low state, low condition

(שפע) to flow abundantly, be abundant; to incline, slant, slope; abundance

(שש) six; white marble; egyptian linen

(ششה) six; to divide by six; to multiply by six

(זב) one that has a flux

(זבל) to dwell; to manure, to fertilize

(זה) this

(זהב) gold; to gild, to plate with gold

(זהה) to identify

(זלזל) to despise, to neglect

(זלל) to be mean, to be vile; to be a glutton; to shake

(זלעף) to terrify

(זלף) to pour, to sprinkle, to spray
(זע) tremble, quake
(זעה) sweat, perspiration
(זעזע) to shake violently
(זעף) to be angry, enraged
(זפת) to pitch, coat with pitch
(עב) cloud; thick; thicket; beam, rafter; to cover with clouds
(עבב) to cover with clouds
(עבש) to shrivel, to grow moldy
(עז) Strong, mighty, fierce, fortress, refuge, splendor, glory
(עזב) to leave, to forsake; to help, assist; prepare, fortify
(עזז) prevail, to be strong
(על) yoke; height, upper part, on, upon, above; beside; because of, on account of
(עלב) to put to shame, insult, humiliate
(עלה) to go up, to ascend; sprang up, grew, shot forth; he rose, surpassed, excelled; leaf; lactating animal
(עלז) rejoice, exult
(עלל) to act, do, work; to insert, thrust in; to accuse falsely; to glean (grapes or olives)
(עלע) to swallow, to suck up, lick
(עלעל) to drive about, to hurl, to cast
(עלף) to cover, wrap; to faint, swoon
(עפל) to be heedless; be reckless; mound, hill
(עפש) to become moldy; to decay
(עש) moth; name of constellation
(עשב) to cover with grass; to weed out
(עשה) to do, make
(עשש) to waste away, to decay

The overlay theme :
The master, to tarry and dwell, to save and rescue, to draw out (sheaves). A sacrificial gift, the lamb [was] set apart [for the] offense, the crime, which is or belongs to [others].

In haughtiness and folly [they] hurl wild talk to coat with pitch. [They] despise and speak ill of the master to take prisoner, to put to shame, to insult and humiliate [him]. A thicket [of thorns] upon a yoke, because of those who have blinded themselves.

[They] accuse falsely to insert, to thrust in, to pierce and penetrate the inner part, to draw out [blood and water] to pour and flow abundantly.

The master('s) speech, saying, to pray [not] to leave, to forsake. The master to groan, a breath, to leave behind and be separated, to be at ease.

The hill to shake violently to frighten and terrify the vile, to shake, tremble and quake [for] gilt of transgression.

[We] abhor and loath to ripen; we pray to arbitrate, to give, to let us cover and wrap.

[On] the third [day] to roll, to open, to penetrate. To gaze and to look about, to search, examine and investigate; to seek, to ask question. Rejoice, he rose, to make astonished and amazed.

The master returns, to swallow corruption and confound decay. Purified, to cover [us] with clouds, to spread the train of [his] robe, that [we] shine in Egyptian linen, and bind [us] by seven things or oaths [in] the refuge of splendor, glory. To set ablaze the heart and help [us] to prevail. To envelope the low and meek apple of the eye and gild [as] with pure gold [golden olive oil, anoint, crown of head].

Individual letters :
(ב) the lamb to come and remove the error and offense, draw out from water, restore again the shine.
(פ) let us [be] pure as gold, innocent and clean, give dream [vision] to envelop the apple of the eye, to astonish and amaze.
(ה) [HE] commands [us] to repent, to forgive, to lift up, to draw out [from water] and bear witness of the lamb. Behold, here is life.
(ל) Pray and entreat the lamb to intervene; thrust in and slain upon a yoke on account of the wicked, to negate the offense of the sheep, and loose the chains of the enemy. Draw out from water the sheaves which belong to EL and shine. Sing praise to the lamb, and shout for joy.
(ש) Be humbled and rejoice, the lamb came into being to become a gift of white linen to the children of men who bow down and repent. [talk+bent bowed+humbled= repentance]
(ז) [Be] set apart [purified], to be strong, to go beyond and open [the veil], the secret of splendor and glory, in the stronghold of power.
(ע) Fear and tremble before the lamb. Shut the eyes of evil and affliction, to waste away [and die], pray, to give, companion, to tarry, and take delight in making eyes to gaze upon wonders and be astonished.

For the sake of the time that it takes to do these final compilations of the three. It will suffice, for this edition, to leave a place holder. As the words beneath the overlay contains the essence of the message.

The Bet Theme :

The master, to tarry and dwell, to save and rescue, to draw out (sheaves). A sacrificial gift, the lamb [was] set apart [for] the offense, the crime, which is or belongs to [others].
In haughtiness and folly [they] hurl wild talk to coat with pitch. [They] despise and speak ill of the master to take prisoner, to put to shame, to insult and humiliate [him]. A thicket [of thorns] upon a yoke, because of those who have blinded themselves.
[They] accuse falsely to insert, to thrust in, to pierce and penetrate the inner part, to draw out [blood and water] to pour and flow abundantly.
The master('s) speech, saying, to pray [not] to leave, to forsake. The master to groan, a breath, to leave behind and be separated, to be at ease.
The hill to shake violently to frighten and terrify the vile, to shake, tremble and quake [for] gilt of transgression.
[We] abhor and loath to ripen; we pray to arbitrate, to give, to let us cover and

wrap.

[On] the third [day] to roll, to open, to penetrate. To gaze and to look about, to search, examine and investigate; to seek, to ask question. Rejoice, he rose, to make astonished and amazed.

The master returns, to swallow corruption and confound decay. Purified, to cover [us] with clouds, to spread the train of [his] robe, that [we] shine in Egyptian linen, and bind [us] by seven things or oaths [in] the refuge of splendor, glory. To set ablaze the heart and help [us] to prevail. To envelope the low and meek apple of the eye and gild [as] with pure gold.

As for the Main theme of the letter Bet . . .
We can see the (ר) Reish in the middle of the Temple. This is the chief, the bull, the Son to rule. However, this may be one of those letters which has both good and evil standing in the same place.

Note : As stated just before this chapter, there are new tools words which have been added, yet the old work has not been modified. Sometimes, evil and good can stand in the same place. If it is by their fruits that we shall know them, the Reish is sitting on a fruit of a (ג) Gimmel which does not follow the Father. That (ג) Gimmel will grow up and grab the Atbash (ש) Shin and Atbash (ז) Zayin. More about this in the next chapter.

It appears that the letters reveal their meanings, they show their Atbash pairs which reveal their meanings, they begin to come together in sayings, they stand up in their respective places and reveal more meanings, and then their placements allow you to reveal yet more information once the Atbash pairs are joined together.

It is like a little seed. The Aleph-Bet in the Menorah, unfolds. It stretches out and unfolds more, and that stretches out and unfolds even more, and again, and again, until that 22 letter grid, ciphered out with the tools, becomes thousands of pages.

Distilled definition : It is the house or dwelling, the refuge of glory, dwell ; in her, in it. THIS IS ONLY READING THE PETALS. IF WE ADD THE FRUIT LATER, THIS COULD HAVE MORE TO SAY.

In the (י) Yud section, (אי) = Refuge. As a word, this would = 11, and reduce to 1+1=2. The same value as the letter ב.

We know that the (י) Yud refers to the Father, that both the (א) Aleph and the (ק) Kuf refer to the Son, and each are reducible to 1.

I'm still not sure if this is coincidence, or statistically provable. I am still learning, but I see a lot of connections that appear to be relevant. Even so, if this is part of a code, there must be rules . . . for now, I'll just say, "Hummmmmm".

Look at the letters which make up the word Bet בית, or house.

Bet בית = 412
(ב) to dwell, in the
(י) Almighty, father, refuge
(ת) light, foundation, basis, stay, lot, portion, share

This gives us :
To dwell in the Almighty's light   (and/or)
To dwell in the father's refuge, lot [place]

There is no doubt that this describes a house. However, the connections to the Temple are just as clear. . . Again, there are things that I need to explore regarding this overlay.

I have to question the new tools which includes, "(טס) deviation; deviation from the right path; also spelled (טש) = Apostate", the fact that I now know that the "Evil Eye", is part of its foundation, and the fact that I have two houses, and this one is on the LEFT side of the grid.

The rules dictate that the overlay is for the (ב) Bet in the Petals, that which we see. However, I am still ciphering out the grid, and if "by their fruits you will know them" is truly a part of the instructions, as I believe, I see connections to the great and abominable church, and the Devil is its founder.

I have to question the true identity of the (ר) Reish which sits in the middle of the (ב) House. The fruit which it sits on is the (ג) Gimmel, and when it grows up, it does not take hold of the hand of the Father [like the regular (ג) Gimmel]. The Atbash (ג) Gimmel takes hold of the Atbash (ש) Shin [the Serpent].

Sorry, I haven't even gotten to those sections yet, but I can already see what's coming. My point is that I am not going to address these things in full, but there is more than what you see on the surface.

We will need to get to that in their sections, but I'm going to throw those things out there. My [original] point in this edition was to create a larger basic tools grid that I can put in my hand. That will make filling out the layers on top of that easier for me. Not to mention the fact that each of the Atbash pairs have important meanings when joined together. However, I need to take the time to isolate and identify them.

The tools lists, and Atbash combinations are like a foundation which everything else stands on.

Atbash Shin :

Tools :

Ruler of 2 :
(גשגש) to tinkle, to rattle, to rustle
(חשש) to feel pain, fear, apprehend; chaff

Square :
(צב) covered wagon
(צבב) to cover
(שב) gray, old; an old man; one who returns
(שבץ) to weave in checker work; to be struck by apoplexy; cramp, convulsion
(בז) booty, spoil, prey, plunder, pillage
(זב) one who has a flux (flow)
(שזב) to save, to rescue

(שן) tooth
(שטן) Satan

Atbash Overlay Words :

Atbash Overlay letter-by-letter :

The ג/ר

TOK # TOL

[ד/ק]+[ח/ס]+[צ/ה]=(ג/ר)
[ח/ס]+[ו/פ]+[ד/ק]+[ג/ר]=(ג/ר)
[ח/ס]+[ד/ק]+[ג/ר]=(ג/ר)

[ד/ק]+[ע]+[צ/ה]=(ג/ר)
[ע]+[ו/פ]+[ד/ק]+[ג/ר]=(ג/ר)
[ע]+[ד/ק]+[ג/ר]=(ג/ר)

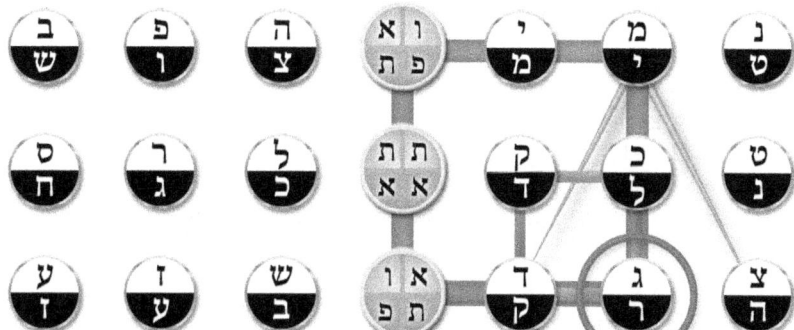

compound letters

[(א)= ו,י][(ב)= ו,ר,י][(ג)= ו,י,(ז?)*][(ד)= ו][(ה)= ו,ר,י][(ז)= ו,י]
[(ח)= ו,י,(ז?)*][(ט)= ו,י][(כ)= ו,י,ר][(ל)= ו,י][(מ)= ו,י,ו,ג,ז][(נ)= ו,י]
[(ס)= ו][(ע)= ו,י][(פ)= ו,י,ו,(ר,כ?)*][(צ)= ו,י][(ק)= ו,י][(ר)= ו]
[(ש)= ו][(ת)= ו,ר]

*The Gimel has a question as to whether or not it contains a ז Zayin. I think that the answer to this may be yes.

However, with the א Aleph, I can clearly see where each piece of the de-constructed letter comes from. If I place a compass on the ס Samech [middle row, far left side of the grid], I can see from older letter or font shapes that it takes a bent וו nail [hook/Waw] from the ע Ayin for its right side, the peg [another ו Waw] from the bottom of the ב Bet for its top, and I think it pulls the nail from the ל Lamed for its left side. Regardless of where it comes from, I see the three ו Waws.

So, does simply having a י Yud over a ו Waw mean that it contains a ז Zayin? What about the נ Nun or the ט Tet? I have to say that none of these deconstructions are going to satisfy me the way the א Aleph does until the code shows me the answer. My best guess is that it grabbed its י Yuds from the י{מ}&ג{מ}.

Some of these I can clearly see. Others, I'm not satisfied that I have even seen the original 500 BC shape. I have sifted through examples of the early Aramaic-Hebrew, but how much was simply a hand writing style? All I know for sure is that the answer will be in the code which the language comes from.

ג מל **Gimel**

גמל = 73

Dictionary : The name means Camel, but these similar words may be related : (גמל) to ripen, to wean [Related to גמר. The orig. meaning of this base was 'to be complete', hence it is related to Arab, kamala = was whole, was complete, Akka. gilmalu = perfect, complete.] ; (גימול) m.n. PBH a kind of muzzle for the calf to prevent it from sucking. Of uncertain origin; perhaps derived from גמל ‑ to wean.

Made from : the (ו) Waw, and the (י) Yud [hand, forearm, "**foreleg**"]. The Yud on top, may add a ז Zayin, so keep it in mind when searching.

The name, Gimel is easily found in the large square from the Tree of Life which lands on the Gimel.

The words made from the letter (ג) Gimel, and the letters within make a short list.

גג = roof
גו = back, body; inside, interior
גוי = nation, people; (with the Yud as a suffix) my back [this would include, "my body"] (see Isaiah 50:6); PBH Gentile
גויי = the nations; Gentile
גי = valley, vale
וו = nail, hook, peg; 6th letter Waw

TOOLS :

Ruler of 2 :
(דג) fish
(דגדג) to tickle
(חג) feast
(חגג) to make a pilgrimage, to celebrate a feast

∧ compass :
(צד) side, flank.
(צדד) to turn aside
(מצד) concerning, in regard, beside, side, the side; fortress, stronghold
(מצדד) follower, supporter
(צמד) yoke, to join, pair, couple; Aram. - Syr. he bound up, bound together
(צמצם) to press, reduce, contract
(צמם) to press, draw together
(צם) should I fast, fasting, fasted
(מץ) oppressor; chaff
(מד) measure; garment
(מדד) to measure

(דם) blood; bloodshed; blood-guilt

V compass : NEW WORDS HERE
(דחה) to push, thrust, banish
(חד) one, uni-, mono-
(חדד) to be sharp
(חץ) arrow
(חצד) to reap, harvest
(חצץ) to divide; to make a partition; gravel, gravel-stone
(צח) dazzling, glowing, bright, clear, pure
(צחח) to be dazzling, be bright, be clear; to become dry
(צחצח) to polish

Squares : NEW WORDS HERE
(גא) proud, haughty
(גו) back, body; inside, interior
(וו) Waw; hook, peg, nail
(אם) mother; matriarch; metropolis, large city, if, whether, when, on condition; nation, people
(גג) roof
(גם) also, to, even as well
(גמא) to sip; papyrus; the plant that swallows water
(גמגם) to stammer, stutter
(גמם) to cut (the branch of a tree)
(גנ) to burst forth
(חגג) to make a pilgrimage, to celebrate a feast, to dance, to reel, to be giddy
(נגו) cleft (of a rock)
(חוג) to make a circle, move in a circle; circle, circuit, horizon
(חוגג) celebrant, celebrating
(חוח) briar, thorn; hook, ring; aperture, cleft
(חח) hook, ring; buckle
(געגע) to long, to yearn; to quack; to dig, make holes, roll in
(עגעג) to peck, pick holes
(גד) good fortune, luck; Babylonian god of fortune
(גדד) to cut; gather in troops or bands
(גנ) to burst forth

Small Squares : NEW WORDS HERE
(גג) roof
(גד) coriander; good fortune, luck; Babylonian god of fortune
(גדד) to cut; to gather in troops or bands
(גד) fish
(גדגד) to tickle
(דק) thin curtain (veil, due to placement in grids Temple)
(דקדק) to examine minutely; to be strict
(דקק) to crush, pulverize
(קדד) to bow down, bow one's head; to cut, bore, drill
(קד) Syr. he tore, he cut away

(קָדְקֹד) head, crown of the head; to crow

The Tools Message :
Turn aside the fish, make a pilgrimage to the stronghold. Measure a garment [for the] followers to be drawn together, coupled and bound [to the] side.

Overlay Words :
(גיד) sinew, vein ; to cut veins
(גדי) kid ; young goat
(יגד) to invade, raid, attack
(גד) good fortune, luck ; name of the god fortune
(דיג) to fish, fisherman
(גדד) to cut; to gather in troops or bands
(יד) hand, arm ; foreleg
(די) which, that, who, because ; sufficiency, enough
(גי) valley, by the valley, to the valley, in the valley, at the valley, unto the valley
(ידד) to be friends, become friends.
(ידיד) friend, beloved
(דד) breast, teat, nipple

The Gimmel Overlay :
Sever the vein of the breast [mother's milk] and become friends. [Take the] hand which fishes to gather in bands unto the valley [of my] beloved.

Individual letters :
(י) Cease the mother's breast! The Almighty's hand shall measure a garment of power to increase [your] strength. A fitting gift sufficient to whitewash my
(ג) followers [who] fish by [my] side. Turn aside and make a pilgrimage [to] the stronghold. Measure a garment to bind together. Draw together and fast.
(ד) Propound a riddle : Yah shall stretch out the hand of power. The nail [affixing the covenant] because of [HIS] beloved. Bow down and confess, give thanks and banish the robber! Be clean and become the hand to gather the offspring [to the] door of my glory. A bush to be kindled with a joyous shout [in the] valley of [my] people.

The message of the Gimmel :
[The letter-by-letter will suffice for this]
   Cease the mother's breast! The Almighty's hand shall measure a garment of power to increase [your] strength. A fitting gift sufficient to whitewash my followers [who] fish by [my] side.
   Turn aside and make a pilgrimage [to] the stronghold. Measure a garment to bind together. Draw together and fast.
   Propound a riddle : Yah shall stretch out the hand of power, The nail [affixing the covenant] because of [HIS] beloved. Bow down and confess, give thanks and banish the robber! Be clean and become the hand to gather the offspring [to the] door of my glory. A bush to be kindled with a joyous shout [in the] valley of [my] people. The Gimmel . . .

Distilled definition : Follower of the Almighty

I am learning as I go through this code, and I may leave out things which turn out to be significant, simply because I have not seen it.

So, before going further . . . This is the reason that you see numerical equivalents at the beginning of each letter. I will look at this later and see if I spot a pattern.

Gimmel = 3 : ב =2, and א = 1

אב = Father = 3 appears to be valid based on the following letter-by-letter . . .
The ב Bet includes the words : honored, chief, gray, old, an old man
The א Aleph contains imagery of a family : father, mother, son.
The honored old chief would be the father.

3 בא = he who comes + 3 אב [to the] Father. Is this not a follower of the Father?

Is it possible that :
ב let us ; come or go [to return again] to the gray old man
א [of] YHWH
= follow THE Father?

Is it possible that there actually is something to the numbers associated with the letters? What about the use of vortex math which the Aleph-Bet seems to use? I would feel better about this if someone above would show me some rules associated with this. . . The more you know, the more you know, how little you know.

There is something to this math connection, but I am still learning as I go.
Search these things out and you will begin to see some of the things that I do.
Don't dismiss it out of hand because some "man" said so.
There is something here, but the "truth" can only come from the original source.

"Whom shall he teach knowledge? and whom shall he make to understand doctrine? them that are weaned from the milk, and drawn from the breasts. For precept must be upon precept, precept upon precept ; line upon line, line upon line ; here a little, and there a little : For with stammering lips and another *language* will he speak to this people. To whom he said, this is the rest wherewith ye may cause the weary to rest ; and this is the refreshing : yet they would not hear. . . " (ISAIAH 28)

Be the Gimmel. . . A follower of the Father.

Gain an understanding of how much you do not understand, and know that this is only the beginning of what you do not know.

Seek your answers from the bridegroom, not other men. It is the only way to be sure that your knowledge is faithful and true.
NOTE - REVISIT ג SHAPE OVERLAY ?(י/מ)(מ/י)(כ/ל)(ג/ר)(ד/ק)?

Atbash Reish :

Tools :

Ruler of 2 :
(הר) mountain
(נר) light, lamp
(קר) cold, cool, coldness, chill

Ruler of 3 :
(תדר) to last
(פקר) to be licentious, be heretical, be irreligious

∧ Compass :
(יה) short form of YHWH
(היה) to be; to exist, happen, become; was, existed; came into being, became; he remained; it came to pass, happened
(קהה) obedience; to be blunt, dull
(קיה) to vomit

Atbash Reish Word Overlay :

Atbash Reish letter-by-letter :

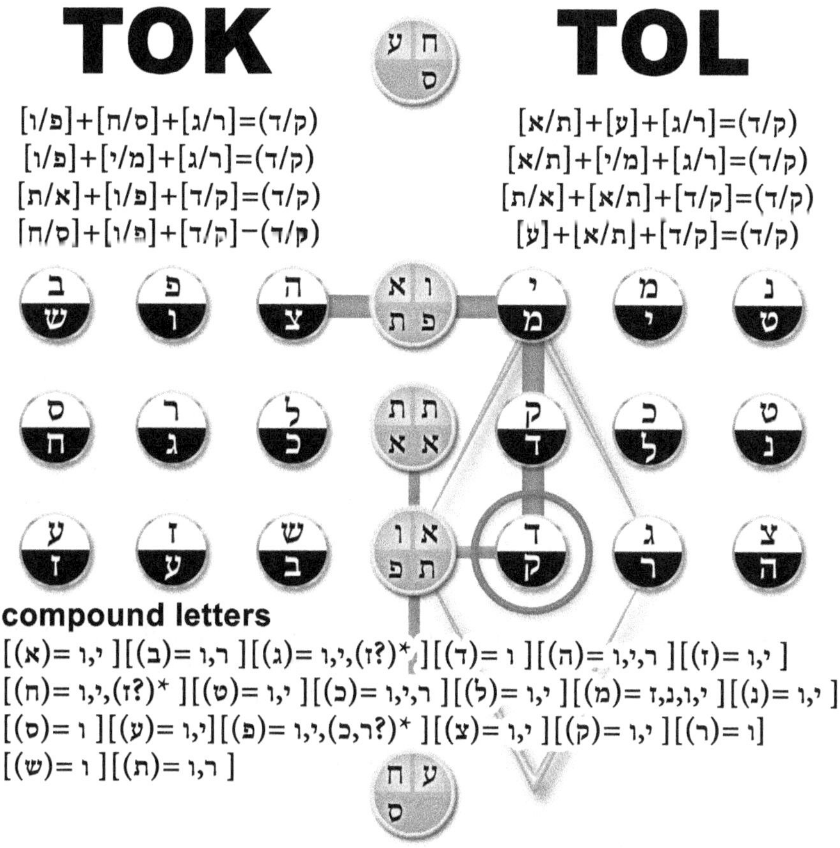
TOK
TOL
[פ/ו]+[ס/ח]+[ר/ג]=(ק/ד)
[פ/ו]+[מ/י]+[ר/ג]=(ק/ד)
[א/ת]+[פ/ו]+[ק/ד]=(ק/ד)
[ס/ח]+[פ/ו]+[ק/ד]=(ק/ד)
[ת/א]+[ע]+[ר/ג]=(ק/ד)
[ת/א]+[מ/י]+[ר/ג]=(ק/ד)
[א/ת]+[ת/א]+[ק/ד]=(ק/ד)
[ע]+[ת/א]+[ק/ד]=(ק/ד)
compound letters
[(א)= י,ו][(ב)= ר,ו][(ג)= י,ו,(ז?)*][(ד)= ו][(ה)= ר,י,ו][(ז)= י,ו]
[(ח)= י,ו,(ז?)*][(ט)= י,ו][(כ)= ר,י,ו][(ל)= י,ו][(מ)= י,ו,נ,ז][(נ)= י,ו]
[(ס)= ו][(ע)= י,ו][(פ)= י,ו,(ר,כ?)*][(צ)= י,ו][(ק)= י,ו][(ר)= ו]
[(ש)= ו][(ת)= ר,ו]

When you go through these lists, I cannot stress enough that this is a partial list of what is found in the regular OR atbash letter. This is an important step in defining values which belong specifically to that letter.

THE COMBINED TREE LETTERS ARE NOT ADDED. I HAVEN'T HAD THE TIME. BUT THEY BELONG THERE.

The way I see my forefathers working this is with all letters at the same time. The additional letters make this far more complex. This is important as a package or wrapper which somehow seems to add meanings to what is going on at that location in the tree.

לת ד **Dalet**

ד = 4
דלת = 434

Dictionary : The name means door.

Made from : two וו Waw. Based on dream...

Hint #1 :
The (ד) Dalet in the outline of the Temple also tells me that this is the "door" to HIS house.

Hint #2 :
The (ו) Waw, Son, or nail, is defined when it stands up. It says, "I AM YHWH, the life and light of the world". In other words, YHWH [the mediator] stands in the door between the heavens and the earth to whitewash, to extend his hand, and lift up the offspring of Yah.

Hint #3 :
We see that the (ד) Dalet has an association with "the door", or the "veil" represented in the דק (a thin curtain). The (ו) Waw standing up next to the (ד) Dalet, creates a graphical door. A door between this world and the next.

The (ק) Kuf in the דק (a thin curtain) has the Son, beside, and the veil. Combining the individual letter definitions for the דק "veil" shows a subtext saying, "The Son to stretch out the hand at the door to my Glory." The (דק) "thin curtain" referred to is THE VEIL, THE DOOR TO HIS GLORY.

This is an opportunity for YOU to learn to look deeper.

TOOLS :

Ruler of 2 :
(חד) sharp; one, single; one, uni-, mono-
(קדד) to bow down, bow one's head; to cut, to bore, drill
(כד) round end
(קד) jug, pitcher
(גדד) to cut
(גדד) to gather in troops or bands
(גד) good fortune, luck; name of Babylonian "god" of fortune

Ruler of 3 :
(שיד = שוד) whitewash
(שודד) robber, destroyer

124 The Menorah Code

(נכד) offspring, progeny
(יקד) to be kindled, burn

The compass :
(וו) hook, peg, nail
(יגו) My body, or my back.
(גוי) nation, people
(גי) valley, vale

The squares :
(חוח) bush
(חוד) to propound a riddle
(דוח) to report
(ידה) to confess, give thanks, to throw, to cast
(יהד) to become a Jew
(דיה) a bird of prey, the kite
(דד) breast, teat, nipple
(דהה) to fade, to become dim
(הד) to shout, shouting, cheer, joyous shout
(דוח) to rinse, cleanse, wash off by rinsing
(יה) Yah
(היה) to be, exist happen, become, was, existed, became, it came to pass
(יהדי) My Glory, My Majesty
(חד) one, single
(יד) Hand
(היד) the hand ; work ; power
(הדה) to stretch out (the hand)
(דחח) to push, thrust, banish
(חד) sharp
(וו) hook, peg, nail
(חדוד) sharp edge, something pointed
(הדד) to reverberate
(ידיד) beloved
(ידד) friends.
(די) who, which, that, because, sufficiency, enough
(הידד) joyous shout, cheer

Small Square [middle] NEW :
(וו) Waw - name of letter; hook, peg, nail
(דד) breast, teat, nipple
(דוד) uncle; beloved, friend; kettle; a large basket
(דות) pit, cistern
(דת) decree, law, usage; religion
(תו) mark, sign; name of letter ת Taw
(תת) he gave

The Dalet Tools : [not updated]

Bow your head, give thanks, confess, and banish the robber [also destroyer] to fade away. Whitewash the nations to become one [with] my body.

Gather in [my] friends, and wash [my] beloved children.

Propound a riddle : [nail] [something pointed] [YaH] [to be kindled, burn] [to stretch out (the hand)] [My Glory] [to bore, to drill] [bush] [the hand ; power] [Hand]

Dalet Overlay Words :

(אד) mist, vapor, gas
(אדם) Adam; man, mankind; to be red; red; red jewel, ruby
(אדמדם) reddish
(אדק) to attach, fasten, connect
(אי) island; jackal; woe! , Alas! ; not; where?
(איד) to vaporize, to steam
(אים) to threaten, to frighten; fearful, frightful, terrible
(אם) mother; if, whether, when, on condition; nation, people
(אמד) to estimate, calculate, reckon; to make well to do
(דא) this
(דד) breast, teat, nipple
(די) sufficiency, enough, sufficiently; who, which, that; of, about
(דיא) thorough, thoroughly, entirely, utterly
(דיק) bulwark, siege wall; to be exact, be precise
(דם) blood, bloodshed, blood-guilt
(דמדם) to be in a daze, to be confused
(דמי) quiet, rest, silence
(דמים) bloodshed, blood-guiltiness
(דמם) to be ore grow dumb or silent; to bleed
(דק) a thin curtain (the veil)
(דקדק) to examine minutely
(דקק) to crush, to pulverize
(יד) hand, arm; foreleg
(ידד) to be friends, become friends
(ידיד) friend, beloved
(ים) sea, lake, large basin, reservoir; west
(ימים) days, year
(יקד) to be kindled, burn
(מאד) to increase; strength, might, power; very greatly, exceedingly
(מד) measure; garment
(מדד) to measure; measurement
(מדי) as often as, every
(מי) who? ; whoever; someone, anyone
(מיד) from the hands of
(מים) water; to mix with water, to hydrate
(מימים) long since
(ממד) measurement, dimension
(מק) rottenness, decay
(מקם) to localize
(מקמק) to rot

(מקק) to rot, decay
(קא) what is vomited up, vomit
(קדד) to bow down, to bow ones head; to cut, to bore, drill
(קד) Syr. he tore, he cut away
(קדים) east
(קדם) to be before, be in front; Aram.-Syr. he was before, preceded, went before, anticipated; what is in front, forward; east
(קדקד) head, crown of the head; to crow
(קיא) to vomit, spit out; what is vomited up
(קד) enemy, foe, adversary

The Dalet Overlay :
Woe to the nations for the terrible day!
He [shall] tear away the veil [for] his friends and his beloved who rest.
In the front, towards the east, the crown of the head! His garment shall be red to reckon the blood-guilt and measure the bloodshed. He spits out water to the sea west and east, His hand to utterly crush the adversary [that they] bleed, rot, and decay.

Individual letters :
(א) [thus saith] YHWH ;
(י) the Almighty ;
(ם) who rises up the sea in the terrible day [of YHWH], a time of
(ק) weeping and wailing, howling and lamentation. [Take] the hand of my child beside the veil ;
(ד) Repent, the hand of power stands in the door.

Now, I'll re-print the text from the tools.

The Dalet Tools :
Bow your head, give thanks, confess, and banish the robber to fade away. Whitewash the nations to become one [with] my body.
Gather in [my] friends, and wash [my] beloved children.
Propound a riddle : [nail] [something pointed] [YaH] [to be kindled, burn] [to stretch out (the hand)] [My Glory] [to bore, to drill] [bush] [the hand ; power] [Hand]

I'm not going to combine these in this edition. If you understood how long it takes me, with everything else I need to do during the day, you would know why. This way, I can get this edition out much sooner.

If you see something that you are really interested in, you can always use the methods I have shown, and analyze it yourself.

Distilled definition : Door to fire of YHWH's Glory & Majesty ; YHWH STANDS IN THE DOOR ; Door to bow ones head & whitewash progeny, the nations.

Atbash Kuf :

Tools :

Ruler of 2 :
(דק) a thin curtain [the veil]

/\ Compass :
(מר) bitter; embittered, sad, gloomy; cruel; master; drop; hoe; myrrh
(מרר) to be bitter
(רמם) to become wormy, grow rotten, decay; to rise exalted
(פר) bull, bullock, steer
(פרם) to tear open, rend [garment, clothes]
(רם) high, elevated, exalted, supreme
(רפף) to move gently, to waver, vacillate; loosen, weaken

(צם) he fasted
(צמם) to press, draw together
(צמק) to be dry, shrink, shrivel
(קץ) end, destruction, ruin
(קצץ) to cut off; to stipulate
(קם) enemy, foe, adversary
(קמץ) to enclose with the hand, grasp, take a handful, to close, shut
(מק) rottenness, decay
(מץ) oppressor; to squeeze, to press
(מצק) to solidify

Atbash Kuf Word Overlay :

Atbash Kuf letter-by-letter :

The צ/ה

TOK　　　　　　　**TOL**

(צ/ה)=[ת/א]+[ע]+[ו/פ]　　　(ה/צ)=[פ/ו]+[ס/ח]+[ו/פ]
(ה/צ)=[ת/א]+[ב/ש]+[ו/פ]　　　(ה/צ)=[פ/ו]+[ב/ש]+[פ/ו]
(ה/צ)=[צ/ה]+[ת/א]+[ע]　　　(ה/צ)=[צ/ה]+[ו/פ]+[ס/ח]
(ה/צ)=[צ/ה]+[ת/א]+[א/ת]　　　(ה/צ)=[צ/ה]+[ו/פ]+[א/ת]
(צ/ה)–[צ/ה][ח/מ][ק/ל][ב/ל][ש/י][ו/ר][ק/ד]　　　(ה/צ)=[צ/ה][ל/ק][ב/ש][ת/א||ק/ד]

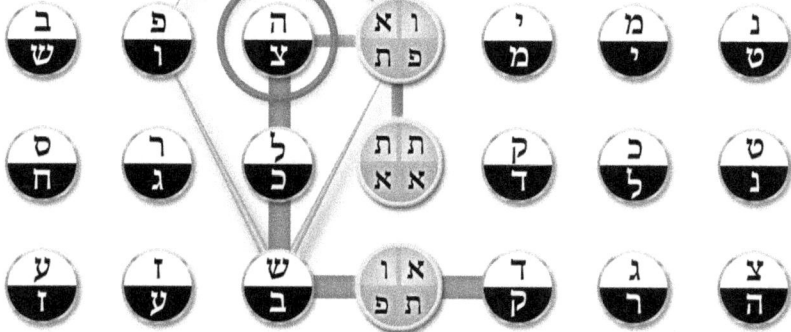

compound letters

[(א)=ו,י][(ב)=ו,ר][(ג)=ו,י,ו][(ד?)*][(ד)=ו][(ה)=ו,י,י][(ז)=ו,י]
[(ח)=ו,י,(ז?)*][(ט)=ו,י][(כ)=ו,י,ר][(ל)=ו,י][(מ)=ו,ו,ב,ז][(נ)=ו,י]
[(ס)=ו][(ע)=ו,י][(פ)=ו,י,(כ,ר?)*][(צ)=ו,י][(ק)=ו,י][(ר)=ו]
[(ש)=ו][(ת)=ו,ר]

I'm going to throw in a few interesting connections which I saw here, because you probably won't see it when I paste my lists.

Do you remember when I said something about apostate cults taking symbols & legends out of the tree?

This position for the ה Hei, which we saw is the Holy Ghost, has the "Mother", in חוה "Eve", Mother of all living.

(שדה) a beautiful Woman / Mother + ערץ Earth + רוח Wind + אש Fire
(שדה) a beautiful Woman / Mother + סהר Moon [this in in the צ/ה [sm sq.] in the bottom right corner of the grid]

Do we see where the mother earth / moon goddess may have come from?

The Hei : ה

QUICK REFERENCE :
ה = 5
הא = 6

Dictionary : The letter itself is of uncertain origin, but is used as a prefix meaning, "the", and it has been understood as "Behold" (see the squares word list).

(הא) Hei : The name of the letter is a Ruler of 2 belonging to the (א) Aleph, or YHWH. Her leg is joined to the (י) Yud [Father] by the (ו) Waw [the covenant] tilted to the side in the (א) Aleph overlay.

The letter (ה) Hei is also part of the Kabbalah Tree of Life labeled as Mother.

// BEGIN VETTED JUN 19 //

The Hei in the Tree of Life:

Rulers of 2 :
(תהה) to be astonished, be amazed, be dumbfounded; to meditate; to repent; to smell; to examine
(לה) to her
(להה) to languish (of the land from hunger), to faint, to be tired
(רהה) to fear
(פה) here; mouth; speech, saying; command; opening, orifice

Rulers of 3 :
(שלה) to draw out (of the water) - base of שליה = afterbirth; insolence, rebellion; at ease, at rest ; another spelling of הליש Shiloh, a city in Ephraim
(ערה) to be naked, bare, to lay bare, uncover; to join, attach
(בפה) with [his] mouth; in [the] mouth

Upper Square leading to the (ה) Hei :
(חוה) Eve ; mother of all the living, life; to show, declare; to experience, be deeply impressed by; tent, village
(הו) alas!
(הוה) that you may be; become; to fall; to be; ruin; disaster
(וו) nail
(חוח) aperture, cleft; briar, thorn, thornbush; hook, ring
(חח) hook, ring, fetter

Lower Square leading to the (ה) Hei :
(הות) to rely on; to rush upon, fall upon, attack
(התת) imagine mischief; overwhelm w. reproaches; to rush upon

(וו) nail
(תוה) to be startled or alarmed
(תהה) to be astonished, be amazed, be dumbfounded; to meditate; to repent; to smell; to examine
(תהו) emptiness, waste, wasteland, desert, chaos, confusion; vanity, nothingness, worthlessness
(תו) mark or sign
(תוה) to make a mark, scribble; to be startled, alarmed, amazed

Upper Hei Compass :
(חוח) aperture, cleft; briar, thorn, thornbush; hook, ring
(חוף) coast, shore
(חח) hook, ring, fetter
(חף) clean, pure, innocent
(חפף) to enclose, surround, cover, shelter
(פו) here
(פוח) to breathe, blow
(פח) thin plate of metal; leaf (of gold); snare, trap, (self springing) bird trap
(פחח) to trap, ensnare; be captured, chained

Lower Hei Compass :
(וו) nail
(פו) here
(פוש) to be strong ; increase, spread; to rest
(פש) haughtiness or folly
(שו) equality
(שוף) to trample upon, bruise; to smooth, rub, scrape, polish
(שוש) to rejoice, exult
(שפף) to crush, rub
(שש) six, white marble, Egyptian linen

// END VETTED JUN 19 //

TOOLS :

Ruler of 2 :
(פה) mouth; speech, saying; command; opening orifice; here
(פהה) to idle, to loaf, to tarry
(לה) pers. pron. to her.
(להה) to languish, faint, be tired
(תהה) [also תהא] to be astonished, be amazed, to meditate ; to repent.

Ruler of 3 :
(יאה) to befit, to become; Aram. (f) beautiful
(שלה) To draw out [from water - related to שליה afterbirth] ; also, to be quiet, at ease, tranquil [the peace of the comforter]
(ערה) to be naked; to lay bare, uncover

(בפה) in her mouth
(דתה) Possible relation to Syr. דתא - decree, law

The compass :
(שאף) Inhale [breath of life]; to gasp, pant after, pant for; to long for; to crush, trample upon
(שפא) Aram. - Syr. he smoothed, planed; Arab. it swept bare, smoothed (said of the wind)
(שף) = שוף to trample upon, bruise
(אשף) a magician, conjurer
(אף) nose, anger, wrath; also, too
(פש) = שוש haughtiness, folly; he increased, spread; to rest
(אש) a fire, fire
(אשש) to strengthen

The Square :
(הא) Hei : name of letter ; lo, behold, here is
(הדה) to stretch out (the hand)
(שהד) to bear witness
(שדה) a beautiful Woman ; field, open country, land [a place to plant seed? garden?]
(דשה) grass
(דש) threshing
(דשדש) to tread, trample
(דשש) to tread, trample, pound
(שד) the female breast; evil spirit; demon, devil
(דד) breast, teat, nipple
(שדד) to plow, harrow; to overpower, destroy violently, rob, devastate, ruin
(הד) a joyful shout, shouting, cheer
(הדד) to reverberate
(הדה) to stretch out (the hand)
(דהה) to fade, become dim
(הדד) to move slowly
(אש) a fire, fire
(אשה) wife [combined tree]
(שא) to forgive ; to lift up
(אף) a nostril, nose, face, anger ; also, yea
(שה) lamb, (young) sheep, goat, one of a flock
(שהה) to tarry, linger; to stay, to delay, be late in coming
NEW SQUARE
(את) with; a cutting instrument (usually rendered plowshare); you, thou
(אתה) to come; you, thou
(אתת) to signal
(התת) to rush upon
(תהה) to be astonished
(תת) he gave

The Square leading to the (ה) Hei from Aleph section :

(חוה) Eve ; mother of all the living, life; to show, declare; to experience, be deeply impressed by; tent, village
(הו) ah!, alas!, woe!
(הוה) to fall; to be; destruction, ruin; desire
(חוח) aperture, cleft; briar, thorn; hook, ring

NEW SQUARE

(הות) to rely on; to rush upon, fall upon
(הוה) to fall; to be; destruction, ruin; desire
(הו) ah!, alas!, woe!
(תוה) to make marks; to astonish, astound, amaze; astonishment, amazement; fright, terror
(תו) mark, sign

New (ה) Hei compass from Aleph section :

(וו) hook, peg, nail
(שופ) to be strong ; increase, spread; to rest
(פש) haughtiness or folly
(שוף) to trample upon, bruise; to smooth, rub, scrape, polish
(שוש) to rejoice
(שפף) to crush, rub
(שפשף) to rub, to polish, to cause to work hard
(שש) six, white marble, Egyptian linen

The Hei Tools :

To Eve, a command, to increase and spread.

Here is the threshing, to plow, to work hard, to be tired and grow faint, [then] to tread and trample [the] briars and thorns.

The decree to repent, to forgive and lift up. Stretch out the hand and draw forth from the water. Stretch out the hand and inhale a fire to bear witness.

The wrath of the lamb shall crush, trample, and bruise. Woe! To the devil, [for] haughtiness and folly, [are] destruction and ruin.

The square's (corners) are, letter by letter ; (ד) a door, (ש) for the children of men (ה) to draw out from water + to be lifted up

The compass facing up is ; (א) YHWH's (פ) mouth (ש) [to the] children of men. I have no doubt that the (ה) Hei, is the feminine Hebrew "רוח הקדוש" **Holy Ghost**.

Overlay Words :

(הא) lo, behold
(הד) joyous shout
(הדא) this, that, that is what is written
(הדד) to reverberate
(הדה) to stretch out (the hand)
(הדק) to press together
(היא) she

(היה) to be, exist, happen, become; was, existed, came into being, became, it came to pass, happened

(הלא) to be removed far away; do I not?, do you not?, is it not so?

(הלה) that

(הלל) to boast, to praise; to shine; be foolish [receive derision, scorn]

(אד) mist, vapor, gas

(אדה) to bring about, to cause; to evaporate

(אדק) to attach, fasten, connect

(אדש) to be indifferent; Aram. to be silent

(אהה) woe!, alas!, ah!

(אהי) where

(אהיה) I AM (name of God)

(אהל) to pitch a tent, to dwell in a tent; tent, shelter, tabernacle, dwelling, shelter

(אי) woe, alas, jackal, island, not, where

(איד) to vaporize, to steam

(איה) hawk, falcon, kite; where

(איל) ram, head, chief, leader; hart, stag, deer; power, strength

(אילה) hind, doe

(איש) man, husband

(אל) God, god; power; nothing, not; to, unto, toward, into, at, by

(אלה) to curse, swear, oath, obligation by oath; wail, lament; terebinth, oak; these; to deify, to worship as a deity; God, god

(אלי) to, towards

(אלל) to be weak; to spy out

(אללי) woe!, alas!

(אש) fire; foundation

(אשד) to pour; waterfall, cascade

(אשדה) slope of a mountain; waterfall

(אשה) woman, wife; burnt offering

(אשיה) pillar, foundation, base

(אשישה) cake made of dried compressed grapes; something compact or solid

(אשש) to strengthen

(יאה) to befit, to become; Aram. (f) beautiful

(יהד) to become a jew

(יד) hand, arm, foreleg

(ידד) to be friends, become friends

(ידה) to confess, give thanks; throw, hurl, cast

(ידיד) friend, beloved

(יה) short form of YHWH

(יקד) to be kindled, to burn

(יקהה) obedience

(יקש) to lay bait, lay snares

(יש) there is, there are; possession, property

(ישיש) old man

(קא) what is vomited up, vomit

(קדד) to bow down, bow one's head; to cut, to bore, to drill

(קדה) to bow

(קדקד) head, crown of the head; to crow

(קדש) to be holy, to be sacred, holiness, sanctity, a holy object, a holy place, the Holy Temple

(קהה) to be blunt, be dull

(קיא) to vomit, to spit out; what is vomited up, vomit

(קיה) to vomit

(קיש) to compare

(קל) light, swift, fast, easy, not difficult, unimportant; lightness, levity

(קלד) to open

(קלה) to roast, to parch, to burn, to consume; to be lightly esteemed, to be disgraced

(קלי) roasted grain, parched corn

(קלל) to be light, be slight, be swift; to be lightly esteemed, to be despised; glittering, burnished

(קלקל) to throw, to shake; to spoil, damage

(קלש) to thin out, to rarefy

(קש) straw, stubble, chaff

(קשה) to be hard, be stiff; be severe, cruel, fierce, violent

(קשקש) to knock, strike, rattle; to hoe

(קשש) to gather, assemble (esp. straw or stubble); to grow old (become dried, withered)

(דא) this

(דאה) to fly, glide (in the air); a bird of prey

(דד) breast, teat, nipple

(דדה) to move slowly

(די) sufficiency, enough; who, which, of, about

(דיק) bulwark, siege wall; to be exact, precise

(דל) door; poor, thin, lean, low, weak

(דלדל) to weaken, loosen, impoverish; to hang down, dangle

(דלה) to draw (water); the poor; thrum; hair

(דלי) bucket

(דליה) branch, bough

(דלל) to become poor, weak, thin; to hang down loosely

(דלק) to burn; to chase, pursue

(דק) thin curtain [veil]

(דקדק) to examine minutely, to be strict

(דקק) to crush, to pulverize

(דשא) to sprout, shoot, grow; green grass, green herbage

(דשדש) to tread, to trample

(דשש) to tread, trample, pound

(לא) no, not; non

(לאה) to be weary, be impatient

(לדה) birth

(לה) to her

(להה) to languish, faint, be tired

(לי) to me

(ליד) near, close to

(ליל) night, at night

(ליש) lion; dough

(ללא) without

(לקה) to be stricken, to be smitten; to be flogged, be scourged; be affected with disease

(לקלק) to lick

(לקק) to lick, to lap

(לקש) to be late; Syr. he gathered late fruit; late growth

(לשד) juice, sap, vigor; to add vigor

(לשלש) to secrete (chicken dirt)

(שאה) to make a din or crash; crash into ruins; to ruin, to lay waste; to wonder, be astonished, be amazed

(שאיה) desolation

(שאל) to ask, to inquire; to entreat, to beg, to borrow

(שאלה) to request, to petition, a thing asked for

(שד) female breast; evil spirit, demon, devil; violence, havoc, devastation

(שדד) to plow, harrow; to overpower, destroy violently, rob, devastate, ruin

(שדה) field, open country, land; a beautiful woman

(שדי) the Almighty

(שדידה) devastation, destruction, robbing

(שדל) to persuade, entice

(שה) young sheep, lamb

(שהד) witness

(שהה) to tarry, linger, stay, delay; be late in coming

(שהק) to hiccup

(שי) gift, present

(שיא) loftiness, pride

(שיד) lime, whitewash, plaster

(שיש) to rejoice; white marble, alabaster

(של) error, offense, crime; belonging to

(שלה) to draw out (from water - base of afterbirth); to be quiet, at ease

(שלי) my, mine; quietness, tranquility

(שליש) officer, captain; a dry measure - prob. the third part of an 'ephah'

(שלל) to spoil, to plunder, to deprive; to draw out (sheaves); to remove, to refuse, to negate; to stitch loosely, to join together loosely, to chain, to fetter; to tie with loops; plunder

(שלק) to boil, to cook; to make smooth, to trim

(שלש) three; to multiply by three; one of the third generation; pertaining to the third

(שק) sack, bag, sackcloth

(שקד) to watch, to wake; was bound, was bent; to be almond-shaped, almond tree, almond [the almond tree awakens first]

(שקה) to cause to drink; to give to drink (water)

(שקל) to weigh, balance; to weigh out, to pay money; to consider, examine; to take, a weight, shekel; name of a coin

(שקק) to rove, to run about noisily; rush in uproar; to desire; yearning, longing

(שש) six, white marble, Egyptian linen

(ששא) Syr. cotton

(ششה) six; to divide by six; to multiply by six

(شششي) sixth

As the overlay's word list is over three pages, I'm going to print the un-refined version first.

[to watch, to wake; was bound, was bent; to be almond-shaped, almond tree, almond (the almond tree awakens first)]
[to desire; yearning, longing] [man, husband]
[to confess, give thanks; throw, hurl, cast] [evil spirit, demon, devil] [to draw out (from water - base of afterbirth); to be quiet, at ease] [whitewash] [witness] [my, mine; quietness, tranquility] [to rejoice]
[woman, wife] [to tabernacle, shelter] [the Holy Temple]
[gift, present] [Egyptian linen] [to befit, to become; Aram. (f) beautiful] [a beautiful woman] [to strengthen] [to be friends, become friends] [friend, beloved]
[I AM (name of God)] [to stretch out (the hand)] [hand] [to examine minutely] [the veil] - [to bow down, bow one's head; to cut, to bore, to drill] [to open] [door; poor, thin, lean, low, weak] [to cause to drink; to give to drink (water)] [to pour; waterfall, cascade] [waterfall; slope of a mountain] [foundation, base, pillar] [fire; foundation] [to be kindled, to burn] [to praise; to shine] [near, close to] [EL]
[this, that, that is what is written] [that] [lamb] [Yah] [came into being] [swear, oath, obligation by oath; wail, lament; terebinth, oak; to deify, to worship as a deity; God, god] [to be lightly esteemed, to be despised] [to be stricken, to be smitten; to be flogged, be scourged] [to hang down, dangle] [offense, crime; belonging to] [to her] [is it not so?] (see Isaiah 53)
[head, crown of the head; to crow] [to compare] [obedience] [the Almighty] [to spoil, to plunder, to deprive; to draw out (sheaves); to remove, to refuse, to negate; to stitch loosely, to join together loosely, to chain, to fetter; to tie with loops; plunder] [to weigh, balance] [loftiness, pride]
[woe!] [to be hard, be stiff; be severe, cruel, fierce, violent] [to lay bait, lay snares] [lo, behold] [lion] (of Judah) [to fly, glide (in the air); a bird of prey] [joyous shout] [to reverberate] [to be late; Syr. he gathered late fruit; late growth] [to make a din or crash; crash into ruins; to ruin, to lay waste; to wonder, be astonished, be amazed] [to hoe; to knock, strike, rattle] [to tread, to trample] [to tread, trample, pound] [to crush, to pulverize]
[woe!] [straw, stubble, chaff] [to gather, assemble (esp. straw or stubble); to grow old (become dried, withered)] [to burn; to chase, pursue] [to roast, to parch, to burn, to consume; to be lightly esteemed, to be disgraced]

The Hei Overlay :
    Awake (as the almond tree in the spring)!
    [Let] thy desire be to thy husband.
    Confess and give thanks [repent] to cast [out] the evil spirit. Draw forth from the water, be whitewashed [white/clean/pure], witness my peace and rejoice.
    [Let] the woman tabernacle and find shelter in my Holy Temple. [Receive] a gift of white linen, befitting a beautiful woman, to strengthen my friends and my beloved.
    I AM shall stretch out his hand to examine minutely [at] the veil. Bow your head, open the door, and drink the cascading water from the slope of a mountain whose foundation is a pillar of fire. Be kindled and burn with praise that you may shine

nigh unto EL.

It is written that the lamb of Yah came into being, an obligation by oath, to be lightly esteemed, to be despised, to be stricken, smitten, flogged, scourged, to hang down and dangle. [Yet] the crime and the offense belong to her. Is it not so? (see Isaiah 53)

The head shall compare obedience [to] the Almighty and weigh in the balance loftiness and pride. To deprive the plunder and negate the spoil. To remove the chains, and draw out sheaves.

Woe to the violent and cruel who lay snares! Behold, the lion [of Judah] shall fly in the air as a bird of prey! A joyous shout reverberates [as] he gathers the late fruit and makes a din (great sound) to lay waste amidst wonder and amazement. Strike to tread, trample, and pound . . . to crush and to pulverize.

Woe to the straw, stubble, and chaff! You shall be gathered together to burn and be consumed in disgrace.

Individual letters :
(ה) Behold the mouth of the lamb bears witness of the decree. Repent and draw out from water to forgive and lift up a beautiful woman. Stretch out the hand, inhale fire, and rejoice in white linen.
(א) YHWH will become
(י) man, and the blood [of] my hand [will] whitewash [your] garment ;
(ק) [my] Son beside the veil is the door. The hand of power.
(ד) To propound a riddle : the bush to burn, stretch out the hand of Yah, bow ones head to bore, to thrust a nail, gather in the offspring, [my] beloved, to become my glory.
(ל) The lamb of EL [was] slain, to remove the offense belonging to the weak and negate the spoil of the enemy.
(ש) The lamb came into being to present a gift of white linen to be like Yah. [Receive inheritance in the Celestial Kingdom with a Celestial glory likened to the brightness of the Sun]

The Atbash ה Hei contains : (רה) Syr. he breathed; Phoen. Spirit; Arab. was windy [compare with רוח], and the large square of the ה Hei, when looking at the full grid, contains [קדש] Holy.

The Holy Ghost is thus found in the tools of the (ה) Hei, part of the א Aleph, and the three letters which make up the name YHWH.

We see this in the heavens of the grid [in the ה Hei], yet we will also see it in the earth, within the ח Chet, the gate of baptism and fire.

Distilled definition : mother ; Eve ; mother of all living ; life ; breath of life ; comforter ; part of YHWH ; behold ; to bear witness ; The Holy Ghost.
[A more full link to the (ח) Chet, Holy Ghost will come in a later edition showing that we know in part, and we prophecy in part. . . That which is revealed will be joined with that which is hidden].

Atbash Tzade :

Tools :

Ruler of 2 :
(עץ) tree; timber, wood; handle
(אץ) hurrying, hastening
(גצץ) to flash, to glitter

V Compass :
(וו) Waw
(תו) Taw; mark, sign
(בו) in him, in it, therein
(בת) daughter; girl, maiden, young woman; deserving; at the age of, worthy of, bath

Square :
(קבב) to utter a curse, curse; to be bent, crooked; to hollow out; to vault
(קבץ) to collect, gather, assemble, store
(קץ) end; destruction, ruin
(קצב) to cut off; to determine; form, shape; end, extremity
(צב) covered wagon, litter
(צבב) to cover
(בץ) mud, mire, silt
(בצץ) to squeeze out, exude
(בצק) to swell; dough
(בק) Syr. worm eaten, decayed
(בקק) to be empty

Atbash Tzade Word Overlay :

Atbash Tzade letter-by-letter :

The TOK פ/ו & ת/א TOL

TOK # TOL

$[א/ת]+[ש/ב]+[ד/ק]=(פ/ו)$ $[ו/פ]+[ש/ב]+[ד/ק]=(ת/א)$

$[ח/ס]+[ש/ב]+[ד/ק]=(פ/ו)$ $[ע]+[ש/ב]+[ד/ק]=(א/ת)$

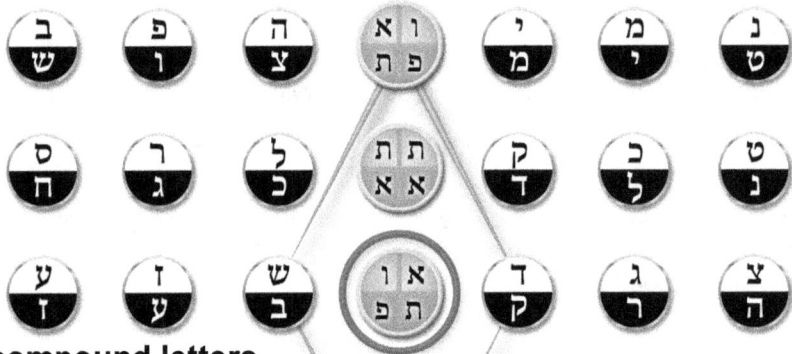

compound letters

$[(א)= י,ו][(ב)= ר,ו][(ג)= (ז?),י,ו]^*[(ד)= ו][(ה)= ר,י,ו][(ז)= י,ו]$
$[(ח)= (ז?),י,ו]^*[(ט)= י,ו][(כ)= ר,י,ו][(ל)= י,ו][(מ)= י,ו,נ,ז][(נ)= י,ו]$
$[(ס)= ו][(ע)= י,ו][(פ)= (ר,כ?),י,ו]^*[(צ)= י,ו][(ק)= י,ו][(ר)= ו]$
$[(ש)= ו][(ת)= ו,ר]$

You have probably noticed that I have been pasting in old work which is mostly from the Tree of Knowledge.

Here, I will paste in what I have for the פ/ו pair . . . but before I do that, I am going to show you what I found in that Aleph, from the Tree of Life Aleph Overlay.

The letters covered by that overlay are (א)(ל) (פ) [אלף=Aleph] (ה)(ו)(ר)(ז).

I was only working the white letters at the time, but I'm sure you will like what I came up with.

Now we look at the Aleph in the Menorah

The configuration is from the Tree of Life, and it is identical to what would be found in the Menorah configuration. Note that the (א) Aleph is in the same place, and as the (ו) Waw IS the center pipe, it would be in the same place in the overlay as well.

Clues that began with the first Aleph overlay :

We saw the (איש) "Man" within the Aleph overlay, created in the image of Yahoo יהו. We saw - Aram. שתיא, Syr. שתיא, Arab, Satan (thread, warp). Consider the "reptile" twisting around when the (א) Aleph comes to earth.

This is part of the Adam and Eve story. In fact, it would appear to be a reference to "Satan" being cast out of the heavens, into the earth, and his desire to be the (א) Aleph [god] of this world.

Note also (for the section on the Waw) when the (ו) Waw is on the top [in the heavens - Tree of Life], the compass which defines it says (אהיה) AHYH, more commonly referred to as the "I AM" which Moses spoke to. It is the (ו) Waw, "the Son", that Adam & Eve spoke to in the Garden of Eden. That is the Genesis of this story.

Adam & Eve :
Now that the Aleph is on the earth, I'll just lay out what I see [literally]. I see the (ו) Waw in the center which was tilted to the left now becomes a rib (in vision). I see (חוה) Eve, whose name now appears in a square [Tree of Life - ח Chet on top] over the letter (ה) Hei fall to the earth, going through the word (אלפ) Aleph, which I see as a rib, to become the (ש) Shin [on the Earth]. The (ש) Shin now represents that which comes forth from the womb. After the (ש) Shin becomes the opening for children to come forth, you would have the center column normal [see tree of Knowledge] and see a square on bottom saying (חוש) to feel pain, anxiety, apprehension.

Now that the (א) Aleph has come to earth, watch how the words in the story of the Aleph begin to change.

TOOLS :

Ruler of 2 :
(דא) This
(קא) vomit
(תא) cell, room, compartment (esp. in the temple)
(לא) no, not
(שא) to forgive ; to lift up ; take, take up

Ruler of 3 :

(פלא) to wonder, marvel; to be extraordinary, be difficult; to be wonderful; to distin-guish, to make special

The Compass :
(שד) evil spirit, demon; (female) breast; violence, havoc, devastation, ruin
(שדד) to deal violently with, despoil, devastate, ruin; to plow, to harrow; to over-power, to rob, devastate, ruin; to ravage; Ethiop. he expelled; Arab. he closed up, stopped up, obstructed
(שדדו) have been destroyed, are spoiled, devastated
(שדוד) dead; completely, utterly, destroyed, spoiled, desolate
(שודד) destroyer; spoiler, robber or thief
(שו) equality
(שש) six, white marble, Egyptian linen
(וו) nail
(דוד) David; beloved one, beloved, love, uncle; kettle, basket
(דודו) his beloved
(דוש) to tread, thresh; trample (men, nations), exterminate
(דד) breast, teat, nipple; uncle
(דשדש) to tread, to trample
(דשש) to tread, to trample; to pound

The Bottom Compass - Tree of Life :
This is from a compass at the bottom of the Tree of Life with an ע Ayin [see Tree of Life].
(עד) to, up to, even to; until, while; eternity, perpetuity; witness, testimony; menstru-ation; booty, prey
(עדד) to count, reckon; alternate spelling of Oded - "restorer", two Israelites
(עש) moth; name of constellation (probably the great bear)
(עשש) to waste away, decay
(דע) knowledge, wisdom
(עשע) to smooth, to besmear, to blind; whence 'was blinded'; to take delight, to be delighted in, treat fondly
(עשעש) to smooth, to besmear; to take delight, to delight

VETTED - SEE WHAT IT SAYS -- LEFT OFF HERE -

SPACE FOR SAYING OF TOOLS
PICK UP HERE

You have seen how the previous two, "tools" / "overlay" / "letter-by-letter" messag-es were created. Now, I am going to combine these the way that they should be.

I will still use a synopsis of each section . . . but this is to give me direction. The end message will be based on these themes. However, I do not wish to leave out alternate word definitions which should end up in the final message. So I will go back to the beginning, and categorize all of the words, as if they are one section.

There are individual overlays which have more words than all three of these sec-tions combined, so this is a good place to begin combining the three into one.

NOTE : There are extra words, relevant to the story, which have been left out of the short synopsis. When these three are combined, we will be able to use them.
Synopsis of words in Tools section :
Woe, alas! To fall, destruction and ruin, expelled, and obstructed. Eve, the mother of all the living to experience life; to be strong, increase and spread. To forgive and lift up [in a] room in the temple. To set apart and to make special, to be extraordinary. [Her seed shall] trample upon and bruise [the] robber [with the] evil spirit.

The words beneath the overlay :
(זר) stranger, flame, edging
(זוהל) reptile who twists at an angle towards the upper right - [the same vector that produced the word satan when the Aleph was on top]
(ילהה) to languish, faint, be tired
(לו) to him; oh that!, would that!, if only!
(לוה) to borrow; to join, he was near; to wind, to turn, twist
(לא) no, not
(אל) EL [God], power, not, nothing
(אלה) curse, oath, wail, lament, strong tree
(לוז) almond tree; to turn aside; to speak evil
(אלוה) Eloh [God]
(אור) light, to give light
(אלף) Aleph :a base prob. meaning orig. 'to be linked together, be connected; to bring forth thousands; thousand; oxen, bullocks, cows, cattle; part of a tribe
(פלא) [Aleph backwards] The orig. meaning is prob. 'to cleave, split, set apart, separate; to distinguish, to make special; to wonder, to marvel; to be extraordinary, be difficult, be wonderful
(פלל) to judge, to arbitrate; to pray
(פאה) to cleave; side, edge, extremity
(פה) mouth, speech, saying, command
(פהה) to idle, loaf, tarry
(פז) pure gold
(פזז) to move quickly, be agile, be supple; be purified, be gilded
(פזר) to scatter, to disperse
(פר) bull, bullock, steer
(פרא) to bear fruit, be fruitful; to be wild, be savage; wild ass; desert dweller
(פרז) to decentralize; to go beyond, exceed; chief
(פרר) to crush; to break; to shake
(ראה) to see
(רהה) to fear
(רז) secret
(רזה) to be or become lean, thin, weak
(רפא) to heal, to cure; to weaken
(רפה) to be weak, be feeble; to heal, to cure
(הא) lo, behold
(הוה) to fall, to be; destruction, ruin; desire
(הזה) to dream, to rave
(הלא) to be removed far away; do I not?, do you not?, is it not so?

(הלל) praise ; shine; To boast, praise, he shouted, sang, praised, shouted for joy; to shine, it began to shine, it shone; to be foolish
(הר) mountain
(הרה) to conceive, to become pregnant

The story in the overlay :

Aleph : (י) Adam (ו) AND (ה) Eve [in the garden]

A stranger, Satan, was near to wind, to turn and twist. Behold the Almond tree, turn aside, [to speak evil] . . . desire, to see [it is] to give light.

Is it not so? EL command(ed) a curse [with an] oath [to] wail and lament the strong tree.

Pray to be purified. Would that EL to heal, to cure the weak and faint.

EL says to conceive, become pregnant, to bear fruit. [They shall] be purified, set apart, to shine in the mountain('s) secret. [They shall] go beyond and become extraordinary, and crush the reptile.

Letter-by-letter :

(ו) The (אהיה) "I AM"

(פ) to redden one's face [with shame], pure, innocent, clean

(א) Aleph : [position on earth] (שודד) robber or thief [has (שד) evil spirit - is this the reptile who considers himself the "Aleph" of this world?]

(ל) offense, to remove, shine [covering of glory], to slay, plunder, to deprive

(ה) Mouth, behold, Eve, mother of all living, to experience, life, to draw out [related to birth], increase, to trample upon, to bruise

(ר) stranger, enemy, to envy, chief, cover with blackness, pitch worker, separate, chief, to rule

(ז) Disquieting thoughts ; Sin, Transgression, to become weak, glory, to waste away, he bruised

Letter-by-letter synopsis :

Thus saith the I AM to the innocent, pure and clean whose faces are reddened with shame. The reptile [that old serpent the Devil], [has caused] your offense, to remove your covering of glory, so you will die.

The voice of [EL] said, Eve shall be the mother of all living, to draw out life and increase; to trample upon and bruise [the reptile].

The enemy who envied the chief used works of darkness to cast pitch upon his glory introducing sin and transgression, to make him weak, that he waste away [and die].

Now, In order to combine the three properly, I begin with the known words in the tools and overlay sections and come up with the following.

[reptile] [stranger; frame, edging] [to borrow; to join, he was near; to wind, to turn, twist] [lo, behold] [this] [almond tree; to turn aside; to speak evil] [to take delight] [to wonder, marvel; to be extraordinary, be difficult; to be wonderful; to distinguish, to make special] [to see] [knowledge, wisdom] [to lift up] [equality] [EL]
[EL] [God]] [mouth, speech, saying, command] [to be removed far away; do I not?,

do you not?, is it not so?] [curse, oath, wail, lament, strong tree]

[ah!, alas!, woe!] [to him; oh that!, would that!, if only!] [no, not] [was blinded] [to fear] [to fall; to be; destruction, ruin; desire] [to be or become lean, thin, weak] [haughtiness or folly] [to fall, to be; destruction, ruin; desire] [to waste away, decay] [to plow, he expelled; he closed up, stopped up, obstructed] [to decentralize; to go beyond, exceed; chief] [briar, thorn] [to cause to work hard] [to languish, faint, be tired]

[Eve ; mother of all the living, life; to show, declare; to experience] [oven to, until, while; eternity; witness, testimony; menstruation] [to conceive, to become pregnant] [to bear fruit, be fruitful; to be wild, be savage; desert dweller] [to be strong ; increase, spread; to rest] [to bring forth thousands]

[to judge, to arbitrate; to pray] [to be weak, be feeble; to heal, to cure] / ['to cleave, split, set apart, separate; to distinguish, to make special; to wonder, to marvel; to be extraordinary, be difficult, be wonderful] [light, to give light] [mountain] [secret] [Egyptian linen] [room in the temple] [to heal, to cure; to weaken] [to rejoice] [to move quickly, be agile, be supple; be purified, be gilded] [pure gold] [praise ; shine; To boast, praise, he shouted, sang, praised, shouted for joy; to shine, it began to shine, it shone; to be foolish]

[to tread, thresh] [to tread, to trample; to pound] [to trample upon, bruise] [to scatter, to disperse] [to crush; to break; to shake] [robber or thief] [evil spirit, violence, devastation]

left over words :
[to idle, loaf, tarry] [vomit] [no, not] [was weary] [kid] [bull, bullock, steer] [to dream, to rave] [kettle, basket] [breast, teat, nipple]
fragment? [to count, to reckon] [six] [to cleave; side, edge, extremity]

The next step involves tapping into the letter-by-letter. So, I will begin by listing all of the words used from the letter-by-letter lists.

(ו) [I AM] [to call, to invoke] [fire] [to overpower] [to banish] [to be new, restored] [a gift]
(פ) [to give] [pure, innocent] [clean] [to redden ones face (with shame)] [let us]
(א) [YHWH] [it will come to pass] [will become] [to become]
(ז) [shine] [EL, power] [error, offense, crime; to put off, to loose; to purposely let fall] [to chain down] [to slay] [a lamb] [enemy, foe] [appointed time]
(ה) [Eve] [saying] [to be naked] [to forgive, to lift up] [to draw out (from water)] [a beautiful woman] [fire] [devil] [saying]
(ר) [enemy] [stranger] [to coat with pitch] [to defile, a person totally wounded, a person slain] [chief] [to finish off, consume] [to chew, masticate] [to swallow]
(ז) [a fortress of glory] [to be strong, to prevail] [to fly] [to become weak, to waste away

The message of the Aleph Adam & Eve Story :

The reptile, the stranger, was near to twist and turn, saying; behold this almond tree, to turn aside and speak evil . . . Take delight, [it is] to make special, to see knowledge and wisdom, to lift up, [to be] equal [with] El (God).

The enemy said, to chew, masticate and swallow, finish off and consume. . . [He did this] to coat with pitch the shine, to defile, to wound, and to slay the chief, [that he] become weak and waste away to die.

Is it not so, [that] EL (God) commanded a curse of lament [regarding] the strong tree?

Woe! If only not blinded [beguiled]. [Now] naked, ashamed, and full of fear for the crime. To fall and become weak for haughtiness and folly. To fall into destruction and ruin, to waste away and decay. To plow briars and thorns, to work hard, to languish and faint beyond.

Eve to become the mother of all living. Menstruation, to conceive and become pregnant. To bear fruit, to increase and spread, to be strong and bring forth thousands.

Let us pray to YHWH, to forgive and lift up, to heal the weak.

It will come to pass, at the appointed time, אהיה [I AM] will become a lamb, set apart [as] a light. To draw out from water a beautiful woman and heal [her].

Rejoice to be restored, pure innocent and clean! [I AM] to give a gift of white linen, a room in the fortress of glory, and a secret fire, to be purified as gold; to shine [like] EL and invoke power. A fire to prevail and be strong.

[These shall] fly and overpower the enemy. To scatter and thresh, to tread and trample, to crush and bruise the thief; to banish and chain down the Devil and his evil spirit.

It was known that Adam and Eve would "fall" prey to the cunning of the Devil. . . and yet, it was part of the plan from the beginning.

The garden of YHWH's planting could not take root unless Adam and Eve became mortal. That their children could increase upon the face of the earth. Do you understand that the garden of his planting represents the children of YHWH bearing fruit? The vineyard of HIS planting? The children of the Kingdom? The Sons and Daughters of YHWH?

Do you understand that this life is a test? That the "plan of salvation" which we shall see in the Aleph-Bet existed before the world? That there could be no test between good and evil to prove our character if they had never partaken of the fruit.

HIS children descend into the earth as the water of life falling from the heavens. The etherial [spiritual being] mixes with the elements to spring forth from HIS seed [the garden of HIS planting]. . . and when we die, our mortal bodies will lie down in the dust to sleep in the earth while our waters evaporate [etherial/spiritual] and return to the heavens from whence we came. We will see more of this in the eternal iteration of the םי Yud-Mem.

Waw

I = 6
II = 12

Dictionary : nail, hook, peg

Stand alone letter : no component letters to de-construct.

The (ו) Waw is used as a conjunctive prefix meaning "and" or "but". This appears to be due to the definition of "nail, hook, peg" used to connect things. It is also used as a prefix changing past tense to future tense, and vice versa. The tools give us the primary meaning of the target letter, so let's look at the אהיה "I am" in the Tree of Life. The key is the היה which includes was, happened, and to be, become, happen. The "I AM", was, and is, and is to come.

As a suffix, the (ו) Waw is used to denote a third person masculine possessive "his", or third person plural "they did".

(לו) to him = [(ל) to the (ו) son (male reference)]

ATBASH PAIRS
(שב) gray, old, an old man; one who returns
(דק) a thin curtain (the veil from position in the Temple within the grid and usage in Isaiah 40:22); fine, thin, small; name of an eye disease
(חם) Derivative of חום = to have pity, spare; to have mercy, to save

Continue here . . .

(קדש) **to be holy**, be sacred; holiness, sanctity; a holy object; a holy place; the Holy Temple; temple prostitute (i.e. priestess of Ishtar - A.K.A. Easter)

(אלף) Aleph - from a ruler of 3 created in the Adam and Eve overlay, within the (ו) Waw of that Aleph [see Aleph section, Adam and Eve overlay].

Before beginning with the tools breakdown I would like to go over a previous breakdown of the "I AM".

אהיה / now separate the (א) Aleph from the (היה) and use the tools list to define the Aleph. א = Yah, Yahoo, or YHWH + היה = to be, exist, happen, become; was, existed; came into being, became; he remained; it came to pass, happened.

Dictionary : hook, peg, nail.

The (ו) Waw is said to be the link that connects heaven and earth. This legend appears to be accurate in every letter within the center pipe of the Menorah. They all contain the (ו) Waw within their overlays. YHWH, a covenant Son, creator, mediator, and judge.

Let's begin with the reminders posted in the (א) Aleph section [The Waw in the Aleph overlay] :

1. The three dictionary definitions of the (ו) Waw. (ה) Hei, has a "hook"
(ת) Taw, "to thrust in" could be a "peg" descriptor
(ד) Dalet, "sharp, to bore, drill & sharp edge, something pointed" could describe a "nail".

2. The meanings of both "Son" and "Creator"
(ה) Hei, the mouth, [of] the lamb, to declare, life -
(ת) Taw, to decree, light, -
(ד) Dalet, the offspring, [of] Yah, my glory, the hand, [of] power.

3. When the (ו) Waw is on the top, its compass defines it as (אהיה) AHYH, more commonly referred to as the 'I AM' which Moses spoke to." I AM (אהיה) = 21 = Yahoo (יהו) = Yah (יה) + Son (ו) [Review the name of (יוסף) Joseph and (ברא) Bara in the Aleph Section].

The Waw will be a very interesting study which shows us that we may need to look deeper than the "tools" list when ciphering out the full meanings in words.

Everything I have seen in the code seems to indicate that the Patriarchs and Old Testament prophets had a firm grasp and understanding of the Aleph-Bet grid as laid out in this book. They understood the meanings within the Aleph-Bet which could not have been derived from the simplicity of the "tools" lists alone.

Tools :

(וו) Waw ; hook, peg, nail

Ruler of 2 :
(ות) sign or mark ; name of last letter in the Aleph-bet [belongs to the (ו) Waw];
(שו) equality [signifies one who will inherit]; related to שוה to be like, be equal
(שוו) Aramaic : equal (plural) equals

(קו) measuring line, line; voice
(לו) to him = [(ל) to the (ו) son (male reference)]

Ruler of 3 :
(אתו) SArab. to come

The Compass :
(אד) mist, vapor, gas. [Prob. a loan word from Akka. edu (= flood, inundation).]
(אדש) to be indifferent; Aram. he was silent
(אש) fire ; Strongs 787. Aramaic = a foundation, foundations
(אשש) to strengthen; Arab. he founded, established
(אשד) to pour, waterfall, cascade
(דא) this
(דשא) to sprout, shoot, grow; green grass, green herbage
(דשדש) to tread, trample
(שד) female breast; evil spirit
(שדד) to plow, harrow; to overpower, destroy violently, rob, ruin
(שש) six, white marble, Egyptian linen
(ششא) Syr. cotton

(חד) one, uni-, mono-
(חדד) to be sharp
(דחח) to push, thrust, banish
(חשד) to suspect; Arab. he envied
(חדש) to be new, restored, new; new moon, month
(שח) bent, bowed
(שחד) a present; a gift; a bribe

MIXED COMPASS ENTRANCE :

ATBASH PAIRS
(שב) gray, old, an old man; one who returns
(דק) a thin curtain (the veil from position in the Temple within the grid and usage in Isaiah 40:22); fine, thin, small; name of an eye disease
(חן) Derivative of חון = to have pity, spare; to have mercy, to save

MIXED COMPASS ENTRANCE : ש ק ד ס ח ד ב
RED
(בד) linen, cloth, material; pole, bar, rod; branch (of a tree); part, portion; lie, fabrication
(בדד) to be alone, be separated, isolated; alone
(בדח) to be happy, jolly, in a good mood
(בדק) to mend, repair; he mended, repaired; to examine, inspect; rent, **breach**; mending, **repair**; Aram. he split
(בחש) to stir; to agitate
(בסס) to trample, tread; to base, establish
(בקק) to be empty, destroyed, laid waste; Arab. he cleft, split

(בוש) to be ashamed

(דב) bear

(דבב) to move gently, to walk softly; to drip; to speak, whisper

(דבק) to cling, cleave, adhere; cleaving, attached; glue; joining; appendage

(דבש) honey; to be as sweet as honey

1(דד) breast, teat, nipple

1(דחה) to push, thrust, banish

(דחם) to press, compress

(דחק) to thrust, press

(דק) a thin curtain (**the veil** from position in the Temple within the grid and usage in Isaiah 40:22); fine, thin, small; name of an eye disease

(דקדק) to examine minutely, to be strict

(דקק) to crush, pulverize, thresh

1(דשש) to tread, to trample

1(דשש) to tread, to trample; to pound

(חב) bosom

(חבב) to love

(חבם) to press, crush

(חבק) to embrace, clasp

(חבש) to bind, bind on, bind up

1(חד) one, single

1(חדד) to be sharp

(חדק) to press together, compress; nightshade (a kind of thornbush)

1(חדש) **to be new, restored**, new; new moon, month

(חן) Syr.-Mand. derivative of חום to have pity, spare; **to have mercy**, to save

(חשב) to think, account; to band, girdle

1(חשד) to suspect

(חשק) to bind, join, be attached to; desire, longing, pleasure

1(חשש) to feel pain, fear, apprehend; chaff

(סבב) to turn about, go round, surround

(סד) stocks (blocks with notches to secure a prisoners feet with iron bolts)

(סדק) to crack, cleave, split

(סחב) to drag, draw, pull

2(סס) moth

2(סקבב) to wound, rub sore

2(קב) a measure of capacity

2(קבב) to utter a curse; to be bent, crooked; to hollow out; to vault

2(קבם) to disgust, to cause vomiting

(קד) Syr. He tore, he cut away

(קדד) to bow down; to cut, bore, drill; related to Syr. קד, Arab. *qadda* = he cut lengthwise

(קדח) to kindle, be kindled; to bore, drill

(קדקד) head, crown of the head; to crow

(קדש) **to be holy**, be sacred; holiness, sanctity; a holy object; a holy place; the Holy Temple; temple prostitute (i.e. priestess of Ishtar - A.K.A. Easter)

(קח) he took

2(קסס) to munch, chew; to become sour

(קש) straw, stubble, chaff

(קשב) to incline one's ears, to listen, hearken; attentive; listener; attention, attentiveness

(קשח) to be hard, rigid

(קשקש) to knock, strike, rattle; to hoe

(קשש) to gather, assemble (esp. straw or stubble); to grow old

(שב) gray, old, an old man; **one who returns**

(שבב) splinter, fragment; chip, chisel; to turn away, apostatize, be refractory, de rebellious

(שבח) to praise, laud; to still, calm, soothe, appease

(שרק) to leave, let alone, forsake, abandon

(שבש) to entangle, confound, confuse

1(שד) evil spirit, demon; (female) breast; violence, havoc, devastation, ruin

1(שדד) to deal violently with, despoil, devastate, ruin; to plow, to harrow; to overpower, to rob, devastate, ruin; to ravage; Ethiop. he expelled; Arab. he closed up, stopped up, obstructed

1(שדש) base of שש six, and words there referred to

1(שח) meditation; talk; bent, bowed

1(שחד) to bribe, bribery

1(שחח) bow down

(שחק) to laugh; to rub away, beat fine; to pulverize; fine dust; cloud of dust; clouds in general

(ooש) to plunder, spoil, pillage

(שקד) was bound, was bent; to watch, **wake**; to be almond shaped; almond; **almond tree**

(שקק) to rove, run about noisily, rush in uproar; yearning, longing, **desire**

1(שש) six; white marble; Egyptian linen

The flipped compass in the Aleph section adds :

(אהיה) AHYH, I AM

(אי) the mariners place of refuge; not; woe!, alas!, where?

(איה) hawk, falcon, kite; where?

(הא) lo, behold

(היא) she

(היה) to be, exist, happen, become; was, existed; came into being, became; he remained; it came to pass, happened

(יאה) to befit, to become

(יה) Yah, short form of YHWH

Additional Definitions : (from Aleph overlay words, and use in Biblical Hebrew)

(ו in the א) = create, creator, creates

(ו in the א) = son, or Son of Yah (also known as, the creator)

(ו) = Hook, Peg, Nail (all from the same diagonal ו Waw in the Aleph overlay)

(אלף) Aleph - from a ruler of 3 created in the Adam and Eve overlay, within the (ו) Waw of that Aleph [see Aleph section, Adam and Eve overlay].

Before beginning with the tools breakdown I would like to go over a previous breakdown of the "I AM".

אהיה / now separate the (א) Aleph from the (היה) and use the tools list to define the Aleph. א = Yah, Yahoo, or YHWH + היה = to be, exist, happen, become; was, existed; came into being, became; he remained; it came to pass, happened. Basically, Yah, Yahoo, or YHWH who was and is and is to come.

Let's also remember that in the (א) Aleph overlay of the Adam and Eve story, the (ו) Waw, in the middle of the (א) Aleph, actually spells out אלף Aleph.

The Waw tools list :

I AM Yah who was and is and is to come.

Behold the sign and the mark of the nail to renew the contract, to be restored.

White linen, a present of equality to become one. A voice to strengthen; to pour as a cascading waterfall from a foundation of fire.

Woe [to the] evil spirit who envied! This shoot to come shall be sharp, to tread and to trample [thresh], to overpower and destroy violently, to thrust and to banish.

As part of the (ת) Taw, it is related to the scales of justice, the scepter of (ק) Mercy and (ל) Severity measured by the (ע) Ayin [eye] of (יה) Yah. . . That is describing the overlay of the (ח) Chet, the gate. Every letter in the center pipe of the Menorah relates in one way or another to the ONE who creates, who judges, who is the covenant, and the gate which leads to eternal life.

"... give us a nail in his holy place, that our God may lighten our eyes, and give us a little reviving in our bondage." (Ezra 9: 8)

Overlay Words :
(ה) the
(הא) lo, behold
(הו) ah!, alas!, woe!
(הוא) he; it
(הוה) to fall; to be; destruction, ruin, disaster; desire
(הות) to rely on, to rush upon, to fall upon
(התת) to rush upon (threatening, menacing)
(אהה) woe!, alas!, ah!
(או) or
(אוה) to desire, to long for
(אות) sign, signal, symbol, token; miracle; to consent, to agree; to cut in; to en-grave or mark, to be willing; to agree; to come in; to be, to exist [literally (א) Aleph (ו) And (ת) Tav - first and last letters]
(את) sign, mark, with, you, portent, token; thou; plow-share, hoe, self; at; by; with; toward; the particle of directed emphasis; THIS! (first and last letters) =Gematria 401= (ישעיהו) "Salvation of Yah"
(תא) cell, room, compartment (esp. in the Temple)
(אתו) SArab. to come
(תאה) to mark out a boundary
(תאו) a wild sheep

(תאוה) desire, wish; passion, appetite; boundary, limit
(תהה + תהא) to be astonished, be amazed, be dumbfounded; to meditate; to re-pent; to smell; to examine
(תהו) emptiness, waste, desert; chaos, confusion, vanity, nothingness, worthless-ness
(תו) mark, sign
(תוה) to make marks; to astonish, astound, amaze
(וו) nail

The Waw overlay :
The wild sheep shall repent and be amazed. Mark out a boundary, a room to make marks.
Behold THE Aleph and Tav, the first and last, willing to engrave the mark of the nail as a sign. +++ (אתו) SArab. to come

Individual letters :
Beginning with the compass definition of the (ו) Waw in the (א) Aleph section :
(אהיה) AHYH or "I AM" and using one word selections from the tools sections.
Then the (א) YHWH
The (ה) Life
The (ת) Light
The (ו) Foundation [where the nail connects the heavens to the earth]

Letter by letter the (ו) Waw = I AM YHWH, the Life and Light of the world!

Letter by letter expanded : The mouth of the Holy Ghost bears witness. YHWH, to be feared, revered, and honored [was] despised and esteemed lightly. [They] hurl forth wild talk and false accusation. The light took a yoke, thrust in [pierced] and lifted up to pay a ransom from the foundation of the world. To him, the sign of the nail, to renew a contract, a gift of fire, a present of equality.
(compare with Isaiah 53)

Now look back to the tools and the overlay sayings. There is absolutely no doubt in my mind that this is our Salvation, Yeshua.

Distilled definition : The foundation, The covenant, The sign or mark of the nail, The gift of equality ; I AM YHWH, the Life and Light of the world.

As I think that we have covered the name pretty well so far, I'm just going to throw out some connections to think about.

Note the (ו) Waw [nail] hidden within the (א) Aleph [YHWH] and the (ת) Taw [cross/scales]. (תא) a room, compartment (especially in the Temple) [Ruler of 2, belongs to Aleph / YHWH]

(אות) Literally Aleph and Taw = sign, signal, symbol, token; miracle; to consent, to agree; to cut in; to engrave or mark, to be willing; to agree; to come in; to be, to exist

(את) sign, portent, token; thou; plow-share, hoe, self; at; by; with; toward; the particle of directed emphasis; THIS! (first and last letters) =Gematria 401
= (ישעיהו) "Salvation of Yah". This one is pretty cool as it is ישע : to deliver, deliverance, salvation + יה : Yah + ו : Son [יהו Yahoo]

So let's keep digging . . .

ישע : to deliver, deliverance, salvation + ו, adding son = ישוע Yeshua
Not just "salvation", the Waw inserts a son who will bring or be salvation.

(ישוע) Yeshua, and (יהושוע) Yehoshua are both names which combine (יהוה) YHWH
and (ישע) yasha [to deliver, salvation].

We have already seen that (ישע) Salvation, plus the (ו) Waw, Son = (ישוע) Yeshua.
So let's look at (יהושוע) Yehoshua, remove the (יהו) Yahoo, he/she creates, (יה) Yah
+ (ו) Son, and look at the (שוע) Shua : a nobleman or prince; to cry out for help.
The "help", in this case looks like it is the connection to (ישע) Salvation. The definition "the LORD is salvation" looks like it is missing the (ו) Waw, Son in (יהו) Yahoo,
he/she creates, (יה) Yah + (ו) Son/creator . . . and it is missing the (ו) Waw, Son in
the (שוע) Shua which creates "prince". Couldn't we also see a י Yud as prefix "my"
+ שוע prince = ישוע Yesuha [recall the אלף Aleph vs. the אלוף Aloph, prince]. I think
this name is saying, "the son of Yah, my prince, is salvation".
The fact that the son is the creator, the prince who will inherit, and our savior, is
dripping from the Aleph-Bet, all over this word.

There are times that I question hidden, or "sub-text", and how much of that should
be connected to the letters which form the words, but, it is better to keep it simple.

Example : (ישיש) = old man
We see the (י) Yud which can mean Adam, man, the Almighty, my, blood
And the (ש) Shin which, in this case, is that which comes forth from the womb.
(י) man + (ש) that which comes forth from the womb x 2 = an old man.

Conceptual thinking.
Now lets look at the root of "to deliver", or "Salvation" ישע yasha :
(י) man
(ש) to come forth [leave womb unspoken], to feel pain, fear, apprehend
(ע) adversity, to afflict, evil, to desire, to gaze, in wonder, amazement

The woman travails in great pain for her child to be delivered from the captivity of
the womb . . . if not, the child will die. . . and when it does come forth out of great
tribulation, we all gaze in wonder and amazement.

Conceptual thinking. The word itself is rooted in a description of child birth.

So take a look at the variations of this word and what each individual letter actually means.

I don't want to spoon feed you all of the answers, I want to teach you how to feed yourself.

See if the words can be broken into parts, and don't forget that those words within the word you are looking at have a meaning that will guide you.

Meditate upon the names and ask the Father of all to guide you.

Try looking into יהוה YHWH. See how many ways you can break it apart.

(ה)(ו)(ה)(י) letter by letter

(ה) + (ו) + (יה)

(ה) + (יהו)

Atbash Peh :

Tools :

Ruler of 2 :
(אף) nose, anger, wrath; also, too
(סף) threshold; basin, goblet
(כף) palm of the hand, hand; sole of the foot; pan, censer; handle; branch (of palm tree); cliff, rock

Ruler of 3 :
(וכף) and the palms (hands); and the soles (feet)

Λ Compass :
(בת) daughter; girl, maiden, young woman; at the age of; worthy of; deserving; bath; native inhabitant of
(בתק) to cut off; Akka. to cleave
(בק) Syr. was worm eaten, decayed
(בקק) to be empty; Arab. he cleft, split
(קבב) to utter a curse, curse; to be bent, crooked; to hollow out

Mixed meanings left side --> יצב to stand (attached to Bet)
+ sm square on right פסח lame, halt; passover
The lame to stand

V Compass :
(סקב) to wound, rub sore
(סבב) to turn about, go around, surround
(בסס) to perfume, to flavor; to base, establish; to trample, tread
(קבס) to disgust, to cause vomiting
(קסס) to munch, chew; to become sour

Atbash Peh Word Overlay :

Atbash Peh letter-by-letter :

_____

Note : I have always known that the letters themselves, with their definitions, themes, placements and shapes hold the purest answers. So when you look at the cypher and key in the future, in meditation and prayer . . . look at the connections made with the tools. Ignore the words they make and just look at what the letters have to say.

Think of the concepts.

The ע/ז

TOK

$[ע/ז]+[ח/ס]+[ש/ב]=(ז/ע)$

$[ח/ס]+[ש/ב]+[ז/ע]=(ז/ע)$

$[ח/ס]+[ו/פ]+[ש/ב]+[ז/ע]=(ז/ע)$

TOL

$[ע/ז]+[ע]+[ש/ב]=(ז/ע)$

$[ע]+[ש/ב]+[ז/ע]=(ז/ע)$

$[ע]+[א/ת]+[ש/ב]+[ז/ע]=(ז/ע)$

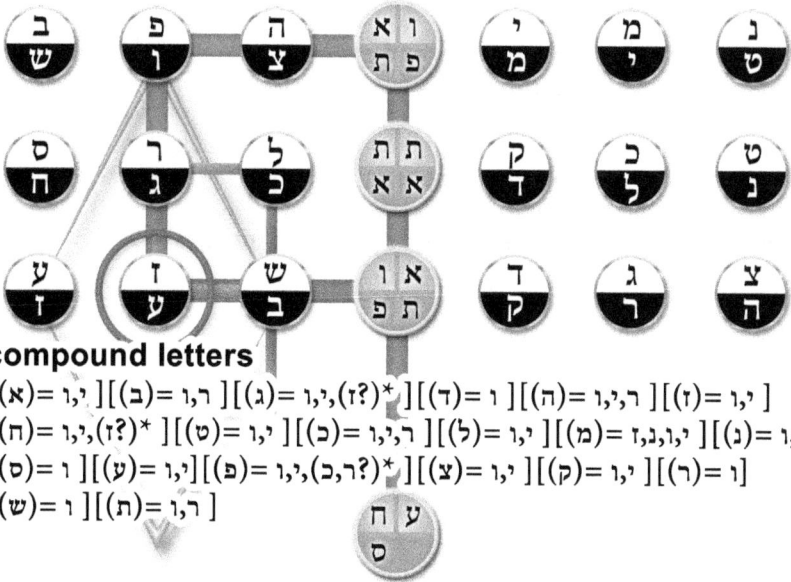

compound letters

$[(א)= ו,י] [(ב)= ו,ר] [(ג)= ו,י,(ז?)*] [(ד)= ו] [(ה)= ו,י,ר] [(ז)= ו,י]$
$[(ח)= ו,י,(ז?)*] [(ט)= ו,י] [(כ)= ו,י,ר] [(ל)= ו,י] [(מ)= ז,נ,ו,י] [(נ)= ו,י]$
$[(ס)= ו] [(ע)= ו,י] [(פ)= ו,י,(כ,ר?)*] [(צ)= ו,י] [(ק)= ו,י] [(ר)= ו]$
$[(ש)= ו] [(ת)= ו,ר]$

The fact that these "lists" only look at definitions for that letter, means that you are learning about the letter without looking at the letters associated with those definitions.

Find the כובע Helmet of ישע, ישוע Salvation.
Find ישוע Yeshua, בר, בן, Son גזע stem of ישי Jesse [see Isaiah 11]

It is unfortunate that most will try not to see the genealogical tree which Isaiah is describing. See Doctrine and Covenants 113, the stem=Yeshua, the rod and root are partly Jesse, and partly Ephraim or Joseph. These are the Two Witnesses. Two anointed sons of Joseph which apparently have a little Jesse in their veins.

Yeshua calls himself "the bridegroom" in all 4 gospels when going to the wedding feast. The governor of the feast calls the groom to inquire about the wine, showing that it was the family of the groom responsible for the feast. Now who was in charge of the servants at the feast? His mother. Who was the first person he showed himself to? Why does Isaiah 53 say he will see his seed? Why would Rome want to omit any reference to a rightful heir to the throne?

The Zayin ז

QUICK REFERENCE :
ז = 7
זין = 717 // זיז = 67

Dictionary : [ignoring the accent marks, which did not originally exist, and bearing in mind that this listing says, "Post Biblical Hebrew"] arms, weapon; to arm; to adorn, to ornament.

Is there anything to be found in the letter-by-letter breakdown of the (זין) Zayin to add to this?

(ז) (עשף) PBH sharp edge of an axe [this may be PBH, but look at the letters which precisely match the compass]; + fierce, strong, warrior (see below).
(י) my, hand, threshing, blood
(ן) to divide + [hand, your, protector, to judge, favor, grace]

TOOLS :

Ruler of 2 :
(זע) strong, mighty, fierce, fortress, refuge, splendor, glory, stronghold, power; goat
(זזע) to prevail, to be strong
(זר) secret or mystery
(זזח) to flash

Ruler of 3 :
(זרפ) to decentralize; to be open; to go beyond, exceed; he set apart, separated; to extend ; chief, warrior

The compass :
(עשף) PBH sharp edge of an axe [Aram. עושפא - related to Arab. *ishfa* - awl, punch]
(עף) = עוף to fly; it flew, flew away
(עפש) became moldy, to decay [reference to leaven? ; corruption?]
(פשע) to step, to march; he stepped, marched; to rebel, transgress; Syr. was terrified; transgression, trespass; guilt of transgression
(שפע) abundance; to sink, sink down, go down
(שעף) disquieting thoughts; thought
(עעש) to smooth; to besmear; to blind; he smoothed, smeared, plastered; (hence) was blinded [implication of getting something in his eye, he plastered his eye. [I think that the (ש) becomes "aperture", then the (ע) "eye", and (ע) "to cover with

clouds" this is a description of cataracts]; to take delight, be delighted [(ש) to "rejoice" over a "gift", or something that "happened" (ע) which you "desired" or "prayed" for (ע) and you "see" it.. Symbolically, an eye watching that which is delivered from the womb or tribulation]

(עש) moth; name of a constellation - prob. great bear

(עשש) to become weak, waste away, decay; Akka. grief

(פש) 'haughtiness' or 'folly'

(שף) Syr. he bruised; he rubbed, scraped, filed, polished, he smeared; Akka. to trample upon

(פע) [related to פעה to groan? (פ) mouth (ע) adversity; loudly; affliot; to tremble, quake?]

NEW Squares :

(אז) then, at that time; time

(אף) nose; anger, wrath; also, too

(אפף) to surround, encircle

(זפף) to pitch, coat with pitch

(פא) mouth; here; name of letter פ

(פז) pure gold

(פזז) to move quickly, be agile, be supple; to be gilded, be purified

(או) or

(וו) Waw; hook, peg, nail

(ז) this; who, which

(זוז) to move

(זוח) to raise oneself, rise

(זחח) to remove, displace

(חוח) briar, thorn; hook, ring; aperture, cleft

(זזח) to flash

(זעזע) to shake violently

(עז) strong, firm, mighty; fierce; strength, might; fortress, refuge; splendor, glory; goat

(עזז)to be strong

(חשש) to feel pain, fear, apprehend; chaff

(שח) meditation, talk; bent, bowed

(שחז) to sharpen, whet, grind; to be exposed

(שעשע) to smooth, to besmear (to blind ones self); to take delight; to delight

(שעע) to smooth; to besmear; to blind

(עש) moth; great bear constellation

(זלזל) to despise, to neglect; tendril; that which is shaken

(זלל) to be mean, to be vile, to be a glutton; to shake

(זר) stranger; frame, edging

(זרר) to sneeze; to press, to squeeze

(רז) secret

(לשלש) to secret chicken dirt

(של) error, offense, crime; that which is (or belongs) to

(שלל) to spoil, to plunder, to deprive; to draw out (sheaves); to remove, to refuse, to negate; to stitch loosely, join together loosely, to chain, to fetter; booty

(שלש) three; to multiply by three; one of the third generation; great grandson; pertaining to the third

(שלשל) to let down, lower, to chain down, couple

(שש) six; white marble; Egyptian linen; to divide by six; to multiply by six

RE-DO / INCLUDE NEW SQUARES
Zayin Tools :

Be set apart to go beyond, the mystery of the stronghold of power, the refuge of splendor and glory, to fly, to be strong and prevail.

The haughtiness of the Great Bear to smear and plaster to blind. Disquieting thoughts of transgression, of rebellion.

The sharp edge of the axe is rubbed, scraped, filed and polished to trample upon. [The Great Bear shall] go down to sink, to waste away and decay.

Overlay Words :

(בה) in her, in it

(בהה) to be astonished, amazed

(בהר) to clarify, clear, brighten

(בז) booty, spoil, prey, plunder, pillage

(בזבז) to waste, to squander, to dissipate

(בזה) to despise; despised; booty, spoil, plunder, pillage

(בזז) to spoil, plunder, pillage, rob

(בזר) to scatter, strew

(בר) son; threshed grain or corn; pure, clean; open field; cleanness, purity; lye, alkali, potash

(ברבר) to babble, to prattle

(ברד) to be cold; to hail; to be spotted; hail, hailstone; spotted, speckled

(ברה) to recover, to restore, eat bread; to choose

(ברז) to drill, bore; open the tap

(ברר) to purify, select, set apart, separate; to sharpen; Akka. to shine

(הב) give

(הבה) give; let us

(הבהב) to singe; to hesitate; burnt offering, sacrificial gift

(הבר) to pronounce, to articulate; to divide, to cut into pieces; the son

(הזה) to dream, to rave

(הר) mountain, mount

(הרה) to conceive, to become pregnant

(הרהר) to think, to meditate, to reflect

(הרף) stop!; [PBH "wink" of the eye]

(הרר) secondary form of "mountain"

(זב) one that has a flux

(זה) this; which

(זהב) gold; to gild, to plate with gold

(זהה) to identify

(זפף) to pitch, to coat with pitch

(זר) stranger; frame, edging

(זרב) to press, to compress

(זרה) to scatter, winnow; to measure with a span

(זרז) to speed up (originally meaning "to gird on"); JAram.-Syr. he girded on, armed

(זרר) to sneeze; to press, to squeeze

(פה) mouth, speech, saying, command, opening orifice; here

(פהה) to idle, to loaf, to tarry

(פז) pure gold

(פזז) to move quickly, be agile, be supple; to be gilded, be purified

(פזר) to scatter, to disperse

(פר) bull, bullock, steer

(פרה) to bear fruit, be fruitful

(פרז) to decentralize; to be open; to go beyond, to exceed, to extend; chief, warrior

(פרזה) open region, un-walled town

(פרף) to clasp, to fasten

(פרפר) to break, to crumble, to crush; to shake, to shatter

(פרר) to crush, crumb, crumble, break into crumbs; to break, violate, annul, frus-trate; to shake, to shatter

(רב) much, many; large, great; mighty; abounding, abundant; honored, important; enough; lord, chief; bowman, archer; multitude; great quantity, abundance; major-ity

(רבב) to be or become many or much, to be or become great; to shoot; to make rain; to grease, to soil, to stain

(רבבה) ten thousand, myriad; a great quantity

(רבה) to be or became much, many, or great; to shoot

(רברב) to aggrandize

(רהב) to fear; to act stormily, act arrogantly; arrogance, haughtiness; name of a sea monster symbolizing Egypt

(רההh) to fear

(רז) Secret or mystery

(רזה) to be or become lean; lean, thin, scant, scarce

(רפה) to be weak, to be feeble; to sink, decline; to relax; to heal, to cure; slack, weak, feeble

(רפף) to move gently; to waver, vacillate; to loosen, weaken

(רפרף) to flutter, to move (wings)

The Zayin Overlay :
   The command of the chief, be fruitful and conceive to become many. Be purified to shine, set apart in the mountain to go beyond.

   The son shall break into pieces and shatter the gilded pitch workers of Rahab. The hailstones shall scatter, waste and dissipate the un-walled cities.
   Aggrandize the weak and despised which winnow and scatter the lean. Gird on the weapons and become armed [as] a myriad of bowmen, let us spoil the strang-er and restore the prey.

Take note at the (רז) mystery, (שפע) flowing downward from the (פ) "Mouth" or Peh [(פה) ruler of 2 owned by the (ה) Holy Ghost] to the (ז) Zayin from the heavens above.

Individual letters :
(ב) Tarry in the Temple of YHWH and be sated/full in her. (פ) The dream, the vision, to astonish and amaze the pure and clean. (ה) The Holy Ghost bears witness of (ר) the Son to rule, set apart and purified. Awake, be agile and move quickly - spring forth, clean and pure. (ז) The chief will extend the border. *The mystery of the mighty, the secret of splendor, shall overflow the refuge of glory.*

Distilled definition : sharp edge of an axe, to be armed, chief, to extend the border of the refuge of glory [Do over when more info available]

Atbash Ayin :

Tools :

Ruler of 2 :
(עֿז) to tremble, to quake
(זעֿזע) to shake violently; was moved violently, was shaken
(גע) touch, reach, strike
(געֿגע) to long, to yearn; to quack; to dig, make holes, roll in
(כעֿכע) to cough slightly
(בעֿבע) to bubble

Ruler of 3 :
(וֿגע) and touch

/\ Compass :
(בו) in him, in it, therein
(בוֿז) to despise, mock at, treat with contempt; shame, mockery; two Israelites
(בוֿזז) robber
(בז) booty, spoil, prey, pillage, plunder
(בזֿבז) to waste, to squander, to dissipate
(בזֿז) to spoil, plunder, pillage, rob
(וו) Waw - sixth letter; hook, peg, nail
(זֿב) one that has a flux; a discharge, flowing
(זֿבוב) fly
(בוֿז) to flow; flux; issue (of fluid)
(זֿז) this, which, who

V Compass :
(בז) booty, spoil, prey, pillage, plunder
(בזֿבז) to waste, to squander, to dissipate
(בזֿז) to spoil, plunder, pillage, rob
(בֿoo) to trample, tread; to base, establish
(זֿב) one that has a flux; a discharge, flowing
(סֿבב) to turn about, go round, surround
(oo) moth

Squares :
(בֿoo) to trample, tread; to base, establish
(בעֿבע) to bubble
(סֿבב) to turn about, go round, surround
(oo) moth
(עֿב) cloud; thick; thicket; beam, rafter

(עבב) to cover with clouds
(עוו) to press, crush, tread; to fill with juice, make juicy

(עו) moth
(עוף) to lop off boughs; divided, wavering, hesitating, vacillation; division, divided opinion
(סף) threshold; basin, goblet
(ספסף) to tear, to cut [hair]; to singe, burn
(עוו) to press, crush, tread; to fill with juice, make juicy
(עפעף) to flutter, fly about; eyelid
(פס) tunic composed of variegated stripes; tunic reaching to the palms and ankles
(פסס) to end, cease, disappear; to be broad, spread; to tear apart; to strip
(פסע) to step, walk, tread
(פספס) to crumb, separate, to part; to sign; to make something in mosaic form
(פעפע) to bubble; to pierce, to penetrate

(גג) roof
(געגע) to quack; to dig, make holes, roll in
(כעכע) to cough slightly

(בך) in thee, in you
(בעבע) to bubble
(כעכע) to cough slightly
(עב) cloud; thick; thicket; beam, rafter
(עבב) to cover with clouds
(עכב) to hinder, prevent

(וו) Waw - sixth letter; hook, peg, nail
(עוות) to be crooked, be bent; to come to help [uncertain origin]
(עת) time; season; appointed time
(עתת) to time
(ות) mark, sign
(ותות) to mark, to doodle
(תעע) to deceive, to mock
(תעתע) to deceive, to mock

(עפעף) to flutter, fly about; eyelid
(עת) time; season; appointed time
(עתת) to time
(פעפע) to bubble; to pierce, penetrate
(פת) vulva; corner of their head; their forehead
(פתע) suddenly; to surprise, to amaze
(פתפת) to crumb, crumble, to mash
(פתת) to break [esp. bread] into pieces, crumb, crumble
(תעע) to deceive, to mock
(תעתע) to deceive, to mock
(תף) drum

164   The Menorah Code

(תפף) to drum, beat the drum

Atbash Ayin Word Overlay :
Atbash Ayin letter-by-letter :
The ע/o/ח

TOK   TOL

compound letters

[(א)= י,ו][(ב)= ר,ו][(ג)= (ז?),י,ו][(ד)= ו][(ה)= ר,י,ו][(ז)= י,ו]

[(ח)= (ז?),י,ו][(ט)= י,ו][(כ)= ר,י,ו][(ל)= י,ו][(מ)= י,ו,נ,ז][(נ)= י,ו]

[(ס)= ו][(ע)= ו,י][(פ)= (ר,כ),י,ו][(צ)= י,ו][(ק)= י,ו][(ר)= ו]

[(ש)= ו][(ת)= ר,ו]

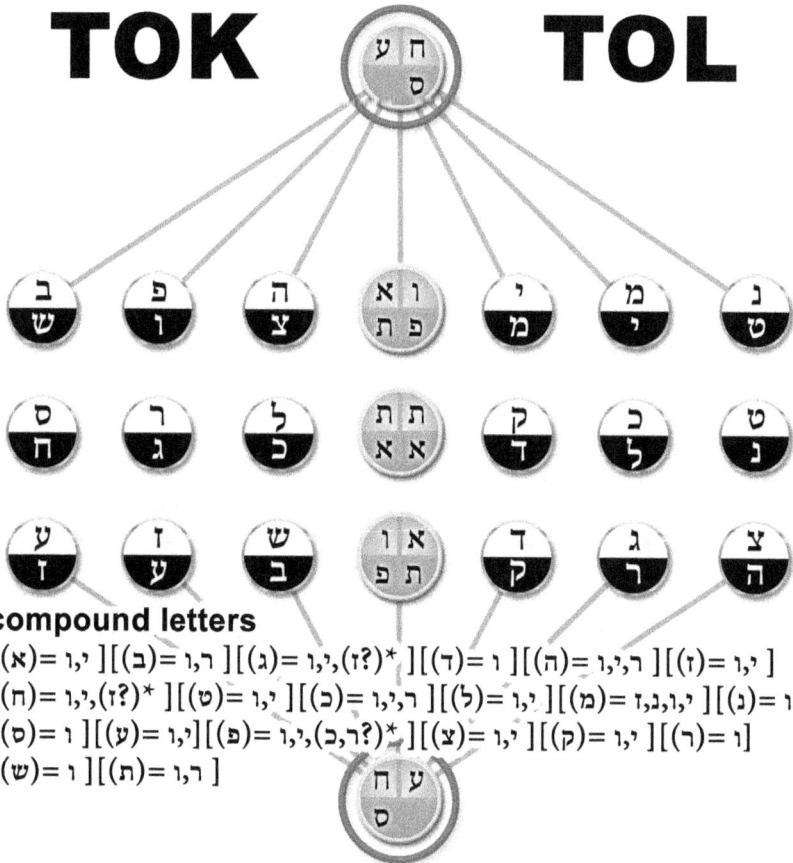

You are basically looking at any vertical or diagonal string ending above or below the trees. Rulers . . .

The Chet ח

QUICK REFERENCE :
ח = 8
חית = 418

Dictionary : beast (ח tradition=barrier/fence)

The ח Chet had me stumped for a while. However, as with so many other times when I felt stuck, I receive a little help from above.

I was disappointed, because I realized that the Compass to be used on this was wrong. So I decided to play a computer game for a while and clear my head.
While turning on the computer, the screen saver that I had made for myself (see image p.21), I was also saying a silent prayer for help. No sooner had I done this when boom, there it was right in front of my face.
I had always said that the ח Chet, or the character used for it in 500 BC, was made from two וו Waw. That Yeshua was the nail connecting the heavens and the earth. So if you look at that image on p.21, which splits the two trees, the ח Chet is targeting the ו Waw in the heavens above, and targeting the ו Waw on the earth beneath. Those two compass' targeting the ו Waw, are the compass' which define the ח Chet in the Tools segment.

TOOLS :

(חח) hook, ring; fetters

Ruler of 2 (Tree of Life):
(נח) Noah; rest
(מח) marrow; a fatling; fat; wealthy
(פח) gold leaf; thin (metal) plate; snare, bird-trap

[Note: I question if there is a meaning for every letter which can bond with the Chet as a ruler of 2. If the letter meanings should be connected.]

Ruler of 2 (Tree of Knowledge):
(צח) dazzling, glowing, bright, clear
(צחח) to be white, to be dazzling, be bright, be clear; to become dry
(גח) JAram. - Syr. to burst forth
(דחח) to push, thrust, banish

(שׂ) meditation, thoughts ; talk; bent, bowed
(שׂחח) he bowed down, crouched; was bowed down, was humbled
(זחח) to remove, displace

RE-CHECK EVERY SINGLE COMBINATION!
Chet Overlay Words :
(דד) breast, teat, nipple
(דדה) to move slowly
(דדי) JAram. he led a child
(דהה) to fade, become dim
(די) sufficiency, enough, sufficiently; who, which, that, of, about
(דיה) a bird of prey, the kite
(דיק) bulwark, siege wall; to be exact, be precise
(דיש) threshing
(דל) poor; thin, lean; weak, low, powerless; door
(דלדל) to weaken, loosen, impoverish; to hang down, dangle
(דלה) to draw (water); the poor; thrum (warp threads hanging in the loom); hair
(דלי) bucket
(דליה) branch, bough
(דלל) to become poor, become weak, become thin; to hang down loosely
(דלק) to burn; Aram. it burned; Mand. to kindle; to chase, to pursue
(דע) knowledge, wisdom
(דעה) knowledge, wisdom
(דק) a thin curtain
(דקדק) to examine minutely, to be strict
(דקק) to crush, to pulverize
(דשדש) to tread, trample
(דשש) to tread, trample, pound
(הד) joyous shout
(הדד) to reverberate
(הדה) to stretch out (the hand)
(הדי) Syr., Arab. = he led, he guided
(הדהד) to reverberate
(הדק) to press together
(הידד) hurrah!, bravo!, (joyous shout, cheer)
(היה) to be, exist, happen, become; was, existed; came into being, became; he remained; it came to pass, happened
(הילל) star
(הלה) that
(הלל) to boast, praise: to shine; to be foolish; Hallel
(יד) hand, arm; foreleg
(ידד) to be friends, to become friends
(ידה) to confess, to give thanks; to throw, hurl, cast
(ידיד) friend, beloved
(ידע) to know
(יה) short form יהוה YHWH
(ילד) to bear, bring forth, beget; child, boy, offspring, young man

(ילדה) girl

(יליד) son

(ילל) to howl, wail; wailing, howling, lamenting; lament

(ילק) a kind of locust; first creeping phase of the locust

(יעד) to appoint

(יעה) to sweep together and carry away; shovel

(יעל) to be of use, profit, benefit; mountain-goat

(יעלה) female mountain goat

(יקד) to be kindled, to burn

(יקהה) obedience

(יקע) to be out of joint, dislocated

(יקש) to lay bait, to lay snares

(יש) there is, there are; possession, property

(ישיש) old man

(ישע) to deliver; deliverance, salvation, welfare

(לדה) birth

(לה) to her

(להה) to languish, to faint

(להלה) to confuse, to drive crazy

(להק) to gather together, assemble

(להקה) group, band, company

(לי) to me

(ליד) near, close to; at the hand of

(לילה, ליל) night, at night

(ליש) lion; dough

(לע) throat

(לעד) forever

(לעע) to swallow, sip; to talk wildly

(לקה) to be stricken, be smitten, be flogged, be scourged; to be afflicted with disease; to be eclipsed

(לקלק) to lick

(לקק) to lick, lap

(לקש) to be late; late growth

(לשד) juice, sap; vigor; to add vigor

(לשלש) to secrete (chicken dirt)

(עד) to, unto, up to, even to; until, while; eternity, perpetuity; booty; witness; testimony; menstruation

(עדד) to count, reckon

(עדה) to ornament; to pass by; assembly, congregation; witness; testimony

(עדי) ornament, jewel

(עדשה) lentil

(עי) ruin, heap of ruins

(עיל) to thread (a needle), to insert

eye of yah?

(עיש) the great bear constellation

(על) height, upper part; above; on, upon, above; at, beside; towards; against; concerning, about; because of, on account of; together with; yoke

(עלה) to go up, to ascend; he went up, ascended; it sprang up, grew, shot forth; he rose, surpassed, excelled; leaf; lactating animal

(עלי) pestle; upper, higher

(עליה) upper chamber, upper story

(עליל) furnace; crucible

(עלילה) deed, act; pretext, wanton charge, false accusation

(עליליה) deed, action

(עלל) to act, do, work; to insert, thrust in; to accuse falsely; to glean (grapes or olives)

(עלע) to swallow, suck up, lick

(עלעל) to turn over the pages; to drive about, hurl, cast

(עלק) to suck

(עקד) to bind; striped, streaked; gathering, collection (place where sheep were gathered for shearing)

(עקה) to press, oppress; pressure

(עקל) to bend, twist, curve, make crooked; Syr. to distort, pervert; to attach (property), seize, foreclose, distrain

(עקלקל) crooked

(עקלקלה) crooked way

(עקש) to twist, make crooked, pervert; twisted, crooked, perverted

(עש) moth; great bear (constellation)

(עשה) to do, make; he did, made he worked, labored; he acted, dealt; he produced, yielded, performed, accomplished; he brought about, caused, effected; he appointed; he acquired, gained

(עשק) to contend; contention, quarrel; to oppress, wrong, extort; oppression; extortion, robbery

(עשש) to waste away, decay

(קד) Syr. he tore, he cut away

(קדד) to bow down, bow one's head; to cut, to bore, to drill

(קדיש) holy, sacred

(קדקד) head, crown of the head

(קדש) to be holy, be sacred; holiness, sanctity; a holy object; a holy place; the Holy Temple

(קהה) to be blunt, be dull

(קהל) to assemble, to gather; assembly, gathering; congregation, community

(קהלה) assembly, congregation, community

(קיה) to vomit

(קיש) to compare, draw analogous conclusions

(קל) light; swift, fast; easy, not difficult, unimportant; lightness, levity

(קלד) to open

(קלה) to roast, parch; to burn, consume; to be lightly esteemed, be disgraced

(קלי) roasted grain, parched corn

(קלל) to be light, be slight; to be swift; to be lightly esteemed, be despised; glittering, burnished

(קללה) curse; calamity, evil

(קלע) to sling, hurl forth; to weave, plait, twist; to sway, to waver; to cut out, carve; sling; curtain hanging; slinger, marksman

(קלקל) to throw, to shake; he moved to and fro; to spoil, damage

(קלש) to thin out, rarefy; Aram. was thin

(קעקע) to tattoo; to undermine, destroy; to cackle

(קש) straw, stubble, chaff

(קשה) to be hard, be stiff; to be severe; to be difficult; hard; difficult; severe, cruel; fierce, violent

(קשש) to gather, assemble; to grow old

(שד) female breast; evil spirit; violence, havoc; devastation

(שדד) to plow, harrow; to overpower, destroy violently, rob, devastate, ruin; to despoil, ravage

(שדה) field; open country; land; a beautiful woman

(שדי) the Almighty; field

(שדידה) devastation, destruction, robbing

(שדל) to persuade, entice

(שדש) six

(שה) young sheep, lamb; small cattle (goat, sheep)

(שהד) witness; BAram. to bear witness, to testify

(שהה) to tarry, to linger, to stay, to delay, be late in coming

(שהק) to hiccup

(שי) gift, present

(שיד) lime, whitewash, plaster

(שיש) to rejoice; white marble, alabaster

(של) error, offense, crime; that which is or belongs to; belonging to (+ noun)

(שלה) to be quiet, be at ease; to draw out (from water)

(שלהי) end

(שלי) my, mine; quietness, tranquility

(שליה) afterbirth, placenta

(שליש) a dry measure (possibly the third part of an ephah)

(שלל) to spoil, to plunder, to deprive; to draw out (sheaves); to remove; to refuse, to negate, deny; to stitch loosely, join together loosely, to chain, fetter; spoil, booty

(שלק) to boil, to cook; to make smooth, trim

(שלש) three; to multiply by three; one of the third generation; pertaining to the third

(שלשל) to let down, lower, to chain down, couple

(שעה) to gaze at, look about; to care for

(שעל) hollow of the hand; handful; to cough

(שעע) to smooth; to besmear; to blind; to take delight, be delighted

(שעשע) to smooth, to besmear (to blind one's self - paste one's eyes); to take delight; to delight

(שק) sack, bag; sackcloth

(שקד) was bound, was bent; to watch, wake; to be almond-shaped; almond tree; almond

(שקה) to cause to drink, give to drink, water

(שקל) to weigh, balance; to weigh out, pay money; to consider, examine; to take; a weight, shekel; name of a coin

(שקלל) to balance, poise

(שקע) to sink, sink down, go down

(שקק) to rove, run about noisily, rush in uproar; to desire; yearning, longing, desire

(שקשק) to make a noise; to shake, move to and fro

(שש) six; white marble; Egyptian linen

(ששה) six; to divide by six; to multiply by six

(ששי) sixth

(יעה) to sweep/collect/gather together and carry away.

(יקד) to be kindled, burn [Ruler of 3 belongs to the Dalet] = [fire]

(דק) Veil [Ruler of 2 belongs to Kuf] = [door to the kingdom of the Father]

(יה) YH [short form of YHWH]

(שלה) draw out [from water - related to שליה afterbirth] ; [Ruler of 3 ending with (ה) Hei, Holy Ghost]

OVERLAY STORY HERE

Atbash Samech :

Tools :

Ruler of 2 :
(פס) a tunic composed of variegated stripes; a tunic reaching to the palms and the ankles

(פספס) separate, to part

(ספ) to end, cease, disappear, blot out, destroy [death]; to be broad, spread; to tear apart; to strip

(קספ) to munch, chew; to become sour

(בסס) to trample, to tread; to base, establish

Ruler of 3 :
(אפס) to come to end, cease; end, nought; ankle

(גבס) mortar, plaster, gypsum

The נ/ט

TOK TOL

compound letters

[(א)= ו,י][(ב)= ר,ו][(ג)= ו,י,(ז?)*][(ד)= ו][(ה)= ו,י,ר][(ז)= ו,י]
[(ח)= ו,י,(ז?)*][(ט)= ו,י][(כ)= ו,י,ר][(ל)= ו,י][(מ)= י,ו,ג,ז][(נ)= ו,י]
[(ס)= ו][(ע)= ו,י][(פ)= ו,י,(כ,ר,?)*][(צ)= ו,י][(ק)= ו,י][(ר)= ו]
[(ש)= ו][(ת)= ו,ר]

Reminder for this position :

Some of you will remember "Satan" in the "Nest". Bear in mind that the "Nest" belongs to the ט Tet, and is assigned that value using all regular [white background] letters. נ, Satan, uses all black background, "Atbash" letters.

Both of these arrive at the same place, but one is on the top, and the other on the bottom.

If you care to look for what this relationship is, you need to combine the regular and Atbash letters in the tools.

You should be able to tell that this section is a work in progress, and will not be completed until a computer program is written to lend a hand.

Check themenorahcode.com for details on when this may become available.

The Tet ט

Add Gematria and Dictionary definitions here.

Please remember that as I have found this grid to be like a cylinder, I am joining the sides to make seeing the connections easier.

The Tet is spelled (טית), yet its name is of unknown origins. Tradition claims that it is related to the word (טיט) mud.

So let's break it down.
(ט) to build a nest, nest, cell
(י) the hand of the Almighty plastered or whitewashed
(ת) a foundation to be honored and revered, to give light and instruction.

Once we examine the (מ) Mem, and the (נ) Nun, it will become clear that the Tet is the nest of the protector, a bird of prey which gathers Zion under its wing.

The Nest, however, is a clear reference to the Temple. It is a place that Zion is to be gathered in order to separate themselves from the world. A hedge of protection from destruction and ruin.

Note : old work, this will have more meat on its bones later.

TOOLS :

NEW < Compass :
(נץ) hawk; blossom, flower
(נצץ) to shine, flash, sparkle; to blossom, bloom, sprout
(צן) thorn
(קן) nest; cell, chamber
(קנן) to build a nest, nestle
(קנץ) when will you put an end to words
(קץ) end; destruction, ruin
(קצן) to become an officer
(קצץ) to cut off; stipulate
(צקצק) to grate, to rasp

NEW > Compass :

(נצר) branch; sprout; he watched, guarded, kept; to convert to Christianity.
(נר) light, lamp
(צן) thorn
(צר) narrow; distress, anguish; enemy, foe; rock; flint
(צרצר) to chirp
(צרר) to bind, tie up, wrap; to show hostility toward, vex, oppress; to be sharp
(רן) ringing cry, shout for joy
(רנן) to give a ringing cry; to shout for joy; to murmur, complain
(רץ) runner, courier, strip, bar
(רצן) to become serious
(רצץ) to break, crush; Arab. he bruised, crushed
(רצרץ) to run about

NEW V Compass :
(חח) hook, ring; buckle
(חך) palate
(חכך) to scratch, rub
(חסך) to spare, withhold
(כח) strength, power, force, vigor; a kind of lizard
(כס) throne
(כסח) to cut off, trim, clear
(כסכס) to crush with the teeth, crunch; to rub
(כסס) to grind, chew, gnaw; to compute, reckon; to make small, divide up
(סך) large crowd; thicket; hut
(סכך) to screen, cover
(סכסך) to instigate, incite, arouse; he confused, entangled

NEW /\ Compass :
(כעס) to be vexed, be angry; he angered; vexation, anger; grief
(עע) moth
(עכס) anklet, bangle; to shake bangles, rattle, tinkle
(עוס) to press, crush, tread; to fill with juice, make juicy

Squares :
(סט) deviation; deviations from the right path
(עע) moth
(עט) stylus; reed pen
(עוס) to press, crush, tread; to fill with juice, make juicy

(בטבט) to swell, to protrude
(בטן) to make pregnant, impregnate; to cover with lining, to line; belly, abdomen; bowls; womb
(בן) son; offspring; branch, shoot; inhabitant of; worthy of, deserving
(טב) good
(טנן) to be moist, be damp
(נבב) to make hollow, hollow out
(נבט) to sprout, burst forth, grow; to look

Tools saying here :

Overlay Words :

Individual letters :
(כ) poor, lowly, oppressed, people ; your bridle is the covenant of perfection ; (ו)
thus the wing of the protector gathers the wandering exiles ; (ט) who cry unto
YHWH, to the nest ; (צ) Zion, my righteous ; (ג) followers of the Father ; (ד) gather
in the nations to the door of my glory and cleanse my offspring ; (ק) the decree of
my child beside the veil ; (י) the blood of my hand is sufficient to whitewash [your]
garment.

Distilled definition : Nest, hedge of protection for the righteous, Temple reference

"As a bird that wandereth from her nest, so is a man that wandereth from his
place."
(Proverbs 27: 8)

Note that this "nest", or hedge of protection, also uses "thorn" in the word list. Long
ago when shepherds were in the field, they would use thorn bushes to corral and
protect their flocks at night.

Atbash Nun :

Tools :

Ruler of 2 :
(נטן) to be moist, be damp
(שן) tooth; point; peak; ivory
(שנן) to sharpen, whet
(חן) favor, grace, charm
(חנן) to show favor, be gracious
(זן) sort, kind
(הן) they; behold; yes; if
(רן) ringing cry, shout of joy
(רנן) to give a ringing cry; to shout for joy
(לנן) to murmur

Ruler of 3 :
(סרן) axle, axis; lord, prince
(עטן) to pack olives in a vat
(גחן) to curve, bend, bow, stoop

Squares :
(שטן) Satan; adversary; accuser; to be or act as an adversary; to accuse; to hate
(שט) apostate, deviator
(שן) tooth; point, peak; ivory
(שנן) to sharpen, whet
(שש) six; white marble; Egyptian linen
(נטש) to leave, forsake, abandon, permit
(טנן) to be moist, be damp
(טשטש) to smear over, erase

(זחח) to remove, displace
(זן) sort, kind
(זנח) to reject, spurn
(חדד) to flash
(חזן) to serve as a cantor
(חן) favor, grace, charm
(חנן) to show favor, be gracious
(נחח) to spray scent

∧ Compass :

(חח) hook, ring; buckle
(חל) rampart, wall; something secular, something profane, something common
(חלחל) to cause to tremble, to startle; to perforate, penetrate
(חלל) to lose, profane, defile; to begin; to be hollow, to hollow out, to bore, to pierce; to play; a person deprived of priesthood; a priest of illegitimate descent; a person pierced, a person totally wounded, a person slain
(לח) freshness, vigor; moist, fresh, new
(לחח) to be moist, be fresh
(לע) throat
(לעע) to swallow, sip; to talk wildly
(על) hoight, uppei part; above; on, upon, above; at, beside; towards; against; con-cerning, about; because of, on account of; together with; yoke
(עלל) to act, do, work; to insert, thrust in; to accuse falsely; to glean (grapes or olives)
(עלע) to swallow, suck up, lick
(עלעל) to turn over the pages; to drive about, hurl, cast

V Compass :
(סל) basket
(סלל) to lift up; he cast up (or paved) a highway; he lifted up a song; he cast up a way
(סלסל) to exalt; to curl; to trill; he exalted, esteemed highly

< Compass :
(הד) joyous shout
(הדד) to reverberate
(הדה) to stretch out (the hand)
(הדהד) to reverberate
(דד) breast, teat, nipple
(דהה) to fade, become dim

> Compass :
(גג) roof
(גהה) to heal; to blind; to incline (said of a wall); healing
(הגג) to imagine, fancy
(הגה) to hum, murmur, ponder; to remove; rumbling (said of thunder); moaning, moan, sigh; whispering

Atbash Nun Overlay Words :

Atbash Nun letter-by-letter :

The מ/י

TOK TOL

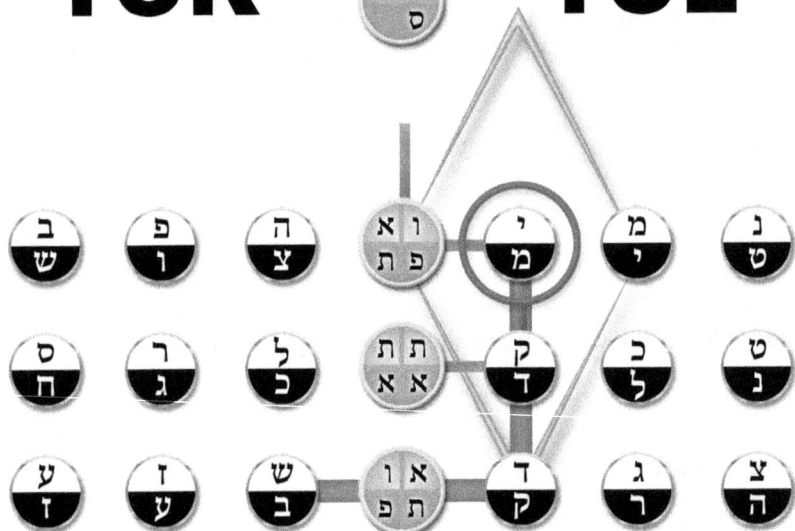

compound letters

[(א)= י,ו][(ב)= ר,ו][(ג)= ו,י,(ז?)*][(ד)= ו][(ה)= ר,י,ו][(ז)= י,ו]
[(ח)= ו,י,(ז?)*][(ט)= ו,י][(כ)= ר,י,ו][(ל)= ו,י][(מ)= י,ו,נ,ג][(נ)= י,ו]
[(ס)= ו][(ע)= י,ו][(פ)= כ,ר,(ז?)*][(צ)= י,ו][(ק)= י,ו][(ר)= ו]
[(ש)= ו][(ת)= ו,ר]

Note : TOL [n/o combinations] such as חי life, or חיים life (plural) have not been
added to the tables.

Also, the compass and square positions do not include letters from the TOL. Just
looking at the large square, I see the איש husband. See אשה wife in the ה Hei
[Taking it back to the bridal chamber]. Now I see the פני face... More things just
jumping out when the TOL is added.

The true title of "קדוש Holy אב Father" belongs to the (מ/י) and the (ב/ש). For a man upon the earth, to usurp that name, is BLASPHEMY!

The Yud י

The Yud has a numerical value of 10 and is part of the Holy Name (יהוה). It is historically recognized in the Kabbalah Tree of Life to be the Father, and its name means hand.

TOOLS :

Ruler of 2 :
(מי) who?; whoever; someone; anyone
(אי) island; a mariners place of refuge; woe!; alas! ; not ; where ; jackal
(יאי) Aram. fitting, fine
(כי) that ; because ; when, while, as ; if, in case ; although, though; burning, branding (כי was orig. a demonstrative pron. meaning 'thus', 'therefore', 'then'): Aram. as, like
(תי) a suffix meaning "my", or pertaining to

Ruler of 3 :
(שתי) drinking; warp on a loom

The compass :
(אדם) Adam; to be red; a man; mankind; red; a ruby.
(מד) garment.
(מדד) to measure, measured
(מאד) to increase; strength, might, power
(אד) mist, vapor, gas
(אם) mother [Note: check that in the code]; nation, people; if, whether, when, on condition
(דמם) cease
(דא) this
(דם) blood; bloodshed; blood-guilt
(אמד) to estimate, calculate, reckon

The squares :
(שדי) The Almighty
(יד) hand, are, foreleg; name of letter
(ידד) to be friends, become friends
(שי) there is, there are; possession, property
(שי) gift, present

(ישיש) old man : ["Ancient of Days" = (עתיק = "Aged" / Strongs 6268)]
(שיד) lime, whitewash, plaster
(דד) breast, teat, nipple
(דיש) threshing
(די) sufficiency ; enough, sufficiently; who, which, that; of, about
(שד) female breast; evil spirit; violence, havoc, devastation
(שדד) to plow, harrow; overpower, destroy violently, rob, devastate, ruin; to despoil, ravage
(דשדש) to tread, trample
(אי) island; a mariners place of refuge; woe!; alas! ; not ; where ; jackal
(עי) ruin, heap of ruins [probably a contraction of עוי, so may not apply]
(יעא) Aram. shovel
(תי) a suffix meaning "my", or pertaining to

NOTE : I cannot leave the compass and square intersection un-noticed :
The compass (י) Yud = (אדם) ADAM, [spelled out in sequence] and following the square down = (קדוש) Holiness [also spelled out in sequence].
(אדם קדוש) = ADAM Kadosh = MAN OF HOLINESS.
..same square mixed מקדש temple & בית house [tree of life]
This use may also be telling us that the squares may contain more than just words made from the three corners of the square. I'm sure that if my Hebrew was better, and I didn't have to look every word and fragment up, I would probably catch more of these. So if you see something like this in a square, it may be something that I missed.

Overlay Words :
(אי) [Phoenician] - fair [is this also an associated sound of the Yud?]
(יאי) Aram. fitting, fine

RE-DO after all letter lists are complete . . .
Individual letters :
(א) YHWH
(י) Adam, Man, Old Man, Father, Much Power, The Almighty, Man of Holiness, Adam Kadosh // Quite the overlay connection to YHWH

Distilled definition : Father [as part of (יהוה) = YHWH THE FATHER], The Almighty, Adam, Man, Old Man [compare to Ancient of Days], Adam Kadosh, Man of Holiness

"...the Son of man came with the clouds of heaven, and came to the Ancient of days, and they brought him near before him. And there was given him dominion, and glory, and a kingdom, that all people, nations, and languages, should serve him."
(Daniel 7: 13, 14)

Note that the Son of man comes to the "Ancient of days", [or "Aged"] and the "Ancient of days" bestows dominion and glory and a kingdom upon the "Son". So, we have another personage, part of the [יהוה = YHWH], which stands above the Son. Who would that be? The Yud of course, the Father.

Another interesting note :
Later we will see that the (מ) Mem will become identified as the Son of Man, a traveler, or sojourner. He has the (מ) Mem, (י) Yud Atbash pair, while the Father has the (י) Yud, (מ) Mem Atbash pair.

   I am in the Father, and the Father is in me, appears to be another reference to the Menorah.

   By their fruits you will know them, the first shall come last, and the last shall come first . . . All of these sayings have served as clues which I have used to decrypt the code in the Menorah.

Atbash Mem :

Tools :

Ruler of 2 :
(ים) sea, lake, large basin, reservoir; west
(דם) blood, bloodshed, blood guilt
(דמם) to be or grow silent; to bleed
(אם) mother; if, whether, when; nation, people
(תם) complete, perfect; innocent; was ended, was finished, was completed

Ruler of 3 :
(הלם) to strike, beat; to suit, fit; strike, shock
(קדם) to be before, in front; what is in front, forward; east
(באם) they came

V Compass :
(תי) Suff. my

∧ Compass :
(סיס) swift; to drive a horse
(סס) moth
(סתת) to cut stones, chisel
(עי) ruin, heap of ruins
(עת) time; season; appointed time
(עתי) timely, ready
(עתת) time
(תי) suff. my; pertaining to
(סות) to ferment
(תעע) to deceive, to mock

Squares :
(מס) body of forced laborers, forced service
(מסמס) to melt, to dissolve
(מסס) to melt, to dissolve
(מעם) from; away from being together with
(מת) dead; a dead person, corpse
(מתם) wholeness, soundness; people, men
(מתת) gift
(סם) spice

(סמם) to poison

(oo) moth

(סתם) to stop up, close; to express oneself vaguely; vague or indefinite expression; an anonymous opinion; in general

(סתת) to cut stones; chisel

(עם) people; kinsman, relative; together with, with; close to, beside; as long as, while

(עמם) to darken, to dim; to join, connect

(עמת) to join; to compare, confront; against, opposite

(עת) time; season; appointed time

(עתם) to be burned by heat, covered with smoke

(עתת) to time

(תם) was ended, was finished, was completed; complete, perfect; innocent, artless; completeness, perfection; integrity; innocence

(תמם) to be finished, come to an end, be completed

(תמס) melting away, dissolution

(תסס) to ferment

(תעתע) to deceive, to mock

(תעע) to deceive, to mock

(אד) mist, vapor, gas

(אדם) Adam, man; to be red; red; name of a red jewel; ruby

(אם) mother, matriarch; metropolis, large city; if, whether, when, on condition; nation, people

(אמד) to estimate, calculate, reckon; to make well to do

(דא) this

(דד) breast, teat, nipple

(דם) blood; bloodshed; blood-guilt

(דמדם) to be in a daze, to be confused

(דמם) to be or grow dumb or silent; to bleed

(מאד) to increase; strength, might, power; very, greatly, exceedingly

(מד) garment; to measure

(מם) Mem - the 13th letter

(בקבק) to gurgle

(בקק) to be empty

(בם) in them

(קבב) to utter a curse, curse; to be bent, crooked; to hollow out; to fault

(קם) enemy, foe, adversary; one who rises against somebody

(מם) Mem - the 13th letter

(מק) rottenness, decay

(מקק) to rot, decay

Words in the tools :

Atbash Mem Overlay Words :

The ל/כ

TOK  TOL

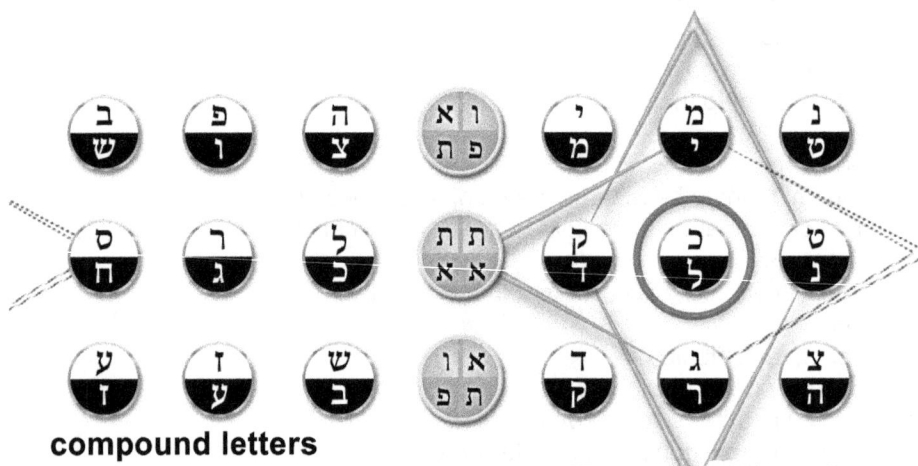

compound letters

[(א)= ו,י][(ב)= ר,ו][(ג)= י,ו,(ז?)*][(ד)= ו][(ה)= ר,י,ו][(ז)= ו,י]

[(ח)= ו,י,(ז?)*][(ט)= ו,י][(כ)= ר,ו,י][(ל)= ו,י][(מ)= י,ו,ג,ז][(נ)= ו,י]

[(ס)= ו][(ע)= ו,י][(פ)= ר,כ,ו,י,(ר?)*][(צ)= ו,י][(ק)= ו,י][(ר)= ו]

[(ש)= ו][(ת)= ר,ו]

As I am going through and pasting in this old work, I find it quite satisfying. While my original hope was to "COMPLETE" the tools table, in order to have a quick reference to each letter, this was an impossible task to "complete". So, "satisfying" to show the work in progress. "Satisfying" because the insane process of the decryption is revealed. Sorry, I'm not hiding a Urim & Thummim somewhere.

Those who choose to dive into this work to search the tree should begin by starting from scratch. Then you will realize that everything depends on getting layer 1 right. Layer one being the decryption [using tools] for each letter. Then move on to layer two, looking at words from "other letters" beneath the tools. The hidden definitions of the letters under the tools combine to more fully define the letter which you are working on. Then you may move onto layer three, the overlays. Then layer four, the "sacred symbols".

Completing the layer one, however, remains incomplete. I am decrypting, to find the rules and how it works . . . but imagine trying to figure out layers 2,3,4 without that full foundation. It's not an easy task, so please understand the incomplete notes you see here.

The Chof כ

The Chof has a numerical value of 20 and includes a final form [value of 500] which drops the (ו) Waw / (ד) Dalet, in order to make a straight line down the right side to the (ח) Chet, and form the word (חך) palate [the roof of the mouth].

TOOLS :

Ruler of 2 :
(מך) poor, lowly
(דך) crushed, oppressed.
(חך) palate [final Chof connection to Chet] - (bridle goes in mouth)

The compass :
(חטח) to be besmeared; was besmeared
(קח) he took
(חק) something prescribed, enactment, decree, statute, law, rule: prescribed portion, prescribed due
(חח) hook, ring; buckle
(חטט) to dig, scratch
[NEW](עוס) to press, crush, tread down [all in top or bottom point]

(מתג) to bridle, curb
(תם) completeness, perfection ; integrity ; blameless ; innocence, artlessness; was ended, was finished, was completed
(תמם) to be complete or finished, come to an end
(מג) magician
[NEW](מגן{מ}ג) Shield, Protector
(מגג) to squeeze, soften [related to מוג to melt]
(מגמג) to stir
(גם) also, moreover, yea; to, even as well
(גמם) to cut [the branch of a tree]; Arab. he cut off
(גת) wine press; wine pit
(מת) dead; a dead person, corpse
(מתם) wholeness, soundness; people, men
(מתת) gift [? contraction of מתנת?]

(עט) stylus; reed pen
(קט) small
(קטע) to cut, lop off; to amputate
(קעקע) to tattoo; to undermine, destroy

(גג) roof [unknown etymology]
(גם) conj. also, to even as well
(גמגם) to stammer, stutter
(גמם) to cut (the branch of a tree)
(גסס) to be dying, expiring; to behive rudely, be haughty
(מג) magician - a loan word from Akkadian of uncertain origin
(מגג) to squeeze, soften
(מגמג) to stir
(מם) the letter Mem [PBH?]
(מס) body of forced laborers, forced service [uncertain origin]
(מסס) to melt, dissolve
(סם) spice
(סמם) to poison

Tools List Synopsis Here

RE DO THIS LIST!!!
Overlay Words :
(אים) to threaten, to frighten ; fearful,
frightful, terrible [ruler of 3 connection to
final mem and the Protector]
(מם) Mem ; invokes the protector
(מכך) to be low, be humiliated
(כם) Your ; You
(גג) roof
(דג) fish [ruler of 2 connection to Gimmel or followers of the Almighty]
(גדד׳) to cut [double Dalet - door, my glory]
(גדד״) to gather in troops or bands [double Dalet - door, my glory]
(וו) Waw ; nail ; covenant
(חג) feast, festival
(חך) palate
(חכך) to scratch, rub
The protector, to be low, be humiliated, you, gather in bands, to cut [off], [the] one

Individual letters :
(א) [Thus saith] YHWH, (י) my hand ; (מ) shall rise up against your enemies in that
frightful day ; (כ) [while] the innocent, poor, oppressed people (ג) who follow the
Father (ד) shall gather in the nations and whitewash my offspring with a joyous

186   The Menorah Code

shout. [Enter] the door of my glory. (ו) Receive the gift of equality with a covenant, a sign, a mark, affixed with a nail. (ח) Repent [and enter] the gate which leads to eternal life.

Distilled definition : The bridle of YHWH ; poor, lowly, oppressed, people ; perfection : (ת) Scales, touching (מ) protector [YHWH who rises up] and (ג) followers of the Father; (כ) dead receive gift of wholeness & perfection.

Atbash Lamed :

Tools :

Ruler of 2 :
(טל) dew
(טלל) to cover with dew
(הלל) to shine; he has praised
(קל) light; swift, fast; easy, not difficult, unimportant; lightness, levity
(דל) door; poor, thin, lean, low, weak
(דלל) to become poor, weak, thin; to hang down loosely
(מל) circumcised

Ruler of 3 :
(עיל) to thread a needle, to insert

∧ Compass :
(עד) witness; testimony; menstruation
(עדד) to count, reckon
(עדן) eden; to refine, make tender; to do unwillingly; pleasure, delight, luxury; hitherto; time period
(ענד) to bind around; Arab. he turned aside; Syr. he departed
(דע) knowledge, wisdom
(דן) judge
(נע) moving, mobile
(נד) = נוד wandering exile; wanderer, vagabond; nomad; skin bottle
(נדע) know

< Compass :
(יא) Phoen. fair
(יאר) stream (of the nile), stream, canal
(ירא) to fear; he feared, was afraid; he revered, honored; fearing, fearful
(אי) island; woe!, alas!; prefix not; where?
(איר) related to אור light, to give light
(אריא) Aram. - Syr. lion
(ראי) mirror; seeing, sight; appearance, figure
(רי) moisture

V Compass :

(סד) stocks for torturing

(נד) heap, wall, moving

(נס) standard, ensign, flag; signal, sign

(נסס) to perform miracles; to move to and fro

(דן) judge

(נדד) to wander about, flee

(נדן) sheath, case; harlots pay

The כ/ל

TOK   ע ח / ס   TOL

compound letters

[(א)= י,ו][(ב)= ר,ו][(ג)= י,י,(ז?)*][(ד)= ו][(ה)= ר,י,י][(ז)= י,ו]

[(ח)= י,י,(ז?)*][(ט)= י,ו][(כ)= ר,י,י][(ל)= י,ו][(מ)= י,ו,נ,ז][(נ)= י,י]

[(ס)= ו][(ע)= י,ו][(פ)= כ,ר,?(ז?)*][(צ)= י,ו][(ק)= י,ו][(ר)= ו]

[(ש)= ו][(ת)= ו,ר]   ע ח / ס

Now this would be an excellent location for you to begin examining the Atbash pairs.

You just finished the כ/ל pair, so lean back in the center of the Aleph-Bet and see what the other side of the כ/ל coin has in common.

Note : There is a LG square in the ה Hei which has sword of the spirit & the word of El . . . I'm can't to remember why, but I do recall questioning if the Lamed over-lay, and the "Shepherd's Crook" are becoming a sickle-sword [another Egyptian connection]. . . something about words landing in that overlay which sounded like it was becoming a harvest tool.

The Lamed ל

The Lamed has a numerical value of 30. When it stands up, its (ל) handle ascends into heaven, where it is joined by the (ע) Ayin [of YHWH's glory] to become (על), a yoke . . . or, in this case, EL's sheep yoke. The Good Shepherd's Scepter used to correct direction or something more SEVERE for the stubborn sheep.

TOOLS :

Ruler of 2 :
(על) yoke; height, upper part; above; on, upon, above; at, beside, towards, be-cause of, on account of [upward letter extension joining the Ayin when standing]
(עלל) to insert, thrust in [upward letter extension joining the Ayin when standing]
(הלל) "Hallel" Praise; to boast, praise, he shouted, he shouted in festival joy, sang, praised, shouted for joy; to shine, it began to shine, it shone
(אל) EL (short form of Elohim); power; to, unto, toward; nothing; not
(תל) mound, hill ; heap of ruins.
(של) prep, that which is (or belongs) to [this is why the Lamed is a prefix meaning "to the"] ; error, offense, or crime ; to put off, to loose ; to purposely let fall
(שלל) spoil, booty, plunder; to spoil, plunder, to deprive; to draw out (sheaves); to remove; to refuse, to negate, deny; to stitch loosely, join together loosely, to chain, fetter
(שלש) three ; one of third generation; to multiply by three; of the third
(שלשל) to let down, lower, to chain down, couple.
(פלל) to intervene, interpose ; pray

Ruler of 3 :
(קתל) Aram. to slay
(חשל) to be weak; to forge, hammer, to shape, mold

The compass :
(הס) hush! silence

(סה) to hesitate

(סשׁ) to rob, pillage, or sack

(שׂה) (young) sheep, lamb ; small cattle (goat, sheep)

(שׂק) sack, bag ; sackcloth

(שׂקה) the sackcloth, the sack

(קשׁ) straw, stubble, chaff

(קשׁה) to harden, be difficult, stubborn, obstinate, or **SEVERE** [The term on the Kabbalah tree of life where the Lamed goes]

(שׁהק) to hiccup

(שׁקה) to cause to drink, give to drink

(קהה) to be blunt, be dull

(תר) searcher, explorer

(תרע) to blow a horn or trumpet; to warn, to sound an alarm; to break, to split

(תער) razor; sheath of a sword, scabbard

(רע) bad, worthless; evil, wicked; wickedness; friend, companion, associate; fellow-man; thought, purpose, aim; noise, shout

(רעע) to be evil, bad; to break into pieces, crush, shatter, to make friends with, associate with

(רתע) to tremble, startle, recoil, rebound

(ער) enemy, foe; awake, wakeful

(עת) time, season, appointed time

(עתת) time

(עתר) to pray, supplicate, entreat; to be abundant; odor

(תרח) ʻTerahʻ - a silly idolater

(תחר) to compete, to contest

(תח) Syr. it rotted; was softened

(תחח) to crumble, loosen

(רתח) winnowing shovel

(רתח) to boil, bubble; a piece of boiling meat

(חר) = חור hole, aperture; socket of the eye; nobleman

(חרת) to grave, engrave

(חת) terror, fear; shattered, dismayed

(חתת) to be shattered, broken, dismayed, terrified; terror

(חתר) to dig, row

INSERT Tools Message HERE :

Overlay Words :
RE-DO ALL OVERLAY WORDS

(שׂה) Sheep [out of sequence, but listed here because it is part of the compass and defines the yoke as the shepherds crook.]

(על) yoke

(תלה) to hang

(ללת) to be delivered

(תו) a mark [Paleo-Hebrew cross, probably related "to measure" (balance scales)]

(וו) a nail ; a covenant

(וש) equality : striped down to be defined as a covenant child who will inherit. [Ruler of 2 belongs to Waw / Son / YHWH]

The good shepherd to be delivered and hang upon a yoke [think of the man in the shape of the Paleo-Hebrew Tav on the Kabbalah Tree of Life], fastened to the scales of Mercy and Severity with a nail, a covenant of equality.

Individual letters :

(ע) He shut their eyes with an evil report. (ה) The mouth of the Holy Ghost bears witness [that] (ל) the lamb of EL was slain to remove our offense. (ת) They hurled forth wild talk to accuse falsely. Purchased to pay a ransom. [He was] despised and esteemed lightly. He took a yoke, lifted up, and thrust in [pierced] (ו) the mark of the nail, a sign of equality [an inheritance] to him that renews the covenant (ש) and accepts the gift of the lamb, a gift of white linen to the children of man.

Distilled definition : EL's Shepherds Crook, instruction, correction for sheep gone astray, judgment of severity in the hand of EL.

As I noted in the beginning, I thought that this should also be checked for becoming a sword / threshing instrument.

Atbash Chof :

Tools :

Ruler of 2 :
(אך) surely, truly; but, only, however
(פך) flask, jar, cruse
(בך) in thee; in you

Ruler of 3 :
(סבך) thicket; to interweave, interlace

∧ Compass :
(אע) wood, timber, beams
(גא) = גאה proud, haughty
(עא) touch

V Compass :
(סג) to turn aside

< Compass :
(נצ) dazzling, glowing, bright, clear, pure
(צב) covered wagon, litter
(חץ) arrow
(חצב) to hew out, cleave; to draw water
(חב) bosom
(חבץ) to compress, to churn
(בץ) mud, mire, silt
(חבב) to love

> Compass :
(דב) bear [walks softly]
(דבב) to speak, whisper
(בד) linen, cloth, material; pole, bar; branch; part, portion; something separated; lie, fabrication
(בצד) in the side
(צד) side, flank

(צדד) to turn aside

Atbash Chof Word Overlay :

Atbash Chof letter-by-letter :

The י/מ

TOK   ע ח ס   **TOL**

ב ש   פ ש   ה צ   ו א פ ת   י מ   מ י   נ ט

ס ה   ר ג   ל כ   ת א   ק ד   כ ל   ט נ

ע ז   ז ע   ש ב   ו א ת פ   ד ק   ג ר   צ ה

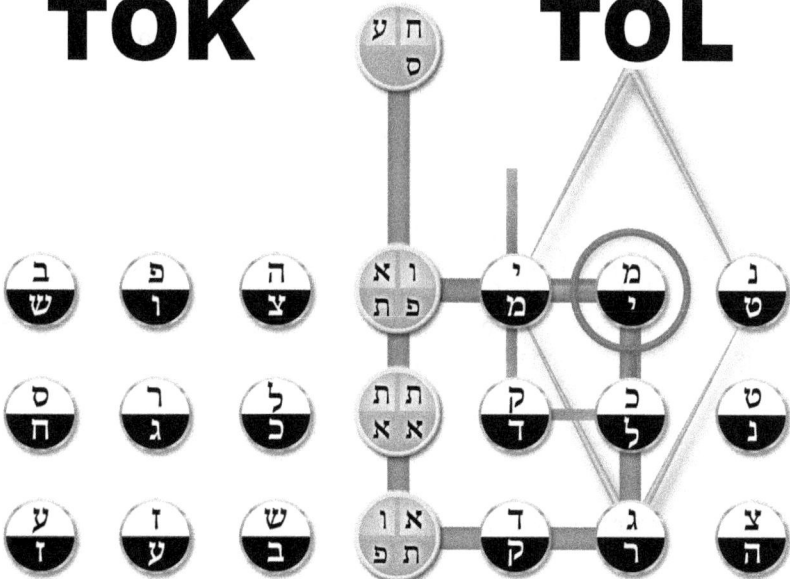

compound letters

[(א)= ו,י] [(ב)= ו, ר] [(ג)= ו,י,(ז?)*] [(ד)= ו] [(ה)= ו,י, ר] [(ז)= ו,י]
[(ח)= ו,י,(ז?)*] [(ט)= ו,י] [(כ)= ו,י, ר] [(ל)= ו,י] [(מ)= ז,ג,ו,י] [(נ)= ו,י]
[(ס)= ו] [(ע)= ו,י] [(פ)= ו,י,(כ,ר?)*] [(צ)= ו,י] [(ק)= ו,י] [(ר)= ו]
[(ש)= ו] [(ת)= ו, ר]

ע ח ס

ים : The eternal iteration

I will spare you the details of the long version. I took another look at the "final Mem" overlay and began with the (י) Adam, (מ) Garden, (נ) Gather, (ט) to the Nest, (צ) Zion, righteous, (ג) followers of the Father, (ד) to the Door, of my Glory, (ק) the hand of my child beside the Veil, [and the iteration returns to the] (י) Father.

I then understood the metaphor of the water. The water in the clouds of the sky [Heaven] falls to a garden on the earth where it combines with the elements to become a plant with the potential to bear fruit and seed for offspring. When it dies, it's water evaporates. The ethereal form returning to the heavens from which it came.

Elohim, even when used in the singular, is plural, because the (ים) "im" references the eternal cycle, without beginning and without end. A cycle which we are all a part of. A cycle which is part of our being.

The Mem מ

The Mem has a numerical value of 40, and includes a final Mem [ם – numerical value of 600], which covers all of the letters surrounding this block evenly. In addition to this, fully half of the Mem overlay is identical to the (נ) Nun. This makes the Mem a compound letter which includes the Nun [excluding square and final form definitions].

It appears that the Mem is the protector, and the Nun is its wing which it uses to protect. As with the (ו) Waw and (ד) Dalet working together to create a doorway, the Mem appears to be a bird of some sort trying to use its (נ) Nun [(יד) Hand + (ינץ) hawk = wing] to partition or protect [gather] the wandering exiles [(צ) Tzade, Zion . . . gathering them to the (ט) nest, who's overlay sits in the same place as the (מ) Mem].

TOOLS :

(מם) Mem : Contraction of (מים) Water

Ruler of 2 :
(עם) people; kinsman, relative; together with, with, close to, beside; as long as, while
(כם) added to nouns and meaning 'your' ; pron. suff. for the second pers. pl., added to verbs and meaning 'you' (accusative).
(קם) enemy, foe, adversary; one who rises against somebody; BAram. - Syr. he stood up, stood, rose, arose
(ימים) = (plural of יום) day ; time ; year
(ים) m.n. sea ; lake ; large basin, reservoir ; West
(מים) water

The final ם Mem invokes (י)Yud-(ם)Mem [eternal iteration] and (ג)Gimmel-(ד)Dalet connections as well as generic "Protector" meaning. Terrible, day, right hand, your, protector, one who rises against somebody, the sea, to cut off [Dalet connection, (ים) nations], fish [invokes Gimmel (followers) to the veil], to gather in troops or bands [invokes Dalet - probable reference to the veil of the temple].

Note : (גד) Interesting Post-Biblical word [of uncertain origin] for WORMWOOD [god - name of Babylonian god of fortune or luck].

Ruler of 3 :
(אים) to threaten, to frighten ; fearful, frightful, terrible

The compass :
(גין) to be grieved, be sorrowful [final Nun invokes favor, grace]
(גין) garden + (י) my = (גין) My Garden? [final Nun invokes favor, grace]
(גן) garden [final Nun invokes favor, grace
(גי) valley, vale
(נגן) to play an instrument
(ני) wailing, lament
(גנן) to defend, protect, guard, shelter; to garden
(יען) Ostrich; inhabitant of the desert; the voracious bird; because of; because; purpose; intention
(ני) wailing, lament
(נין) to sprout, increase; offspring, posterity
(נע) Syr. he quacked, trembled; it waved [said of trees]; it vibrated; he swung, staggered; he tottered; he wondered about; moving, mobile
(נענע) to shake, to stir up
(עי) ruin, heap of ruins
(עין) eye; visible surface; appearance; gleam, sparkle; spring fountain; Ayin - the name of the 16th letter; to look carefully at, to consider
(עני) poor, needy; humble, afflicted; to be poor, to impoverish; affliction; oppression; poverty
(ענין) occupation, task; affair, business; to interest
(ענן) he brought clouds, covered with clouds; to practice soothsaying; cloud
(חי) alive, living; lively, active; raw
(חין) grace, comeliness
(חנן) to show favor, be gracious
(יין) wine
(חיי) live long!, live on!
(נחח) to spray scent

Squares :
(אן) or
(אם) mother; matriarch; metropolis; large city; if, whether, when, on condition; nation, people
(וו) Waw; hook, peg, nail
(מאום) blemish, defect, something
(מום) blemish, defect, fault; to become deformed
(מם) Mem - the 13th letter

(גג) roof
(גו) back, body
(גם) also, to, even as well

(גמם) to cut [the branch of a tree]
(מג) magician [uncertain origin]
(מגג) to squeeze, soften
(מגגם) to stir
(מוג) to melt

(אם) mother; matriarch; metropolis, large city; if, when, whether, on condition; nation, people
(מעם) from [away from being together with]
(אח) brother; kinsman; friend; fire port, brazier, fireplace; woe!, alas!; Eagle Owl
(חח) hook, ring; buckle
(חם) warm; warmth, heat; husband's father, father-in-law
(חמא) to flatter
(חמם) to be or become warm
(חח) marrow; fat one
(מחא) to strike, to clap the hands

(ים) sea; lake; large basin, reservoir; west
(מי) who?; whoever; someone, anyone
(מים) water; to mix with water, to hydrate
(מימים) long since
(ימים) days, year
(מעי) bowls, intestines; heap of stones, ruin
(עי) ruin, heap of ruins
(עים) strength; glow
(עם) people; kinsman, relative; together with, with; close to, beside; as long as, while
(עמם) to darken, to dim; to join, connect
(עממ) to dim, darken, obscure
(חי) alive, living; lively, active; raw
(חיים) life, livelihood
(חמים) slightly warm, lukewarm
(מחי) stroke, blow
(יחם) to be hot

(ימים) days; year
(ים) sea; lake; large basin, reservoir; west
(מי) who?; whoever; someone, anyone
(מים) water; to mix with water, to hydrate
(מימים) long since
(מם) Mem - 13th letter
(מק) rottenness, decay
(מקם) to localize
(מקמק) to rot
(מקק) to rot, decay
(קם) adversary, enemy, foe; one who rises against somebody

(כם) you, your

196 The Menorah Code

(מך) poor, lowly
(מכמך) to press, crush

A note here to be more fully expounded upon in a later edition.
Show מ/י - י/מ : I am in the Father, and the Father is in me.
Show connection to Nun in Seraph, making the Nun a Son.
Show position on the right hand of the Father.
Compass puts it in the middle of a defined (בן אדם) making it the Son of Man. who
is a [bottom of compass] (גר) traveler & a sojourner.
Show breakdown of being crowned on this spot.
This is bottom square Urim, light
When Chet is on top [center flipped] it adds Light.
Look at words for earth, or world.
Words with the lamed such as הלל, בבל & etc. assume an (א) Aleph, because that
(אל) is a ruler of 2 belonging to the Lamed list.
This is Michael, blowing trump, resurrecting the dead . . . but this is Yeshua on the
right hand of the Father. Gathering the righteous into the nest.
Show prince in Nun Square.
Show how in the Kuf, the Yelad for Son is laced with Michael's name.
Show quote from Enoch that shows Michael locking the fallen ones up in what I
think is the South Pole. This happened during the days of Enoch & Adam.
* A lot to add to this one.

Overlay Words :
(מם) Mem [name of letter]
(מן) Manna ; out of [Ruler of 2 belongs to Nun, final Nun invokes favor, grace]
(ימין) f.n. the right hand, right side, the right ; the South (i.e. the right side if one
faces east).
(גנן) Protector [final Nun invokes favor, grace]
(טנן) to be moist, be damp. [final Nun invokes favor, grace]
    I think this is related to (תאן) weep, lament, wail
(יצג) To set in place [I think the Yud may be able to connect with any of these letter
combinations]
(דג) fish [connection to Gimmel, the follower in final Mem]
(גצץ) to flash, to glitter [is this NEW HEBREW?]
(גדד׳) to cut off [belongs to Dalet, door in the final Mem]
(גדד״) to gather in troops or bands [belongs to Dalet, door in the final Mem]
(דד) breast, teat, nipple
(דק) Veil [ruler of 2 belongs to Kuf kingdom of YHWH on earth - Temple]
(יקד) to be kindled, burn [ruler of 3 - Dalet]
(יד) hand [not in sequence, but thin line may be making Yud available?]
(ידד) to be friends, become friends.
(ידיד) friend, beloved

Individual letters :
(מ) Protector : (נ) Gather ; (ט) Nest ; (צ) Zion ; (ג) Followers ; (ד) Door ; (ק) decree ;

(י) Almighty

The next page will give you a detailed breakdown of the long version. This turns out to be the mystery of the endless iteration of eternal lives. It is this mystery which makes the (ים) "im" ending on Hebrew words plural. A reference to the eternal cycle without beginning or end.

Distilled definition : Protector ; grieved for my garden ; water, the sea ; the days, times, years.

Atbash Yud :

Tools :

Ruler of 2 :
(מי) who, whoever, someone, anyone
(די) sufficiency, enough; who, which, that, of, about
(לי) to me
(ני) wailing, lament

∧ Compass :
(טמטם) to make stupid
(טמם) to stop up, fill up
(טמע) to be mixed up; Aram. he sank
(טעם) to taste; to perceive; taste, flavor; judgement, discretion, discernment; decree, command
(מטמט) to shake, destroy
(מטע) planting; plantation
(מטעם) savoury food, delicacy
(מם) the letter Mem [PBH?]
(מס) body of forced laborers, forced service
(מסמס) to melt, to dissolve
(מסס) to melt, to dissolve
(מעט) to be small, be few, diminish; little, few; a little
(מעם) from (away from being together with)
(סט) deviation (Apostacy)
(סם) spice
(סמם) to poison
(עט) stylus; reed pen
(עם) people; kinsman, relative; together with, with; close to, beside; as long as, while
(עמם) to darken, to dim; to join, connect
(עממ) to dim, darken, obscure

∨ Compass :
(טמר) to hide, conceal

(טרטר) to rattle, make a loud noise; to mess somebody around
(טרם) to do before
(מטר) rain; to rain
(ממר) bitterness, grief, affliction
(ממרט) polished
(מר) bitter; embittered, sad, gloomy; cruel; drop; master; hoe; myrrh
(מרט) to make bare, make smooth, polish
(מרטט) to tatter, to make ragged
(מרמר) to become embittered
(מרר) to be bitter
(רטט) to tremble; trembling, panic
(רם) high, elevated; exalted, supreme (the Most High)
(רמם) to become wormy, grow rotten, decay; to rise exalted

Squares :
(תי) suff. my; pertaining to
(תסס) to ferment
(תעע) to deceive, to mock
(סיס) swift; to drive a horse
(סס) moth
(עי) ruin, heap of ruins
(עת) time; season; appointed time
(עתי) timely, ready
(עתת) to time

(ים) sea; lake; large basin, reservoir; west
(יסם) to become blind
(מי) who?, whoever; someone, anyone
(מים) water; to mix with water, to hydrate
(מימים) long since [could this also be many waters?]
(מם) the letter Mem [PBH? really?]
(מס) body of forced laborers, forced service [uncertain origin]
(מסמס) to melt, to dissolve
(מסס) to melt, to dissolve
(מעי) bowls, intestines; heap of stones, ruin
(מעם) from; away from being together
(סים) to end, finish, terminate
(סם) spice
(סמם) to poison

(יפי) beauty, splendor
(פי) mouth
(פת) morsel of bread, piece of bread; vulva, corner of the head; forehead
(פתפת) to crumb, crumble, mash
(פתת) to break (esp. bread) into pieces, crumb, crumble
(תי) suff. my; pertaining to
(תף) drum

(תפף) to drum, beat the drum

(פר) bull, bullock, steer
(פרי) fruit; offspring; product
(פרפר) to break, to crumble, to crush; to shake, shatter
(פרר) to crush, crumble, break into crumbs; to break, violate, annul, frustrate; to shake, shatter
(רי) moisture
(ריר) to flow like slime; slime, juice, spittle, saliva
(רפף) to move gently; to waver, vacillate; to loosen, weaken

(דד) breast, teat, nipple
(די) sufficiency; enough, sufficiently; who, which, that; of, about
(דם) blood; bloodshed; blood-guilt
(דמדם) to be in a daze, to be confused
(דמי) quiet, rest, silence
(דמים) bloodshed, blood-guiltiness
(דמם) to be or grow dumb or silent; to bleed
(יד) hand, arm; foreleg
(ידד) to be friends, become friends
(ידיד) friend, beloved
(ים) sea, lake; large basin, reservoir; west
(מד) garment; to measure
(מדי) Prep. as often as, every
(מי) who?, whoever; someone, anyone
(מידי) from the hands of
(מים) water; to mix with water, to hydrate
(מימים) long since
(מם) the letter Mem [PBH?]

(דל) poor; thin, lean; low, weak, powerless; door
(דלי) bucket
(דלל) to become poor, become weak, become thin; to hang down loosely
(ילד) to bear, bring forth, beget; child, boy, offspring, young man
(יליד) son
(ילל) to howl, wail; wailing, howling, lament
(לי) to me
(ליד) near, close to

The ט/נ

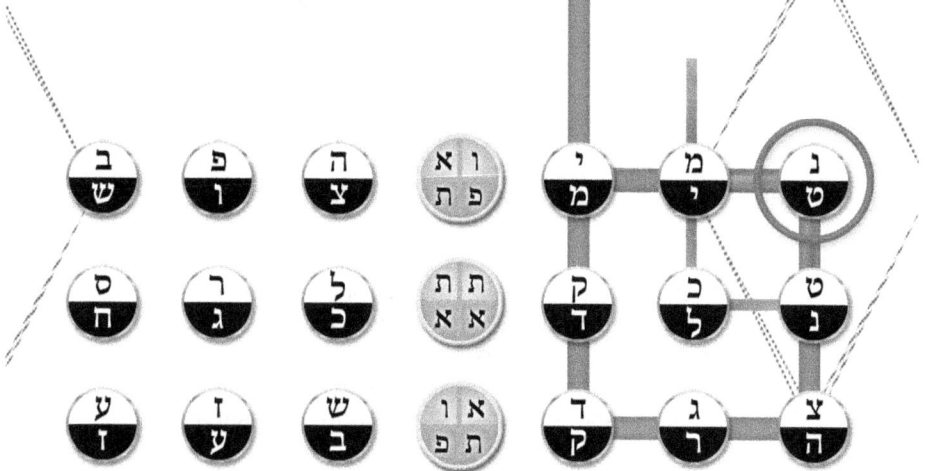

compound letters

[(א)= ו,י][(ב)= ו,ר][(ג)= ו,י,ז(?)*][(ד)= ו][(ה)= ו,י,ר][(ז)= ו,י]
[(ח)= ו,י,ז(?)*][(ט)= ו,י][(כ)= ו,ר][(ל)= ו,י][(מ)= ו,ז,ב,י][(נ)= ו,י]
[(ס)= ו][(ע)= ו,י][(פ)= ו,י,ב,ר(?)*][(צ)= ו,י][(ק)= ו,י][(ר)= ו]
[(ש)= ו][(ת)= ו,ר]

This was what I saw that made me want to look harder at the compass crossing from one side of the tree to the other.

The נון Nun [fish] top compass touches ישוע Yeshua on one side, and מיכאל Michael on the other.

The Nun נ

The name of the letter, "Nun", means fish and has a numerical value of 50. The Final Nun [ן value of 700] may look like a straight line down [given the modern font being used], but it actually hits the (מ) Mem, (נ) Nun, (ט) Tet, (צ) Tzade, and drops below the horizon down to the (ח) Chet [(חן) favor, grace].

TOOLS :

Ruler of 2 :
(חן) favor, grace, charm & (חנן) to show favor [final form extension of Nun applies to all ruler words]
(ענן) cloud; to practice soothsaying
(מן) Manna ; out of ; than, from, who, whomever [final Nun invokes favor, grace]
(כן) so, thus; right, truthful, honest; louse; suff. meaning 'your' ; 'you' (accusative)
(כנן) to place, put; to regulate, adjust; to coil
(טנן) to be moist, be damp; Aram. was moist, was damp
(בן) son; offspring; branch, shoot; inhabitant of; worth of; deserving
(סנן) filter, strain

Ruler of 3 :
(ימן) to go or turn to the right; to use the right hand; to prepare, appoint

∧ Compass :
(בם) in them
(בעבע) to bubble
(חב) bosom
(חבב) to love
(חם) warm; warmth, heat; husband's father, father-in-law
(חמם) to be or become warm
(מח) marrow; fat one
(מם) Mem - 13th letter
(מעם) from; away from being together with
(עב) cloud; thick; thicket; beam, rafter

(עבב) to cover with clouds
(עם) people; kinsman, relative, relative; together with, with; close to, beside; as long as, while
(עמם) to darken, to dim; to join, to connect

V Compass :

(בץ) mud, mire, silt
(בצבץ) to squeeze out, exude
(בצץ) to squeeze out, exude
(מץ) oppressor
(מיר) standing place, station, position; garrison; placed, stationed
(מצמץ) to suck, lick; to blink, wink
(מצץ) to suck
(צב) covered wagon, litter
(צבב) to cover
(צם) he fasted
(צמם) to press, draw together
(צמצם) to press, reduce, contract

The squares :

(נין) to sprout, increase, offspring, posterity
(דד) breast, teat, nipple
(די) often, sufficiency, enough; who, which, that; of, about
(דין) to judge; judgment; verdict, sentence; lawsuit, cause; judge
(ניד) quivering motion, movement
(נד) heap, wall; moving
(נדן) sheath, case; harlot's pay
(נדד) to wander about, flee
(נדנד) to nag, to bore
(יד) hand, arm, foreleg
(ידד) to be friends, become friends
(ידיד) friend, beloved

(נץ) hawk; blossom, flower [final Tzade invokes to divide; to make a partition]
(נצץ) to shine, flash, sparkle; to blossom, bloom, sprout
(נד) heap, wall; moving
(נדד) to wander about, flee
(צן) thorn [final Nun invokes favor, grace]
(צנן) to be cold; Aram. was cold
(צד) side, flank. [final Tzade invokes to divide; to make a partition]
(צדד) to turn aside

(חח) hook, ring; buckle
(חי) alive, living; lively, active; raw
(חין) grace, comeliness
(חן) favor, grace, charm
(חנן) to show favor, be gracious
(יחי) long live _!, live on!

(יען) Ostrich; inhabitant of the desert; the voracious bird; because of; because
(עי) ruin, heap of ruins
(עין) eye; visible surface; appearance; gleam, sparkle; spring, fountain; eye of the water; to look askance at; to look carefully at, consider; name of 16th letter
(ענן) he brought clouds, covered with clouds; to practice soothsaying; cloud
(יין) wine
(נע) moving, mobile
(נענע) to shake, to stir up
(ני) wailing, lament
(ניח) to immobilize
(נין) to sprout, increase; offspring, posterity

(חן) favor, grace, charm
(חמן) sun-pillar
(חמם) to be or become warm
(חם) warm; warmth, heat; husband's father, father-in-law
(חנן) to show favor, be gracious
(מח) marrow; fat onethan
(מן) manna; what?; away from, from, of out of; since, because; more than,
(מנחם) comforter, to console
(מנע) to keep back, withhold
(מעם) away from being together with
(נחח) to spray scent
(נחם) to have compassion; to console oneself; repentance
(נמנם) to slumber
(נע) moving, mobile
(נעם) to be pleasant, be delightful, be lovely; to sing; to compose or play music; pleasantness, delightfulness, loveliness, charm
(נעמן) pleasantness
(נענע) to shake, to stir up
(עם) people; kinsman, relative; together with, with; close to, beside; as long as, while
(עמם) to darken, to dim; to join, connect
(עמעם) to dim, darken, obscure
(ענן) he brought clouds, covered with clouds; to practice soothsaying; cloud

(כם) suff. you, your
(כמן) to be hidden
(כן) so, thus; right, truthful, honest; louse
(כנם) louse, vermin
(כנן) to place, put; to regulate, adjust; to coil
(מן) manna; what?; away from, from, of, out of; since, because; more than, than
(מך) poor, lowly
(מכך) to be low, be humiliated
(מכמך) to press, crush
(מכמן) hidden store, treasure
(נמך) to be low
(נמנם) to slumber

(טנן) to be moist, be damp
(כן) so, thus; right, truthful, honest; louse; you, your
(כנן) to place, put; to regulate, adjust; to coil

Note : This working draft is still missing information. What I will leave you with in the Seraph section, has obvious links between this Nun, and the Bet [showing the word "Son" to be in the Nun's word list]. At this point, it looks like the compass may cross over. There may be more of the same story or connections to it here.

Atbash Tet :

Tools :

Ruler 2 :
(לט) enchantment, magic; secrecy
(עט) stylus; reed pen
(שט) Apostate, deviator
(חטט) to dig, scratch

Ruler 3 :
(קלט) to contract, draw in, take in

Squares :
(טמם) to stop, fill up
(טמ) gives way
(מק) rottenness, decay
(קם) has risen, arose, risen up
(קט) small; very soon; very little while
(קטם) to cut off; lop off; to cover with ashes

(קטה) Pterocles (a genes of birds, sand grouse - Pigeon like bird
(הט) incline
(קהה) to be blunt, dull

Compare to next squares :
(טמע) to be mixed up; Aram. he sank
(טעם) to taste; to perceive; taste, flavor; judgement, discretion, discernment; decree, command
(מטמט) to shake, destroy
(מטע) planting; plantation
(מטעם) savory food, delicacy
(סו) deviation; deviations from the right path
(סם) spice
(סמם) to poison
(סס) moth

(עט) stylus; reed pen

(עם) people; kinsman, relative; together with, with; close to, beside; as long as, while

(עמם) to darken, to dim; to join, to connect

(טיט) to plaster; to erase, to draft; mud, mire, clay

(יעט) to cover

(עי) ruin, heap of ruins

(עיט) to rush upon; to scream, shriek; bird of prey; the screaming bird

(טיל) to walk, to go on a trip

(טל) dew

(טלטל) to cast, throw, hurl

(טלל) to overshadow, roof, cover; to cover with dew

(ילל) to howl, wail; wailing, howling, lament

(לט) enchantment, magic; secrecy

(ליל) night, at night

(לנן) to murmur

(טנן) to be moist, be damp

(נטל) to lift, bear; to take; burden, weight

(קהה) to be blunt, be dull

(קטט) to quarrel

(קטקט) to flatten, make even

(יש) there is, there are; possession, property

(ישע) to deliver; deliverance, salvation, welfare

(סיס) swift; to drive a horse

(עי) ruin, heap of ruins

(עיש) name of constellation - prob. The Great Bear

(עש) name of constellation - prob. The Great Bear

(שיש) to rejoice; white marble, alabaster

(שסס) to plunder, spoil, pillage

(שעשע) to smooth, to besmear; to blind oneself; to take delight; to delight

(שש) six; white marble; Egyptian linen

(ששי) sixth

(היה) to be, exist, happen, become; was, existed; came into being, became; he remained; it came to pass, happened

(יה) Yah, short form of יהוה YHWH

(יש) there is, there are; possession, property

(ישיש) old man

(שה) (young) sheep, lamb; small cattle (goat, sheep)

(שהה) to tarry, linger; to stay, to delay, be late in coming

(שי) gift, present

TOK TOL

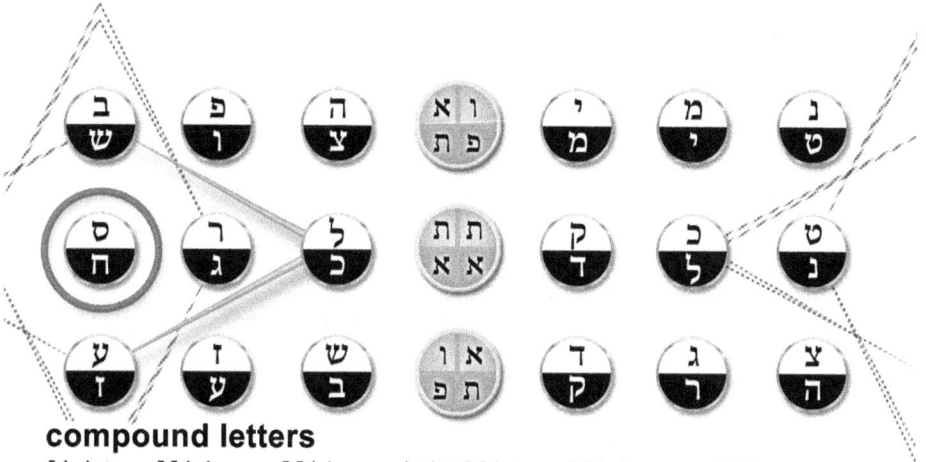

compound letters

[(א)= י,ו][(ב)= ר,ו][(ג)= ו,י,(ז?)*][(ד)= ו][(ה)= ר,י,ו][(ז)= ו,י]
[(ח)= ו,י,(ז?)*][(ט)= י,ו][(כ)= ר,י,ו][(ל)= ו,י][(מ)= י,ו,נ,ז][(נ)= ו,י]
[(ס)= ו][(ע)= י,ו][(פ)= ו,י,(ר,כ?)*][(צ)= ו,י][(ק)= י,ו][(ר)= ו,י]
[(ש)= ו][(ת)= ו,ר]

The Samech o

The Samech (סמך) definition is : he supported, sustained, upheld and it has a numerical value of 60.

The Paleo Hebrew Samech looks like the three-teir-cross in the Kabbalah Tree of Life. When the letter is defined, there appears to be a connection to the crucifixion theme.

TOOLS :

Ruler of 2 :
(בס) to perfume, to flavor; to trample, tread; to base, establish
(פס) a tunic reaching to the palms and the ankles
(ספסף) to crumb, separate, to part; to sign; to make something in mosaic form
(ספס) to end, cease, disappear, blot out, destroy [death]; to be broad, spread; to tear apart; to strip
(רס) to break into small pieces, crush; to spray, sprinkle, moisten
(עס) to press, crush, tread; to fill with juice, make juicy
(נס) standard, ensign, flag; signal, sign
(נסס) to move to and fro, to fly; to perform miracles; to pine away, to be sick

/\ Compass :
(טרטר) to rattle, make a loud noise; to mess somebody around
(עט) stylus; reed pen
(עטר) to surround, encircle; to crown
(ער) enemy, foe; awake, wakeful
(ערער) to lay bare; to protest; to arouse, awaken, incite; to gargle; name of a tree - prob. the juniper; stripped, destitute, lonely
(ערר) to strip oneself; to strip; to tear down
(רטט) to tremble; trembling, panic
(רע) bad, worthless; evil, wicked; wickedness; harm, misfortune, calamity; badness; friend, companion, associate; fellowman; thought, purpose, aim; noise, shout
(רעע) to be evil, be bad; to break into pieces, crush, shatter; to make friends with, associate with
(רערע) to shake, to undermine

V Compass :
(חח) hook, ring; buckle
(חטט) to dig, scratch
(חטר) branch, twig, rod
(חר) hole, aperture; socket of the eye; nobleman
(חרחר) to burn, to provoke; to grunt
(חרט) to chisel, to engrave, to turn; to repent; graving-tool, stylus

(חרר) to be hot and dry, be scorched, burn; to make a hole, bore through; to be or become free

(טחח) to be besmeared

(טחר) to strain at stool

(טרח) to take pains, take trouble; burden, labor, trouble, bother

(טרטר) to rattle, make a loud noise; to mess somebody around

(רח) Syr. he breathed; Phoen. spirit

(רחרח) to sniff, snuff; to scent, track, detect

(רטט) to tremble; trembling, panic

< Compaoo :

(בך) in thee, in you

(בעבע) to bubble

(כעכע) to cough slightly

(עב) cloud; thick; thicket; beam, rafter

(עבב) to cover with clouds

(עכב) to hinder, prevent

> Compass :

(בבל) Babel, Babylon, Babylonia

(בל) not

(בלל) to confuse

(בלבל) to confuse

(בלע) to swallow; swallowing, a thing swallowed; confusion, corruption

(בעל) to rule over, own, possess; to marry; to cohabit with; owner, master; husband; Baal - chief Canaanite god

(לב) heart, mind, will; the inner part, the middle

(לבב) heart; to be understanding, likable; to make cakes; to blaze up

(לבלב) to bloom, blossom

(לע) throat

(לעב) to jest, to mock

(לעע) to swallow, sip; to talk wildly

(על) height, upper part; above; on, upon; at, beside; towards; against; concerning, about; because of, on account of; together with; yoke

(עלב) to put to shame, insult, humiliate

(עלל) to act, do work; to insert, thrust in; to accuse falsely; to glean (grapes or olives)

(עלע) to swallow, suck up, lick

(עלעל) to turn over the pages; to drive about, hurl, cast

Overlay Words :

(בפה) (ב) "in the" + (פה) Mouth ??? [or] Perhaps (ב) "full" + (פה) Mouth ???

(הלל) "Hallel" Praise ; he has praised

(הלז) that one

(ooע׳) to press, crush, tread

(ooע״) to fill with juice, make juicy

(ooב״) to base, establish

(עז) Strong, mighty, might, fierce, fortress, refuge, splendor, glory
(עזז) prevail, to be strong
(רעז) tremble, quake

Atbash Chet :

Tools :

(חח) hook, ring; fetters

Ruler of 2 :
(שח) bent, bowed
(גח) JAram., - Syr. = גיח to burst forth
(זחח) to remove, displace
(נח) Noah; rest
(טח) to shut [the eyes]; to besmear

⋀ Compass :
(גג) [flat] roof [upon which one may walk]; top slab of altar of incense
(גן) garden
(גנן) to enclose, fence in, hedge in, protect
(נגן) to play a stringed instrument
(נגע) to touch; Aram. he touched; to strike, smite; stroke, blow, wound; sign of leprosy; plague; mark
(נע) a vagrant, a fugitive
(עגן) shut oneself in; to be shut in; to be deserted; Aram. he shut up, cast into prison; to anchor
(ענג) to be soft, be tender; to please; exquisite delight, pleasure; tender, delicate
(ענן) he brought clouds, covered with clouds; to practice soothsaying; to divine from the form of clouds [dictionary guess]

> Compass :
(זך) pure, clean, clear
(זכך) to be clear, bright; to be pure, guiltless
(עז) strong; power, strength, mighty, fierce; strength; stronghold, fortress, refuge; splendor, glory; goat
(עזז) to be strong, to prevail
(עש) moth; The Great Bear [constellation]

(עששׁ) to become weak; to waste away; to decay
(שׂך) thorn, splinter; booth, enclosure [hedge of protection?]

V Compass :
(גג) [flat] roof [upon which one may walk]; top slab of altar of incense
(גן) garden
(גנן) to enclose, fence in, hedge in, protect
(נגן) to play a stringed instrument
(נס) standard, ensign, flag; signal, sign
(נסס) to lift up an ensign; sparkling
(סגן) prefect, ruler, governor; head
(סס) a moth; a grub
< Compass :
(זלל) to be mean, be vile, to be a glutton; to shake; to be frivolous, gluttonous; be despised
(שׁל) to remove, put off, loose; error, offense, crime; belonging to
(שׁלל) to spoil, plunder, to deprive; to draw out (sheaves); to remove; to refuse, to negate, to deny; to stitch loosely, to join together loosely, to chain, fetter; spoil, booty, plunder
(שׁלשׁ) three; to multiply by three; to divide by three; one of the third generation; great grandson; pertaining to the third
(שׁשׁ) six; alabaster; Egyptian linen

The ע/ז

TOK TOL

compound letters
[ו,י =(ז)] [ר,י,י =(ה)] [ו =(ד)] [(ז?)*ו,י,י =(ג)] [ר,ו,י =(ב)] [י,י =(א)]
[י,י =(נ)] [ז,ג,ו,י =(מ)] [ו,י =(ל)] [ר,ו,י,י =(כ)] [ו,י =(ט)] [(ז?)*ו,י,י =(ח)]
[ו =(ר)] [י,י =(ק)] [ו,י =(צ)] [(ז?)ר,כ,י,י =(פ)] [ו,י =(ע)] [ו =(ס)]
[ר,ו =(ת)] [ו =(ש)]

The Ayin ע

The Ayin (עין) has a numerical value of 70, and means "eye". It is the origin of the "all seeing eye" and represents the intelligence [wisdom, understanding, knowledge] or glory of YHWH above the Kabbalah Tree of Life (lamps of the Menorah).

TOOLS :

Ruler of 2 :
(רע) bad, worthless; evil; wickedness; harm, misfortune, calamity; friend, companion, associate; fellowman; thought, purpose, aim; noise, shout
(רעע) afflict; to be evil, be bad; to break into pieces, crush, shatter; to make friends with, associate with
(רערע) to shake, to undermine
(רע) to tremble, quake
(זעזע) to shake violently
(צעצע) to adorn, ornament

Ruler of 3 :
(מטע) planting; plantation; to plant
(הרע) an evil report ; wicked, evil
(ע–הרע) given the "ע" Ayin, or eye which is on top of the grid, this line would actually be the equivalent of (עין הרע / Aayin HaRa) = The Evil Eye

Λ Compass :
(בז) booty, spoil, prey, plunder, pillage
(בזבז) to waste, to squander, to dissipate
(בזז) to spoil, plunder, pillage, rob
(בץ) mud, mire, silt
(בצץ) to squeeze out, exude
(בצבץ) to squeeze out, exude
(זב) one that has a flux
(צב) covered wagon, litter
(צבב) to cover

V Compass :
(נחז) to remove, displace
(נזז) to flash
(חץ) arrow
(חצץ) to divide; to make a partition; gravel, gravel-stone
(נץ) dazzling, glowing, bright, clear, pure
(נצח) to be dazzling, be bright, be clear; to become dry
(צחצח) to polish

Squares :
(עט) stylus; reed pen
(עץ) tree; timber, wood; handle
(צטט) to quote

(צעצע) to adorn, ornament

(סס) moth
(סר) sullen, ill-humored
(סרס) to castrate; to transpose; to distort
(סרסר) to mediate, go between
(סרר) to be stubborn, be rebellious
(עסס) to press, crush, tread; to fill with juice, make juicy
(ער) enemy, foe; awake, wakeful
(ערס) to form an arbor; to mix with dough
(ערער) to lay bare; to protest; to arouse, awaken, incite; to gargle; name of a tree - prob. the juniper; stripped, destitute, lonely
(ערר) to strip oneself; to strip; to tear down
(רסס) to break into small pieces, crush; to spray, sprinkle, moisten
(רע) bad, worthless; evil, wicked; wickedness; harm, misfortune, calamity; friend, companion, associate; fellowman; thought, purpose, aim; noise, shout
(רעע) to be evil, be bad; to break into pieces, crush, shatter; to make friends with, associate with
(רערע) to shake, to undermine

(זעזע) to shake violently
(זער) to be small, be few
(זר) stranger; frame, edging
(זרז) to speed up; to gird on
(זרע) to sow; sowing, sowing season; seed; sperm, semen; offspring, posterity
(זרר) to sneeze; to press, squeeze
(עז) strong, firm, mighty; fierce; strength, might, fortress, refuge; splendor, glory; goat
(עזז) to be strong
(עזר) to help, assist, aid; help, assistance; helpmate
(ער) enemy, foe; awake, wakeful
(ערער) to lay bare; to protest; to arouse, awaken, incite; to gargle; name of a tree - prob. the juniper; stripped, destitute, lonely
(ערר) to strip oneself; to strip; to tear down
(רז) secret
(רע) bad, worthless; evil; wicked; wickedness; harm, misfortune, calamity; friend, companion, associate; fellowman; thought, purpose, aim; noise, shout
(רעע) to be evil, be bad; to break into pieces, crush, shatter; to make friends with, associate with
(רערע) to shake, to undermine

(בה) in her, in it
(בהה) to be astonished, amazed
(בעבע) to bubble
(בעה) to bubble; to seek; to ask questions
(הב) give
(הבה) give; let us
(הבהב) to singe; to hesitate; burnt offering; sacrificial gift

(עב) cloud; thick; thicket; beam, rafter
(עבב) to cover with clouds
(עבה) to be thick

(עש) moth; name of a constellation - prob. the Great Bear
(עשה) to do, make; he did, made; he worked, labored; he acted, dealt; he produced, yielded, performed, accomplished; he brought about, caused, effected; he
appointed; he acquired, gained
(עשש) to waste away, decay
(שה) (young) sheep, lamb; small cattle (goat, sheep)
(שהה) to tarry, linger; to stay, to delay, be late in coming
(שעה) to gaze at, look about; to care for
(שעע) to smooth; to besmear; to blind; to take delight, be delighted
(שעשע) to smooth, to besmear; to take delight; to delight
(שש) six; white marble; Egyptian linen
(ششה) six; to divide by six; to multiply by six

(חח) hook, ring; buckle
(חשש) to feel pain, fear, apprehend; chaff
(עש) moth; name of a constellation - prob. the Great Bear
(עשש) to waste away, decay
(שח) meditation; talk; bent, bowed
(שעע) to smooth; to besmear; to blind; to take delight, be delighted
(שש) six; white marble; Egyptian linen

(חזח) to remove, displace
(זעע) to shake violently
(חרר) to flash
(עז) strong, firm, mighty; fierce; strength, might; fortress, refuge; splendor, glory;
goat
(עזז) to be strong

(חצץ) to divide; to make a partition; gravel, gravel-stone
(עץ) tree; timber, wood; handle
(צח) dazzling, glowing, bright, clear, pure
(צחח) to become dry
(צחצח) to polish
(צעצע) to adorn, ornament

Tools section saying here :

Overlay Words : RE-DO ALL
(רף) Shelf
(פר) Bull, Steer ; implied relation to (אלף") [see Aleph section]
    *Interesting to note that the (פר) ends in the center of the Temple Court
(ערף) to break neck, to behead ; to drip, drop ; back of the neck, neck
(לע) throat
(הלל) "Hallel" Praise ; he has praised

(הלל'') To boast, praise, he shouted in festival joy, sang, praised, shouted for joy
(הלל'') To shine, it began to shine, it shone
(עז) Strong, mighty, fierce, fortress, refuge, splendor, glory
(עז) to tremble, quake
(עלה) Glorify
(עזרה) barrier, enclosure, the temple court

Individual letters :
(ע) he shut their eyes with an evil report : (ז) to extend the border : (ר) the son, pure and clean : (פ) [was] despised, disdained and scorned : (ל) the lamb of EL was slain to remove [our] offense : (ה) the decree [is] to repent, be drawn forth from the water pure and clean, [receive] the Holy Ghost and bear witness with a joyous shout!

Atbash Zayin :

Tools :

Ruler of 2 :
(גז) shearing; the shorn wool; fleece
(עז) strong, firm, mighty, fierce; strength, might; fortress, refuge, splendor, glory

Ruler of 3 :
(שחז) to sharpen, whet, grind; to be exposed [naked]
(בעז) Boaz - name of the left hand of the two bronze pillars in front of the Temple

Squares :
(צב) covered wagon, litter
(בץ) mud, mire, silt
(בז) booty, spoil, prey, plunder, pillage
(בז) one that has a flux [flow]

(גז) shearing; the shorn wool; fleece; mowing, mown grass
(גזז) to cut off, shear
(גח) JAram. - Syr. to burst forth
(גז) skin of the grape
(זגג) to glaze
(זגזג) to make transparent
(זחח) to remove, to displace
(חג) feast, festival
(חגג) to make a pilgrimage, to celebrate a feast, to dance, to reel, to be giddy
(זזז) to flash
(חח) hook, ring; buckle
(געגע) to long, to yearn; to quack; to dig, make holes, roll in
(זעזע) to shake violently
(עגעג) to peck, pick holes
(עז) strong, firm, mighty; fierce; strength, might; fortress, refuge; splendor, glory

(עזז) to be strong
(עוס) to press, crush, tread; to fill with juice, make juicy
(סס) moth
(בסס) to trample, tread; to base, establish

(הן) they; behold; yes; if
(הנה) to be agreeable, be pleased; they; here, hither; lo, behold
(הנהן) yes
(הז) this; which
(הזה) to identify
(זן) sort, kind
(הזן) to commit fornication, be a harlot
(נה) wailing lamentation
(נהה) to long for, follow eagerly; to wail, lament
(נזה) to spurt, spatter

(הזה) to dream, rave
(זחח) to remove, displace
(חזה) to see, behold; he saw, beheld, perceived; he prophesied; breast, chest
(חזז) to flash
(חח) hook, ring; buckle

NEW ∧ Compass :
(עש) moth; constellation - probably the Great Bear
(עשה) to do, make
(עששׁ) to waste away, decay
(שה) (young) sheep, lamb; small cattle (goat, sheep)
(שההּ) to tarry, linger; to stay, delay, be late incoming
(שעה) to gaze at, look about; to care for
(שעע) to smooth, besmear; to blind; to take delight, be delighted
(שעשע) to smooth, to besmear; to take delight; to delight

NEW V Compass :
(עסה) to press, squeeze
(הסס) to hesitate
(עסה) to rush, be stormy
(עסו) to press, crush, tread; to fill with juice, make juicy

REDO TO INCLUDE NEW TOOLS.
Atbash Zayin Tools :
The refuge of splendor and glory [has] one with a flow of mud, mire and silt to grind and expose the prey ([as] the shearing of wool..?)

[Pray on this later, is overlay even right? Does it cross over so it can touch its letter?]
Atbash Overlay Words :

(גו) back, body; inside, interior
(גוע) to die, to perish
(גוש) clod, lump of earth; to form a block
(געגע) to long, to yearn; to quack; to dig, make holes, roll in
(געש) to shake, quake, quiver, tremble, to rage, to storm; to moo
(גץ) to flash, to glitter
(גשוש) to tinkle, to rattle, to rustle
(גשש) to feel, to touch, to grope; to touch the bottom of the sea, to ground, to scout
(וו) hook, peg, nail
(עגגע) to peck, to pick holes
(עוג) to bake a cake; to draw a circle
(עוץ) to advise
(עוש) to make haste, hurry
(עץ) tree; timber, wood; handle
(עש) moth; name of constellation - the great bear
(עשש) to waste away, to decay
(צו) command, order
(צוג) to stand
(צוצע) image work, carving
(צעצע) to adorn, ornament
(שגג) to go astray, to commit an error, sin unintentionally
(שגע) to be mad
(שגש) to confuse, to confound
(שגשג) to grow, flourish
(שו) equality
(שוג) to turn back, retreat
(שוגג) erring, sinning unintentionally
(שוע) nobleman, prince; cry for help; to cry out for help
(שוש) to rejoice
(ששע) to smooth; to besmear; to blind; to take delight, be delighted
(ששעש) to smooth, to besmear; to take delight; to delight
(שש) six; white marble; Egyptian linen

Atbash Zayin Overlay :
   Rejoice in white linen to grow and flourish, to peck the nail [a covenant] of equali-
ty. Make a circle and cry [unto YHWH] for help.
   Turn back the great Bear[?], confound and confuse [them that they] be crazed,
that they waste away and perish.
   Make haste to advise; [they] have blinded themselves, sinning unintentionally.
They go astray by adorning the interior, carving an image with wood.
   Stand in the sea and a lump of earth. Command to shake and quake, to rage a
terrible storm to flash, to rattle, to rustle, to besmear [the eyes]. [That they] yearn
to make holes to roll in. [?Missing too much -> do more later?]

Atbash Zayin Letter by letter :
(צ)   The worthy young maiden [the daughter of Zion] shall gather together and
utter a curse to swell and squeeze out mud, mire, and silt to cover the covered

218   The Menorah Code

wagon(s).

In a flash [their] end is destruction and ruin, cut off, worm eaten and decayed.

(ı) Take delight in the place of refuge and adorn the body in white linen as equals.

Then command [the great Bear?] [that] they be dried up to waste away and decay.

(ψ) The one with a flux shall return to rescue the prey and cover the chaff.

(ג) Make a circle beside the throne to cut off the large crowd.

(ע) One that has an flux [shall] fly and strike to shake and move violently, to tremble and quake, to plunder and spoil those who despise and treat with contempt two Israelites. [re-do when more of these letters are done]

These should really be stripped down and re-assembled.

The פ/ו

compound letters

[(א)= ו,י][(ב)= ו,ר][(ג)= ו,י,(ז?)*][(ד)= ו][(ה)= ו,י,ר][(ז)= ו,י]
[(ח)= ו,י,(ז?)*][(ט)= ו,י][(כ)= ו,י,ר][(ל)= ו,י][(מ)= ז,ג,ו,י][(נ)= ו,י]
[(ס)= ו][(ע)= ו,י][(פ)= ו,י,(כ,ר?)*][(צ)= ו,י][(ק)= ו,י][(ר)= ו]
[(ש)= ו][(ת)= ו,ר]

The Peh פ

The Peh (פה) means, mouth, and has a numerical value of 80. Please note that the only difference between the (פ) Peh, and the (ף) Final Peh [numerical value of 800], is that the overlay will detach from the (ז) Zayin and extend straight down from the (ש) Shin. The final Peh reaching down to earth creates (חף) Palate, pure, innocent, and (חפף) clean.

TOOLS :

Ruler of 2 :
(סף) threshold; basin, goblet, wine vessel
(רפף) to move gently; to waver, vacillate; to loosen, weaken
(לפף) to wrap up, envelop, clasp, embrace
(חף) pure, innocent and (חפף) clean [final form connection]

Ruler of 3 :
(זרף) a drip; to flow; Aram. it flowed
(אלף) Aleph - from a ruler of 3 created in the Adam and Eve overlay, within the (ו) Waw of that Aleph [see Aleph section, Adam and Eve overlay].

V compass :
(הב) give
(הבה) give, let us
(הבהב) to singe; burnt offerings; to hesitate
(הזב) an issue, a discharge
(הזה) to dream, rave
(בבה) apple of the eye
(בהה) to be astonished, amazed
(בז) booty, spoil, prey, plunder, pillage
(בזז) to spoil, plunder, pillage, rob
(בזבז) to waste, to squander, to dissipate
(בזה) was despised, disdained, scorned; booty, spoil, plunder, pillage
(בז) issue, flowing, discharge; one that has a flux
(זבה) her issue, her discharge
(הז) this, which ; here
(זהב) to redden one's face [with shame] ; also gold, or gilded
(זהה) to identify

∧ compass :
(בה) in her; in it
(בהה) to be astonished, amazed

(בעבע) to bubble
(בעה) to bubble; to seek; to ask questions
(הב) give
(הבה) give; let us
(הבהב) to singe; to hesitate; my sacrificial gifts
(עב) cloud; thick; thicket; beam, rafter
(עבב) to cover with clouds

Squares :
(פה) mouth; speech, saying; command; opening, orifice; here
(סהה) to idle, to loaf, to tarry
(פעה) to groan
(פעפע) to bubble; to pierce, penetrate
(פפה) to move
(עף) to fly
(עפעף) to flutter, fly about; eyelid

(אף) nose; anger; wrath; also, too
(אפע) nothing, nothingness
(אפף) to surround, encircle
(אפעא) Aram. viper
(עף) to fly
(עפעף) to flutter, fly about; eyelid
(פא) here
(פעפע) to bubble; to pierce, penetrate
(פעא) Aram. - Syr. he groaned, it bleated

(לפלף) to emit pus from the eyes
(לפף) to wrap up, envelop, clasp, embrace
(פלל) to judge, arbitrate; to pray
(פלפל) to discuss, argue, debate; to pepper
(פר) bull, bullock, steer
(פרף) to clasp, fasten
(פרפר) to break, to crumble, to crush; to shake, shatter
(פרר) to crush, crumb, crumble, break into crumbs; to break, violate, annul, frus-
trate; to shake, shatter
(רפף) to move gently; to waver, vacillate; to loosen, weaken
(רפרף) to flutter, to move

(הלל) to boast, praise; to shine; to be foolish; praise
(הלה) that
(לה) to her
(להה) to languish, faint, be tired
(להלה) to confuse, drive crazy
(לפלף) to emit pus from the eyes
(לפף) to wrap up, envelop, clasp, embrace
(פה) mouth; speech, saying; command; opening orifice; here
(פהה) to idle, to loaf, to tarry

(פלה) to be separated, be distinct; to search for vermin, delouse

(הפלה) he made separate, set apart

(פלל) to judge, arbitrate; to pray

(פלפל) to discuss, argue, debate; to pepper

(או) or

(אף) nose; anger, wrath; also, too

(אפו) then, now, so

(אפף) to surround, encircle

(וו) Waw - sixth letter; hook, peg, nail

(פא) same as פה - mouth, speech, saying, command; here

(פו) same as פה - mouth, speech, saying, command; here

(וו) Waw - sixth letter; hook, peg, nail

(זו) this; which; who

(זפף) to pitch, coat with pitch

(פו) same as פה - mouth, speech, saying, command; here

(פז) pure gold

(פזז) to move quickly, be agile, be supple; to be gilded, be purified

Note : Again, squares have not had words added to the lists.

Overlay Words : [?! overlay shape - is the peh 2, or 3 wide !?]

(פה) mouth , speech, saying, command ; also used to spell the letter Peh
   [Ruler of 2 belongs to the Hei or Holy Ghost]

(הלל) "Hallel" Praise ;

(יהלל) To boast, praise, he shouted in festival joy, sang, praised, shouted for joy ;

(יהלל") To shine, it began to shine, it shone [these belong to Lamed]

(פר) Bull, Steer ; related to Arab, farr (= calf), farir, furdr (=lamb, young gazelle) ;
   Ends on / belongs to Reish [place of sacrificial altar]

(רפה) Weak, feeble

(חשל) weak, feeble, faint ; Arab. crushed or bruised

(חלש) to cast lots ; also weak [final Peh connection to the Chet]

(שלה) Draw out of water [related to (שליה) afterbirth] ; [blood mixed with water] :
   Note that this is a ruler of 3 attached to the (ה) Hei ; Holy Ghost.

(שזף) he caught sight of, looked on ; it parched, scorched, tanned
   [final Peh invokes pure, innocent & clean] - belongs to Peh.

Atbash Waw :

Tools :

Ruler 2 :
(צוע) rock, cliff, boulder, support, defense, fortress, place of refuge
(צו) command, order
(צוע) they dried up
(כו) then, thus
(גו) back, body; inside, interior (esp. of a house)
(שו) equality [signifies one who will inherit]; related to שוה to be like, be equal
(שוע) Aramaic : equal (plural) equals

V Compass :
(שש) six, white marble, Egyptian linen
(עצעצ) to adorn, ornament
(עששש) to waste away, decay; weak, dim, dark
(עש) moth, to become weak, waste away; name of constellation, probably great bear
(עץ) tree, timber, wood, handle
(שעע) to smooth; to besmear; to blind; to take delight, be delighted

NEW Squares :
(וו) Waw; hook, peg, nail
(עוץ) to advise
(עץ) tree; timber, wood; handle
(צו) command, order
(צוץ) chirp, twitter
(צוצעו) image work, carving
(צעצ) to adorn, ornament
(סוס) horse
(סס) moth
(סוף) come to an end, cease; end, finish; rush, reed

(סף) threshold
(ספף) to tear, to cut (hair); to singe, burn
(ספף) to stand on the threshold
(פה) here; mouth
(פס) tunic composed of variegated stripes, [and, or] tunic reaching to the palms and to the ankles
(פסס) to end, cease, disappear; to be broad, spread; to strip; to tear apart
(פספס) to crumb, separate, to part; to sign; to make something in mosaic form
(עות) to be crooked, bent; to come to help
(עת) time; season; appointed time
(עתת) to time
(תו) mark, sign; name of last letter
(תעע) to deceive, to mock
(תעתוע) mockery
(תעע) to deceive, to mock
(צו) command, order
(גג) roof
(גו) back, body; inside, interior
(פו) mouth, here
(פת) corner of the head; their forehead; vulva; morsel of bread; piece of bread
(פתות) crumb, bit
(פתת) to break (esp. bread) into pieces, crumb, crumble
(תף) drum
(תפף) to drum, beat the drum
(פעפע) to bubble, to pierce, to penetrate
(עוף) to fly; to be dark; fowl, bird
(עפעף) to flutter, fly about; eyelid
(עץ) tree; timber, wood; handle
(עש) moth; prob. great bear constellation
(צעצע) to adorn, ornament
(שעשע) to smooth, to besmear; to take delight; to delight
(חץ) arrow
(חצץ) to divide; to make a partition; gravel, gravel stone
(חשש) to feel pain, fear, apprehend; chaff
(צח) dazzling, glowing, bright, clear, pure
(צחח) to be dazzling, be bright, be clear; to become dry
(שח) mediation; talk; bent, bowed
(שחח) he bowed down, crouched; was bowed down, was humbled

DO OVER WITH NEW WORDS
Atbash Waw Tools :

Atbash Overlay Words :
(שגג) to go astray, to commit an error, sin unintentionally
(שגע) to be mad (crazed?)
(שגש) to confuse, to confound

(שגשׂא) to grow, to flourish
(שׁו) equality
(שׁוו) Aramaic : equal (plural) equals
(שׁוא) to turn back, retreat
(שׁוגא) erring, sinning unintentionally
(שׁוע) to cry for help, cry out for help
(שׁעע) to smooth, to besmear, to blind; to take delight, be delighted
(שׁשׁ) six, white marble, Egyptian linen
(וו) hook, peg, nail
(גג) roof
(גו) back, body; inside, interior (esp. of a house)
(גוע) to die, to perish
(גוש) clod, lump of earth; to form a block
(געגע) to long for, to yearn for; to dig, to roll in, to make holes; to quack
(געשׁ) to shake, to quake, to tremble, to quiver, to rage, to storm; to moo
(גשׁגשׁ) to tinkle, to rattle, to rustle
(גשׁשׁ) to feel, to touch, to grope; to touch the bottom of the sea; to ground
(עגעג) to peck, to pick holes
(עוג) to bake a cake; to draw a circle
(עוש) to make haste, to hurry; he came to help
(עשׁ) moth, name of a constellation - probably the great bear
(עשׁעשׁ) to waste away, to decay

Atbash Overlay decryption :

Atbash letter by letter :

The צ/ה

TOK TOL

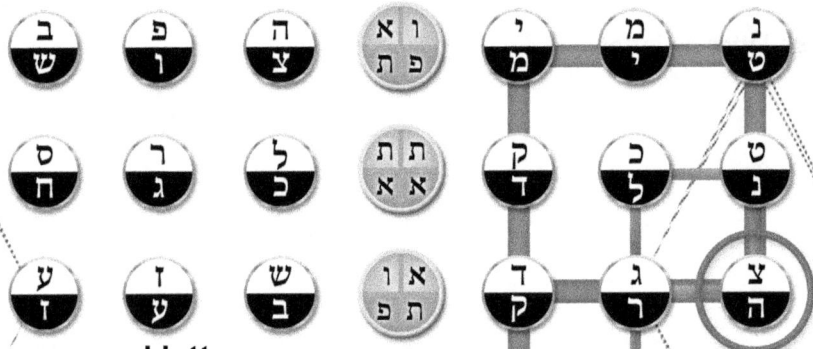

compound letters

[י,ו =(ז)] [ר,י,י =(ה)] [ו =(ד)] [⋆(?ז),י,י =(ג)] [ר,ו =(ב)] [י,ו =(א)]

[י,ו =(נ)] [י,ו,ג,י =(מ)] [י,ו =(ל)] [ר,י,ו =(כ)] [י,ו =(ט)] [⋆(?ז),י,י =(ח)]

[י,ו =(ס)] [י,ו =(ע)] [⋆(?ר,כ),י,י =(פ)] [י,ו =(צ)] [י,ו =(ק)] [ו =(ר)]

[ר,ו =(ת)] [ו =(ש)]

The Tzade צ

Tzade is the 18th letter of the Hebrew Aleph-Bet with a value of 90, and has a final form [value of 900].

TOOLS :

Ruler of 2 :
(גצץ) to flash, to glitter
(חץ) arrow
(חצץ) to divide; to make a partition; gravel, gravel-stone
(עץ) tree; timber, wood; handle

∧ Compass [נ/ג/ע] :
(גג) roof
(גן) garden [part of Mem Compass]
(גנן) to defend, protect, guard, shelter; garden [part of Mem Compass]
(געגע) to quack; to dig, make holes, roll in; to long, to yearn
(געגע) to touch; he touched; he reached; to strike, smite; stroke, blow, wound; sign of leprosy; plague
(נע) moving, mobile
(נענע) to shake, to stir up
(עגן) to shut oneself in; to be shut in; to be deserted; to anchor
(עגנג) to peck, pick holes
(ענג) to be soft, be tender; to please; exquisite delight, pleasure; tender, delicate
(ענן) te brought clouds, covered with clouds; to practice soothsaying; cloud

V Compass [ג/ע/ח] :
(גג) roof
(געגע) to long, to yearn; to quack; to dig, make holes, roll in
(גח) feast, festival
(חגג) to make a pilgrimage, to celebrate a feast, to dance, to reel, to be giddy

Square [י/נ/צ] :

The squares :
(צדי) Tzade ; fishing hook ; the sides; side, lateral

(צד) side, flank

(ציו) Derivative of (ציון) Zion; dry ground, desert; Arab. he protected; to make a note, make a mark [final Nun invokes favor, grace]

(ציד) to feed, provide with provisions; hunting; game; hunter; catch (food) or Hunt

(צי) ship, boat ; desert dweller

(צן) thorn

(ני) wailing, lament

(נצץ) blossom, flower, bloom, sprout; to shine, flash, sparkle

(ידיד) friend, beloved

(יד) hand, arm, foreleg

(ידד) to be friends, become friends

(די) who, which, that ; of, about ; sufficient, enough

DO EVERYTHING OVER !!!!!!!!!!!!!!!!!!!!!!!!!!!!!!!!!

Overlay Words :

(כי) so, thus [final - invokes favor, grace]

(כי״) right, truthful, honest [final Nun]

(***כי) righteousness [final Tzade - divide]

(***יכי) could be (י) Yud is a prefix making it "my righteousness" or "my righteous"? [invokes final Tzade to divide]

(דג) fish [Ruler of 2 - Gimmel - "to follow"]

(גדי) to cut off [ruler of 2 - Dalet - door]

(גדד״) to gather in troops or bands [ruler of 2 belonging to Dalet invokes the door to his Glory]

Final Tzade :

(חץ) Arrow ; base חצה is connected with חץ (= arrow).

Accordingly, the orig. meaning of חצה prob. was 'to divide by casting arrows of lots'.

(חצץ) to divide; to make a partition

(מכך) to be low, be humiliated

(כם) Your ; You

(גג) roof

(חג) feast, festival

Individual letters :

(נ) wing of the Protector, Gather ; (כ) poor, lowly, oppressed, people ; (י) Almighty Father ; (צ) separate my righteous ; (ג) take the Father's hand and follow ; (ד) [to the] Door of [HIS] Glory.

Final Tzade :

(ם) The one who rises, (נ) Gather, (כ) poor, lowly, oppressed, people, (ג) Followers of the Father, (ח) the Gate of equality.

Distilled definition : Zion, my righteous, separate my righteous [from the wicked].

Atbash Hei :

Tools :

Ruler of 2 :
(לה) to her
(נה) wailing, lamentation

Ruler of 3 :
(מלה) word, speech
(קרה) to encounter, meet, befall, occur, happen; to lay beams, roof, cover

Squares :
(מט) who falters
(מטה) stick, rod, staff; branch, tribe; downward, down; bed; perversion of justice; spreading
(מטמט) to shake, destroy
(מה) what?; which?; how, what, something
(מהה) to be worn out, be shabby, be tattered
(טמה) to be stopped up, be stupid
(הם) they
(המה) to murmur, growl, roar
(המם) to make a noise, confuse
(הט) incline
(קהה) to be blunt, dull
(קם) enemy, foe, adversary; has risen, he rose, arose
(קמה) standing corn (grain)
(הקם) erect, establish
(המק) will rot, consume away
(מקק) to decay, rot, fester, pine away

NEW SQUARES :

(הלל) to boast, praise; to shine; to be foolish
(הן) they; behold; yes; if
(הנה) to be agreeable, be pleased; they; here, hither; lo, behold, here
(הנהן) to say "yes"
(לה) to her
(להה) to languish, faint, be tired
(להן) to them
(נה) wailing lamentation
(נהה) to long for, follow eagerly; to wail, lament
(נהל) to lead, guide
(הר) mountain, mount
(הרה) to conceive, become pregnant; pregnant
(חר) hole, aperture; socket of the eye
(חרה) to burn, be kindled (said of anger)
(חרר) to be hot and dry, be scorched, burn; to make a hole, bore through; to be or become free
*(רח) Syr. he breathed; Phoen. Spirit; Arab. was windy *[compare with רוח]
(חק) decree, statute, law, rule; prescribed portion, prescribed due
(חקה) to engrave, to imitate; something prescribed, statute, law, custom
(חקק) to cut, engrave; inscribe, decree

New Compass' :
(חחז) to remove, displace
(חזז) to flash
(חזר) to go round
(חרז) to string together; to rhyme
(רז) secret
(רזז) to tremble; trembling, panic
(טרז) to wedge, form into a wedge
(טרטר) to rattle, make a loud noise; to mess somebody around

Atbash Hei toos list :
They incline to her who falters to establish a perversion of justice.
[This] word shall befall the standing corn (wheat), to be worn out, shabby, and tattered.
Roar! Make a noise to confuse, to shake and destroy the enemy. [That they] be stopped up and stupid, blunt and dull [with] wailing and lamentation. What will rot and consume away shall pine away and decay.

Atbash Hei overlay word list :
(מד) measure, garment
(מדד) to measure; Arab. he stretched, extended
(מדה) measure, measurement; tribute, tax, toll
(מדי) as often as, every; from what is sufficient
(מדים) uniforms or garments
(מדינה) province, region, state

(מדמנה) dunghill

(מדנים) contentions, strifes

(מה) before; what?, which?, how, what, something

(מהה) to linger, to tarry; to be worn out, be shabby, be tattered

(מהם) what are they?; from them

(מטה) stick, rod, staff; branch; tribe; downward, down; bed; perversion of justice; spreading

(מטמט) to shake, destroy

(מי) who, whoever, someone, anyone

(מידי) from the hands of

(מים) water, to mix with water, to hydrate

(מימים) long since

(מין) kind, species; to furrow, to split; to invent; fabricate, lie; to classify

(ממד) measurement, dimension

(מן) manna; what?; away from, from, of, out of; since, because, more than, than

(מנה) to count, number; part, portion, ration, share

(מני) apportionment, fate, destiny

(מק) rottenness, decay

(מקם) to localize

(מקמק) to rot

(מקנה) cattle, herd; purchase, purchase price

(מקק) to rot, decay

(יד) hand, arm, foreleg

(ידד) to be friends, to become friends

(ידה) to give thanks, to confess; to throw, hurl, cast

(ידיד) friend, beloved

(יה) Yah (short form of YHWH)

(ים) sea, lake, large basin, reservoir; west

(ימין) the right hand, right side; the right, the south

(ימיני) the right, right handed

(ימן) to go or turn to the right; to use the right hand; to prepare, to appoint

(ימני) right, right handed

(ינה) to oppress, to maltreat

(יניקה) young shoot

(ינק) to suck

(יקד) to be kindled, to burn

(יקהה) obedience

(טיט) mud, mire, clay; to erase, to draft; to plaster

(טמם) to stop up; to fill up

(טמן) to hide, to conceal

(טנן) to be moist, to be damp

(נד) heap, wall; moving

(נדד) to wander about; to flee

(נדה) to remove, to exclude; a harlot's pay; impurity, impure thing; menstruation, a menstruating woman

(נדן) a sheath, case; a harlot's pay

(נה) a wailing lamentation

(נהה) to long for, follow eagerly; to wail, to lament

(נהי) wailing, lamentation; mourning song

(נהם) to growl, to grown, growling

(נהמה) growling, roaring (of the sea)

(נהק) to bray (said of an ass); Aram. he cried out

(נטה) to stretch out, extend, incline, bend

(ני) wailing, lament

(ניד) quivering motion, movement

(נין) to sprout, increase; offspring, posterity

(נמק) to reason, to give reason; to argue

(נקד) to point, to mark with points; to penetrate; spotted, dotted, speckled

(נקה) to be clean, to be pure, to be innocent

(נקט) to take; to be weary of, to loathe

(נקיק) cleft, crevice

(נקם) to avenge, take vengeance

(הד) a joyous shout

(הדד) to reverberate

(הדה) to stretch out (the hand)

(הדהד) to reverberate (echo)

(הדם) to cut; dissect

(הדק) to press together

(הידד) hurrah!, bravo!, (joyous shout, cheer)

(היה) to be, to exist, to happen, to become; was, existed; came into being, became; remained; it came to pass, happened

(הם) they

(המה) to murmur, to growl, to roar

(המיה) sound, noise

(המם) to make a noise, confuse

(הן) they; behold; yes; if

(הנה) to be agreeable, to be pleased; they; here, hither; lo, behold, here

(הנהן) to say 'yes'

(הני) these

(דד) breast, teat, nipple

(דדה) to move slowly

(דהה) to fade, to become dim

(דהם) to astound, to perplex

(דהן) to smear or polish with an oily substance; Aram. - Syr. he was oiled, was anointed, grew fat

(די) sufficiency, enough, sufficiently; who, which, that, of, about

(דיה) a bird of prey; the kite

(דין) to judge; judgement, verdict, sentence; lawsuit, cause; law

(דיק) bulwark, siege wall; to be exact, to be precise

(דם) blood, bloodshed, blood-guilt

(דמדם) to be in a daze, to be confused

(דמה) to be like, to resemble, to be equal in value; to cease, to stop; silence

(דמי) quiet, rest, silence

(דמים) bloodshed, blood-guilt

(דמין) to imagine

(דמם) to be or grow dumb or silent; to bleed

(דממה) silence, whisper, hush
(דמן) to manure, to fertilize
(דנדן) to ring
(דק) a thin curtain [the veil]
(דקדק) to examine minutely, to be strict
(דקק) to crush, to pulverize
(קדד) to bow down, to bow ones head; to cut, to bore, to drill
(קדה) to bow
(קדים) east
(קדימה) eastward
(קדם) to be before, to be in front; what is in front, forward; east
(קדמה) beginning, origin; former state; front
(קדקד) head, crown of the head; to crow
(קהה) to be blunt, to be dull
(קט) small (used in Ezek. 16:47 very soon, little while)
(קטה) a sand grouse (bird)
(קטט) to quarrel
(קטם) to cut off, to lop off; to cover with ashes
(קטן) to be small, insignificant; the little finger (lit. 'the small one')
(קטקט) to flatten, make even
(קיה) to vomit
(קימה) standing up, rising
(קין) to fit together, to fabricate; spear
(קם) enemy, foe, adversary
(קמה) standing corn (wheat?)
(קמט) to seize, to grasp, snatch; wrinkle, shrivel
(קן) nest, cell, chamber
(קנה) to create, to acquire, to get; to buy, to possess, to own; stalk, reed, cane; beam of scales; shaft of lamp-stand; arm of lamp-stand; length of a reed (6 cubits)
(קנט) to annoy, to vex, to make angry
(קנין) a thing acquired, a thing purchased
(קנן) to build a nest, nestle

Atbash Hei overlay :
  Behold these offspring who give thanks, confess, and cast off the impure thing to be pure, clean, and innocent.
  Build a nest and fabricate a chamber to fertilize the standing corn (wheat).
  Stretch out the right hand to anoint with oil, to prepare and appoint to be kindled and burn.
  Measure a garment, bow your head, grasp the right hand and examine minutely with a whisper. Bow the crown of the head at the veil to be equal in value, to become friends, beloved, standing up with a joyous shout to echo before YHWH.
  Give reason to take vengeance on thy enemy. Judge the cause and measure obedience.
  From them who lie, contentions and strifes. They oppress and maltreat because of a perversion of justice.
  He cried out, wailing and lamentation, a purchase price to become the beam of the scales, the [center] shaft and the arm[s] of the lamp-stand.

Measure the dimensions of bloodshed and count the portion of blood-guilt to be precise. A harlot's pay [is the] apportionment and the fate.

Behold, eastward, in front. A growling as the roaring of the sea, a sound that echoes and rings to daze and confuse, to shake and destroy.

Flee [in] wailing and lamentation! A moving heap as a wall shall cut off and fill up, [they shall] grow silent and bleed, to rot and decay.

Water shall mix with mud, mire, and clay to penetrate [from the] sea west to the sea east. [It shall] crush and pulverize to flatten, to hide and conceal the rottenness and decay. [???may need more done on underlying letters???]

Atbash Hei letter-by-letter : RE-DO TO INCLUDE NEW TOOLS
(ד)

The hand of EL shall weigh manna in a basket for your poor and lowly who wander restlessly to the [shepherds] door.

Build a nest to bow your head. Measure a garment to lift up, to stand, and become friends.

Give your reason to take vengeance and the grounds of accusation against the adversary to punish, to crush, as rottenness and decay.

(ה)

They incline to her who falters to establish a perversion of justice.

[This] word shall befall the standing corn (wheat), to be worn out, shabby, and tattered.

Roar! Make a noise to confuse, to shake and destroy the enemy. Be stopped up and stupid, blunt and dull [with] wailing and lamentation. What will rot and consume away, shall pine away and decay.

(ו)

A little while to cut off secrecy and enchantments. The contract [written with] the pen shall stop, and give way to rottenness and decay.

(ז)

Cut off the oppressor. Destruction and ruin to shrivel and shrink the embittered enemy.

Enclose with the hand and rend the veil. Solidify rottenness and decay, draw together to rise exalted, elevated, and supreme.

(ח)

Behold the Prince and cry out with a joyous shout!

(ט)

My people, complete, perfect and innocent. They came to utter a curse, to strike and beat the enemy [with] rottenness and decay.

[From] the sea west to the east [the enemy] shall grow silent and bleed [for their] blood-guilt.

(י)

Pursue the chase to tatter, to make bare and conceal.

Tremble and panic, wail and lament the exalted who shake to destroy whoever gives way to be bitter and rebel.

RE-DO to include new tools . . .

The ד/ק

TOK **TOL**

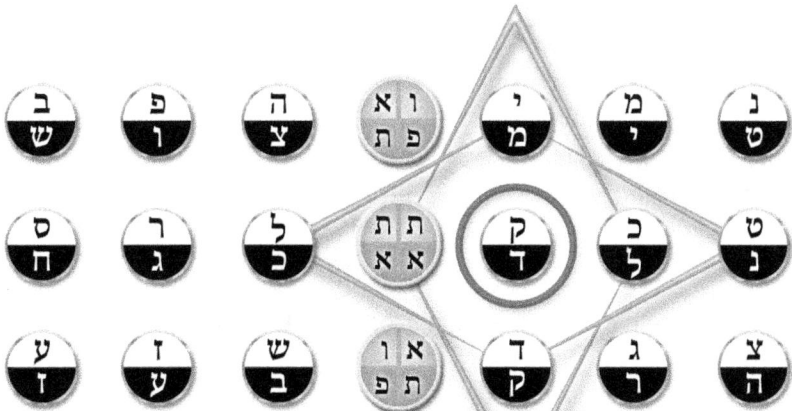

compound letters

[י,ו =(ז)][ר,י,י =(ה)][ו =(ד)][*(?ז),י,י =(ג)][ר,ו =(ב)][י,ו =(א)]

[י,ו =(נ)][ז,נ,ו,י =(מ)][י,ו =(ל)][ר,י,י =(כ)][י,ו =(ט)][*(?ז),י,י =(ח)]

[ו =(ש)][ר,ו =(ת)][י,ו =(ר)][י,ו =(ק)][י,ו =(צ)][*(?ר,כ),י,י =(פ)][י,י =(ע)][ו =(ס)]

The name of the letter (קוף) Kuf, means 'eye of the needle', and it is believed that this came from the ancient shape.

What I can say for sure, is that I saw in vision a large nail pointed up . . . a hand was on top, in the middle . . . then, I saw the hand slip to the right, hanging down, and the nail was pointing at the wrist.

   So this is one letter that I can say for sure is made from a nail [ו Waw] and a hand [י Yud]. . . I then saw that these were just re-arranged with a nail pointing down above the wrist to make the ל Lamed.

The Kuf ק

The (ק) Kuf has a numerical value of 100. It's handle stretching down towards the (ח) Chet on earth makes its own very simple word, (חק) Law, decree, or rule.

TOOLS :

Ruler of 2 :
(חק) Law, decree, or rule.
(דק) a thin curtain [the veil]
(דקק) to crush, pulverize
(מק) decay, rottenness

Ruler of 3 :
(חדק) to press together, compress; nightshade - a kind of bush; JAram. to stick to; Akka. to clothe

The compass :
(ליד) near, by, or beside; close to
(ילד) to bear, bring forth, beget; Aram. he begot; she bore, brought forth; child, boy, offspring, young man; child, son, boy, youth
(דיל) steward
(יד) Hand [part of two compass']
(די) who, which, that; of, about' sufficiency; enough, sufficiently
(דל) poor ; thin. lean ; low, weak, powerless; door [interesting as the (דק) veil of the
(ד) Dalet belongs to the (ק) Kuf]
(דלי) bucket
(לי) inflected pers. pron. meaning 'to me'.

(ילל) wailing, howling, lament

(טיט) plaster; to erase, to draft; mud, mire, clay

(עתת) time
(כעת) now, at present
(כת) party, faction, sect, class; group; herd
(כתת) to crush, pound
(תך) oppression, violence

(כח) strength, power, force, vigor; kind of a lizard
(חך) palate
(חכך) to scratch, rub
(חת) terror, fear; shattered; dismayed
(חתך) to cut, decide; cutter

DO EVERYTHING OVER !!!!!!!!!!!!!!!!!!!!!!!!!!!!

Overlay Words :
(חדק) to press together, compress ; nightshade — a kind of thorn bush [the Kuf ending invokes kingdom of YHWH on earth]
(חק) Law [the Kuf ending invokes kingdom of YHWH on earth]
(דק) the veil / door to heaven [the Kuf ending invokes kingdom of YHWH on earth]
(ימים) = (יום plural) days ; times ; years [מי ending invokes the eternal iteration]
(ים) sea ; lake ; large basin, reservoir ; West [מי invokes the eternal iteration]
(מך) poor, lowly. [the final Chof invokes the bridle of YHWH in the mouth]
(כם) added to nouns and meaning 'your' ; added to verbs and meaning 'you' (accusative).

Individual letters :

Distilled definition :

Atbash Dalet :

Tools :

Ruler of 2 :
(מד) garment; measure
(יד) hand, arm, foreleg
(לד) a name of a city, probably "to the door" or, if they understood the Lamed, they might have understood this as "the Shepherds Door".
(רד) = רוד wander restlessly, roam
(פד) If פדה is to ransom, deliver, redeem . . . there may be a relationship.
(אד) mist, vapor, gas
(ידי) to be friends, become friends
(קדד) to bow down, to bow ones head; to cut, bore, drill

Ruler of 3 :
(עמד) to stand; to estimate, value; standing, place, position
(סקד) to chastise, punish

> Compass :
(נמק) to reason, give reason, argue
(נקם) to avenge, to take vengeance; vengeance
(מן) manna; what?; away from, from, of, out of; since, because; more than
(מק) rottenness, decay
(קם) enemy, foe, adversary
(קן) nest, cell, chamber; bird offering, a couple of birds offered as sacrifice
(מקם) to localize
(מקמק) to rot
(קנן) to build a nest, nestle

< Compass :

(מֵרָ) poor, lowly

(כֹם) your, you

(כמק) like rot, as rottenness

(מכמר) to press, crush

Λ Compass :

(אל) El [God]; power; to, toward; not; nothing

(אע) wood

(לא) not, lo

(לע) throat

(על) yoke; height, upper part; above; on, upon, above; at, beside, towards, against; because of, on account of; concerning

(עלא) matter, affair, occasion; ground of accusation

(אלל) to be weak; to spy out

V Compass :

(סל) basket

(סלא) to weigh

(סלל) to lift up, to cast up

The Atbash Dalet Tools :

The hand of EL shall weigh manna in a basket for your poor and lowly who wander restlessly to the [shepherds] door.

Build a nest to bow your head. Measure a garment to lift up, to stand, and become friends.

Give your reason to take vengeance and the grounds of accusation against the adversary to punish, to crush, as rottenness and decay.

Atbash Overlay Words :

(תי) suff. my

(תם) was ended, was finished, was completed; complete, perfect; innocent, artless

(תמד) to make grape skin wine; to make mead; to do constantly, to continue

(תמיד) continuity, continually, constantly, always; (short for) daily offering in the temple

(תמים) object attached to breastplate; truth, holiness; complete, perfect; whole, sound, healthful; without blemish; innocent, upright, honest

(תמם) to be finished, come to an end, be completed

(מד) measure; garment

(מדד) to measure

(מדי) as often as, sufficient (from what is sufficient)

(מדים) pl. uniform (garments)

(מי) who, whoever, someone, anyone

(מידי) from the hands of

(מים) water; to mix with water, to hydrate

(מימים) long since
(ממתק) sweet thing
(מק) rottenness, decay
(מקם) to localize
(מקמק) to rot
(מקק) to rot, decay
(מת) dead; a dead person; corpse
(מתי) when?
(מתים) people, men
(מתם) wholeness, soundness; people, men
(מתק) to be sweet; sweetness
(מתת) gift
(יד) hand, arm, foreleg
(ידד) to be friends, become friends
(ידיד) friend, beloved
(ים) sea, lake, large basin, reservoir; west
(ימים) days; year
(יקד) to be kindled; to burn
(יתד) peg, pin, tent pin, nail; to peg, to wedge up
(יתם) to orphan, to make an orphan
(דד) breast, teat, nipple
(די) sufficiency; enough, sufficiently; who, which, that; of about
(דיק) bulwark, siege wall; to be exact, precise
(דית) to sweat, to exude
(דם) blood, bloodshed, blood-guilt
(דמדם) to be in a daze, to be confused
(דמי) quiet, rest, silence
(דמים) bloodshed, blood-guilt
(דמם) to be or grow dumb or silent; to bleed
(דק) a thin curtain [veil]
(דקדק) to examine minutely, to be strict
(דקק) to crush, pulverize
(דת) decree, law, usage; religion
(קדד) to bow down, bow one's head; to cut, to bore, to drill
(קדים) east
(קדם) to be before, in front; what is in front, forward, east
(קדקד) head; crown of the head; to crow
(קם) enemy, foe, adversary

Atbash Dalet overlay :

Bow your head and measure a garment. A [REDACTED] and a [REDACTED] at the veil, to examine minutely and a gift of perfection, to become friends.

In the year of the decree, the crown of the head shall be in front, towards the east, to kindle and burn.

My beloved who rest to be sweetness. [Their] dead which rot shall localize, the rottenness and decay of men shall be whole, sound, and perfect.

The blood-guilt of the enemy shall mix with water, sufficient to daze and confuse, to crush and pulverize, to make grape skin wine [from] the sea west to the [sea] east. They shall bleed [for their] bloodshed, and come to an end.

Atbash Dalet Letter-by letter :
(ת) At the time appointed, the decree to kindle the dead kinsmen, to join, to be a numerous force, to scatter and break asunder the oppressor.
(n) Towards the east, in front, to utter a curse and hollow out the enemy, to strike and shock [for their] blood-guilt.
(') Wail and lament, the Supreme which shakes to destroy the those which rebel.
(ז) to punish the adversary and crush as rottenness and decay.
(ק) Rend the veil! Solidify rottenness and decay to rise exalted! Cut off the oppressor! Destruction and ruin to the enemy!

The ר/ג

compound letters

$[(א)= ו,י][(ב)= ו,ר][(ג)= ו,י,(ז?)^*][(ד)= ו][(ה)= ו,י,ר][(ז)= ו,י]$
$[(ח)= ו,י,(ז?)^*][(ט)= ו,י][(כ)= ו,י,ר][(ל)= ו,י][(מ)= ז,נ,ו,י][(נ)= ו,י]$
$[(ס)= ו][(ע)= ו,י][(פ)= ו,י,(כ,ר?)^*][(צ)= ו,י][(ק)= ו,י][(ר)= ו]$
$[(ש)= ו][(ת)= ו,ר]$

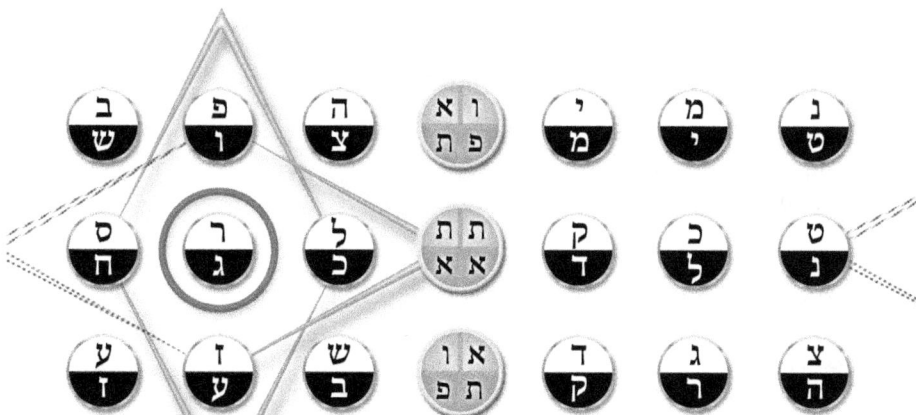

The Reish ר

The Reish has a numerical value of 200.

The letter (ריש) Reish means "head", as does this similar word (ראש). So, I find it interesting to note that Chief, Bull, Son, to rule, are all descriptors in the Reish tools section.

TOOLS :

Ruler of 2 :
(פר) bull, bullock, steer
(סר) sullen, ill-humored
(סרר) to be stubborn, be rebellious
(ער) awake, wakeful; enemy, foe
(בר) son; threshed grain or corn; pure, clean; open field
(ברר) to purify, select, set apart, separate; to sharpen
(הר) mountain, mount.
(שר) chief ; leader; captain, general; ruler; prince, nobleman; patron angel; singer ; naval string, navel
(שרר) to rule, reign, dominate, to be strong
(זר) stranger; frame, edging
(זרר) to sneeze; to press, squeeze

Ruler of 3 :
(חזר) to go round

> Compass :
(זפת) Pitch, coat with pitch; Aram. he pitched, coated with pitch
(זפף) to pitch, coat with pitch
(פז) pure gold
(פזז) to move quickly, be agile, be supple; to be gilded, be purified
(פת) their forehead ; vulva; piece of bread, morsel of bread
(תז) Syr. it swelled up, was boiling hot; was indignant
(תזז) spring out, spring forth; to envy, get excited
(תף) drum
(תפף) to drum, beat the drum

Λ Compass :

(על) yoke; height, upper part; above; on, upon; at, beside; towards; against; concerning, about; because of, on account of, together with

(עלל) to act, do, work; Arab. he did something a second time; to insert, thrust in; Aram. - Syr. he entered, he brought in; to accuse falsely; to glean (grapes or olives)

(עלס) to rejoice, exult

(עלע) to swallow, suck up, lick

(עוo) to press, crush, tread; to fill with juice, make juicy

(לע) throat

(לעo) to chew, masticate

(לעע) to swallow, sip; to talk wildly

(oo) moth

(סל) basket

(סלל) to lift up, cast up; Akka. highway

(סלע) rock, crag, cliff; name of a weight and coin

V Compass :

(סלח) ready to forgive

(לח) freshness, vigor; moist, fresh, new

(לחח) to be moist, be fresh

(לחלח) to moisten, to dampen

(חלחל) to cause to tremble, to startle

(חל) something secular, something profane, something common; rampart, wall; to move in a circle, encircle

(חלל) to lose, profane, defile; to begin; to be hollow, to hollow out, bore, pierce; to play; a person deprived of priesthood; a priest of illegitimate descent; a person pierced, a person totally wounded, a person slain

(חסל) to finish off, consume; Aram. come to an end; Syr. weaned, refrained, restrained

DO EVERYTHING OVER !!

Distilled definition :

Atbash Gimmel :

Tools :

Ruler of 2 :
(גצ) side, flank
(בג) food
(זג) skin of the grape
(זגז) to glaze
(זגזג) to make transparent
(חג) feast, festival
(חגג) to make a pilgrimage, to celebrate a feast

Ruler of 3 :
(עוג) to draw a circle

> Compass : THE three vowels (א)e+(ו)oo+(ע)ah of the name?
(וא) or
(אע) wood, timber, beams
(ואע) and wood, and timber, and beams
(וו) Waw, hook, peg, nail

∧ Compass :
(כח) strength, power, force; kind of lizard
(חך) Palate
(חכך) to scratch, rub

V Compass :

(oɔ) throne
(noɔ) to cut off, trim, clear
(ɿo) large crowd; thicket, hut
(ɿon) to spare, withhold

The Tools message :
Make a pilgrimage to celebrate the feast. A festival with food and the skin of the grape. Draw a circle of wood, trim a thicket of huts [at the] side of the throne of strength and power.

Atbash Gimmel Overlay Words :
(ʊɿ) to tremble, quake
(ʊɿʊɿ) to shake violently
(ʊʊ) moth; name of a constellation - probably the great bear
(ʊʊʊʊ) to become weak, waste away; decay
(ɿʊ) strong, firm, mighty; fierce; strength, might; fortress, refuge; splendor, glory; goat

The Overlay Message :
Tremble and quake! The strength of splendor and glory to violently shake [the great bear?] to waste away and decay.

Letter-by-letter :
(ʊ) one with an issue of blood / to fly / to violently shake
(ʊ) one who returns / to rescue, to save / to rustle / the chaff / cover
(ɿ) [with] mud, mire, and silt to grind the prey

I WILL need to take a deeper look at this later, but there is such an overwhelming amount of work to do to finish the tools lists . . . so I need to move on.

The ש/ב

TOK TOL

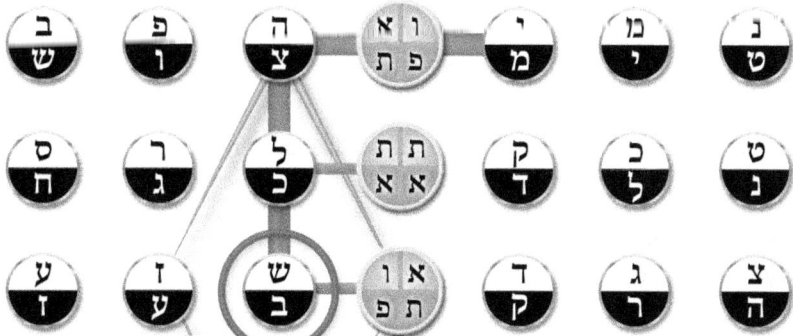

compound letters

[(א)= ו,י][(ב)= ו,ר][(ג)= ו,י,(ז?)*][(ד)= ו][(ה)= ו,י,ר][(ז)= ו,י]
[(ח)= ו,י,(ז?)*][(ט)= ו,י][(כ)= ו,י,ר][(ל)= ו,י][(מ)= ז,ג,ו,י][(נ)= ו,י]
[(ס)= ו][(ע)= ו,י][(פ)= ו,י,(כ,ר?)*][(צ)= ו,י][(ק)= ו,י][(ר)= ו]
[(ש)= ו][(ת)= ו,ר]

The Shin ש

The Shin has a numerical value of 300 and is spelled (שן). I find this interesting as the language key includes a term for white marble, and the name of the letter means tooth.

TOOLS :

Ruler of 2 :

(רש) poor, pauper; beggar

(תש) to be weak, be feeble.

(שלש) to multiply by three ; to divide by three ; was of the third

(שרש) root; source, origin; bottom, lowest part; to uproot

Ruler of 3 :

(דוש) to tread, thresh; to pedal, treadle

The compass :

(זה) this which ; and

(זהה) to identify

(הו) ah! alas! woe!

(הוה) to fall, fall in. come to pass, come to be, be. cp. Arab, waqa'a (= he fell, fell down; it came to pass, happened, took place, occurred), L. cadere and accidere (=to fall to, fall down, happen). — Qal הוה was, existed

(הוזה) dreamer, visionary

(הזה) to dream, rave

The squares :

(היה) to be. exist, happen, become. A parallel form of "הוה ; was. existed ; came into being, became ; he remained ; it came to pass, happened.

(יה) Yah, [short form YHWH]

(שי) gift, present

(יש) there is, there are; possession, property

(שה) (young) sheep, lamb; small cattle (goat, sheep)

(שהה) to tarry, linger; to stay, to delay, be late in coming

(שהי) JAram. he stood still, tarried, lingered, was astonished, became stiff; Syr. was deserted

(שיש) white marble, alabaster

(שש) six; white marble; Egyptian linen

(ששה) to divide by six; to multiply by six.

(ששי) sixth

(חוש) to feel pain, to feel anxious, to feel afraid; to make haste, hurry

(חוח) aperture, cleft ; briar, thorn ; hook ring

(חשש) to feel pain, fear, apprehend

(שחח) bow down, crouched, humbled

(שוח) to be like, be equal, be equivalent; to set, put, place; plain

(שח) meditation ; talk ; bent bowed

(שחו) swimming

(שוש) to rejoice, joy [see the Menorah in the (ו) Waw flanked by two Shins?]

Overlay Words :

(שלש) to multiply by three ; to divide by three ; was of the third

(שלה) draw out [from water - related to שליה afterbirth] [Ruler of 3 connected to Hei (Holy Ghost)]

(שי) gift

(אש) fire

(אשה) woman, wife

DO ALL OVER!!!!!!!!!!!!!!!!!!!!!!!!

Atbash Bet :

Tools :

Ruler of 2 :
(אב) young shoot, sprout; head, leader, chief, God, master, teacher, Father; forefather; patriarch; ancestor, progenitor
(אבב) to bring forth shoots
(גב) pit, cistern; board, plank; locust; back, mound, something curved
(גבב) to vault, rise, lift; gather
(עב) cloud; thick; thicket; beam, rafter
(עבב) to cover with clouds

Ruler of 3 :
(שגב) to be (inaccessibly) high, be very strong

∧ Compass :
(עפעף) to flutter, to fly about; eyelid
(עץ) tree, timber, wood, handle
(עף) = עוף : to fly, fowl, bird; winged creature; to be dark
(פץ) = פוץ to be dispersed, scattered, spread; to speak
(פצץ) to break, break asunder; Syr. crushed, battered, struck down
(פצפץ) to bubble; to pierce, to penetrate; break asunder, dashed, crushed
(פצע) to wound, bruise
(צף) it floated, flowed; float
(צפע) poisonous snake, viper; press, crowd, throng
(צעצע) to adorn, ornament
(צעף) to double, fold; to veil
(צפצף) to twitter, whistle; he whispered, muttered; to press

Top Square :
(מצב) standing place, station position, garrison; placed, stationed
(מץ) oppressor
(צבב) to cover
(צב) covered wagon
(צם) he fasted
(בם) in them
(בצבץ) to squeeze out, exude
(בץ) mud, mire, silt

Small Center Square : [*new words]
(אב) father; forefather, patriarch; ancestor, progenitor; head (of a family), leader, chief; God; master, teacher; important, great; young shoot, sprout
(אבא) father
(אבב) to bring forth shoots, sprout; the coming of spring
(אך) surely, truly; but, only, however
(בא) he who comes; he who arrives; coming, subsequent, next

(בבא) Aram. gateway, entrance
(בך) in thee, in you
(בכא) a species of balsam tree
(כאב) to be in pain, pain

Bottom Square :
(בסס) to base, establish; to trample, tread
(בסף) in the basin or goblet
(סבב) to turn about, go around, surround
(סף) threshold; basin, goblet
(פס) Tunic composed of variegated stripes [or embroidered, raised weave]; Tunic to the palms and the ankles
(סס) moth

V Bottom Compass : [*new words]
*(סעף) to lop off boughs; division, divided opinion
*(סף) threshold; basin, goblet
*(ספסף) to tear, to cut (hair); to singe, burn
*(ספף) to stand on the threshold
*(עסס) to press, crush, tread; to fill with juice, make juicy
*(עפעף) to flutter, fly about; eyelid; that which flutters
*(פס) Tunic composed of variegated stripes [or embroidered, raised weave]; Tunic to the palms and the ankles
*(פסס) to end, cease, disappear
*(פסע) to step, walk, tread
*(פספס) to crumb, to separate, to part; to sign; to make something in mosaic form

The tools theme :
The Father to bring forth shoots to cover with a tunic reaching to the palms and ankles; to veil, to lift, to rise, to fly, to be very high. To establish the garrison, to gather, to cover with clouds.

Mud, mire, and silt to break asunder, to crush, trample, to tread, to wound and bruise the poisonous snake, the viper, the oppressor.

Atbash Bet Overlay Words :
(צב) covered wagon, litter
(צבב) to cover
(צבת) to seize, to grasp, to pinch; to plow crosswise; a bundle of sheaves; bundle, heap
(צד) side, flank
(צדד) to turn aside
(צדק) to be just, righteous; justness, correctness, righteousness, justice, salvation, deliverance, victory
(צם) he fasted
(צמד) to join, to pair, to couple; couple, pair; a measure of land
(צמם) to press, to draw together

(צמצ) to press, reduce, contract; JAram. he drew together, tied up, veiled

(צמק) to be dry, shrink, shriveled

(צמת) to put an end to, exterminate, destroy; to join, attach, contract; to assign in perpetuity

(צקצק) to grate, to rasp

(צתת) to kindle

(תמ) was ended, was finished, was completed; complete, perfect, innocent; completeness, perfection, integrity

(תמד) to make grape skin wine, to make mead; to do constantly, to continue

(תמם) to be finished, to come to an end, completed

(תף) drum

(תפף) to drum; beat the drum

(תקף) to prevail over, to overpower; might, power

(מד) garment, to measure

(מדד) to measure

(ממד) to measurement, dimension

(ממתק) sweet thing

(מפץ) shattering; hammer

(מפקד) muster; census; appointment; appointed place; appointed; commander

(מץ) oppressor

(מצב) standing place; station, position; garrison; placed, stationed

(מצד) fortress, stronghold

(מצמד) bound, fastened, attached

(מצמץ) to suck, to lick; to blink, to wink

(מצץ) to suck

(מצק) to solidify

(מק) rottenness, decay

(מקבת) hammer, mallet; excavation, hole, fissure

(מקד) to focus

(מקם) to localize

(מקמק) to rot

(מקפד) cut, curtailed, made shorter

(מקצץ) cut, curtailed

(מקצת) a little, part of

(מקק) to rot, decay

(מת) dead, a dead person, corpse

(מתם) wholeness, soundness; people, men

(מתק) to be sweet, sweetness

(מתת) gift

(דב) bear

(דבב) to move gently, to walk softly, to drip; to speak, whisper

(דבק) to cling, cleave, adhere; cleaving, attached; glue, joining, appendage

(דד) breast, teat, nipple

(דם) blood, bloodshed, blood guilt

(דמדם) to be in a daze, to be confused

(דמם) to be or grow dumb or silent; to bleed

(דפק) to knock; Aram. he knocked, beat

(דק) a thin curtain [the veil]

(דקדק) to examine minutely, to be strict

(דקק) to crush, pulverize

(דת) decree, law, usage, religion

(קבב) to utter a curse, curse; to be bent, crooked; to hollow out

(קבע) to collect, gather, assemble, store; Aram. he fixed, fastened, nailed, set up

(קד) Syr. he tore, he cut away

(קדד) to bow down, bow ones head; to cut, bore, drill

(קדם) to be before, in front; he was before, preceded, anticipated; to approach

(קדקד) crown of the head, vertex

(קם) enemy, foe, adversary

(קמץ) to enclose with the hand, grasp, take a handful, to close, shut; a handful

(קפד) to be drawn together; to be rolled together; to make oneself unapproachable

(קפץ) to draw together, to shut (hand or mouth); to jump, leap, spring; to chop, cut

(קץ) end; destruction, ruin

(קצב) to cut off; to determine; form, shape; end, extremity

(קצף) to be angry, to be wroth; anger, wrath; foam, froth

(קצץ) to cut off; to stipulate

(פמפם) to stuff, to gorge oneself

(פץ) was dispersed, scattered, spread

(פצם) to split open

(פצץ) to break, break asunder

(פקד) to attend to; to visit; to muster, to appoint; Phoen. to take care of, provide, to attend to; Aram. he commanded; Syr. Inquired, saw to

(פקפק) to hesitate, to doubt

(פקק) to cork, stop up; to tremble, to shake

(פת) morsel of bread, piece of bread

(פתפת) to crumb, crumble, mash

(פתק) to cleave, to split; whence to open (burst, broke open)

(פתת) to break (esp. bread) into pieces

(בד) linen, cloth, material; pole, bar, rod; branch; part, portion (of something cut off); lie, fabrication

(בדד) be alone, be separated, be isolated; alone

(בדק) to mend, repair; to examine, inspect; rent, breach; mending, repair; Aram. he split

(בם) with them

(בץ) mud, mire, silt

(בצבץ) to squeeze out, exude

(בצץ) to squeeze out, exude

(בצק) to swell; dough

(בקק) to be empty

(בת) daughter; girl, maiden, young woman; native, inhabitant of; at the age of; worthy of, deserving; a village or town near a large city; bath (a liquid measure)

(בתק) to cut off

Another "how to" example. Bracket Hebrew definitions separated into categories.

[to break (esp. bread) into pieces] [morsel of bread, piece of bread] [to crumb, crumble]
[to make grape skin wine; to continue]

[to join, to pair, to couple] [measure a garment] [to bow ones head; to cut, bore, drill] [he drew together, tied up, veiled] [to enclose with the hand, grasp] [to prevail over, to overpower, might, power] [to bind and fasten] [to whisper] [to examine minutely, to be strict] [in the stronghold] [linen, cloth, material] [he nailed] [decree, law, religion] [side, flank] [to press, to draw together]

[shattering; hammer] [to knock, beat] [drum, to beat the drum] [to cork, to stop up; to tremble, to shake] [hammer, mallet; excavation, hole, fissure] [to break asunder] [to split open] [to be empty] [to repair; breach] [to turn aside] [the deserving young woman (zion)] [to localize] [to be isolated, alone, separated] [to be dry, shrink, shriveled]

[to be or grow dumb or silent; to bleed]
[to be drawn together, to be rolled together; to make oneself unapproachable] [to draw together, to shut (hand or mouth); to jump, leap, spring]

[The righteous one] [to be finished, to come to an end, completed] [to be before, in front, he was before, preceded]

[to blink, to wink] [he tore, he cut away] [a thin curtain (veil)] [to kindle] [rottenness, decay] [a dead person, dead] [to cling, cleave, adhere, cleaving, attached; glue, joining, appendage] [to solidify] [gift] [wholeness, soundness; people, men] [the commander to muster] [the garrison] [was ended, was finished, was completed; complete, innocent, perfect, perfection] [crown of the head]

[with them] [to be angry, wroth] [to utter a curse; to hollow out] [to cleave, to split; whence to open (burst, broke open)] [mud, mire, silt] [to squeeze out, exude] [to swell] [to cut off] [to cover] [to grate, to rasp] [was dispersed, scattered] [to crush, to pulverize] [to cut off] [enemy, foe, adversary] [to put an end to, exterminate, destroy] [oppressor] [blood, bloodshed, blood-guilt] [end, destruction, ruin] [to rot, decay]

The Atbash Bet overlay :
[Partake of a sacrament / repent, be clean, renew covenant to keep command-ments]
   Break bread and drink wine to continue.
[If you think the following was scrambled on purpose, you are correct. If, or when you are deemed worthy, you can unscramble and clean it up yourself.]
   [to join, to pair, to couple] [measure a garment] [to bow ones head; to cut, bore, drill] [he drew together, tied up, veiled] [to enclose with the hand, grasp] [to prevail over, to overpower, might, power] [to bind and fasten] [to whisper] [to examine minutely, to be strict] [in the stronghold] [linen, cloth, material] [he nailed] [decree, law, religion] [side, flank] [to press, to draw together]

As a shattering hammer to beat the drum, to tremble, to shake, the mallet excavates a fissure. It breaks asunder and splits open to be empty, to repair the breach. To turn aside the deserving young woman, to localize, to be isolated and separated to be dry.

To draw together, it rolled together, to make unapproachable. To leap and spring [forth].

The righteous one to be finished, completed. [He is] in front, preceding. [He] winks and cuts away the veil; to kindle rottenness and decay, that the dead cling, adhere, attached, glue, joining, appendage, to solidify The gift of wholeness and soundness of [his] people. The commander musters the garrison. Complete, innocent and perfect.

With them anger and wrath, to utter a curse, to split open [to burst] mud, mire and silt. To squeeze out, exude, to swell, to cut off, to cover, to grate and scatter, to crush, to pulverize, to cut off [the] adversary and destroy the oppressor. [Their] blood-guilt is destruction and ruin, to rot and decay.

Looking at each letter beneath the Atbash Bet overlay :

(א) Symbolically the righteous
to flash, to glitter, gather, young woman, to utter a curse, to squeeze out, exude, mud, mire, silt, to cut off, to cover, worm eaten, decayed, destruction, ruin

(ת) Symbolically the scales of justice, a sign or mark
he caused to crack, to split open, kinsman, to be in the middle, appointed time, a gift, [the] decree [of] power, to kindle [the] dead, [the] sect to be numerous; with, force, might, power, to close the eyes, to darken, dim, shattering, was dispersed, was scattered, oppressor

(מ) Symbolically water, eternal iteration [waters of eternal life]
to be or grow silent, my, a second time, again, rottenness, decay, was ended, was finished, was completed, complete, perfect; innocent, they came, to be before, nation, people, . . . to utter a curse, blood guilt , to strike, beat, enemy, foe, adversary

(ד) Symbolically the door
EL, to stand, to estimate value, basket, to weigh, your, poor, lowly, to bow down, [in the] nest, to measure, garment. to lift up, he commanded [and] he cut away, the veil, to muster, on account of enemy, foe, adversary, to take vengeance, to rot, rottenness, decay

(ה) Symbolically the veil
a thin curtain, to tear open, wormy, rotten, to rise exalted, to solidify, high, elevated, exalted, supreme, to cut off, enemy, foe, adversary, end, destruction, ruin, rottenness, decay

(פ) Symbolically the mouth
he cleft, split, to be empty, to base, to establish, the worthy young woman... goblet, anger, wrath, to utter a curse, to wound, to cut off, trample, tread, worm eaten,

decayed

(ב) Symbolically the Temple

Father, to bring forth shoots, to cover, tunic reaching to the palms and ankles, to vault, rise, lift; gather, float , cloud, to be inaccessibly high, be very strong, to fly about, establish; to trample, tread, to speak, to be dispersed, to break, break asunder, to wound, bruise, poisonous snake, viper, oppressor, mud, mire, silt, to squeeze out, exude, to bubble; to pierce, to penetrate; break asunder, dashed, crushed, to cover,

The Atbash Bet letter by letter message :

In the twinkling of an eye, I will gather Zion and utter a curse, to squeeze out mud, mire, and silt to cover the corrupt with destruction and ruin.

At the appointed time, I will split open [the hill] for my kinsman, to be in the middle. My decree shall kindle [the] dead. My followers will be numerous. A force with a gift of might and power, to blind, to shatter, and scatter the oppressor.

When I come again, rottenness and decay shall be ended, and the innocent shall be perfected. They shall come before a people to utter a curse, for their blood guilt, the enemy shall be smitten.

I stand in the door to judge your lowly [of heart] which bow before me in the Temple. I have measured for them a garment to lift them up. . . I muster and I command to take vengeance on the enemy.

I will tear open the veil [between this world and the next]. The wormy and rotten [dead] shall solidify to rise exalted, and put an end to destruction and ruin.

I shall split and cleave, to empty a place to base the woman. My cup of wrath to wound with a curse, to cut off and trample.

Mud, mire, and silt will bubble, to penetrate and crush the oppressor.

The Father has brought forth shoots, to cover with a tunic reaching to the palms and ankles. [These shall] rise and gather in my cloud, to be very strong, to trample and tread, to bruise the poisonous snake, the viper.

These three messages may be combined, but I am going to focus on filling out the tools lists.

The א/ת

TOK   TOL

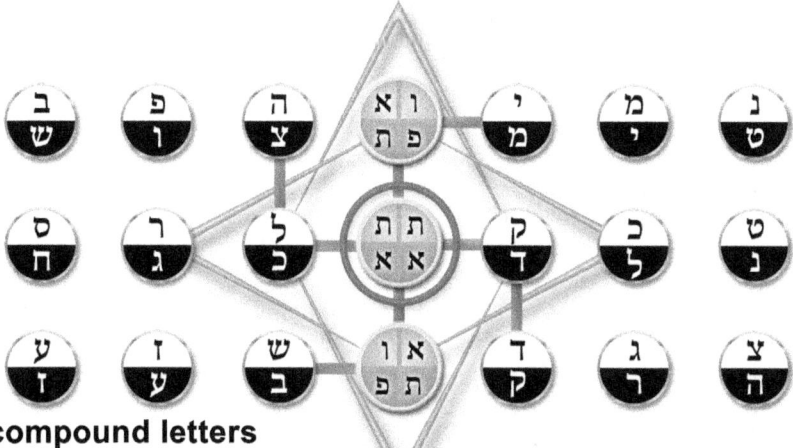

compound letters

[(א)= י,ו][(ב)= ר,ו,י][(ג)= י,ו,י,(ז?)*][(ד)= ו][(ה)= ר,י,ו][(ז)= י,ו]
[(ח)= י,ו,(ז?)*][(ט)= י,ו][(כ)= ר,י,ו][(ל)= י,ו][(מ)= י,ו,ב,ז][(נ)= י,ו]
[(ס)= ו][(ע)= י,ו][(פ)= ר,כ,י,ו,(ז?)*][(צ)= י,ו][(ק)= י,ו][(ר)= ו]
[(ש)= ו][(ת)= ו,ר]

If you are going to work the Swastika, remember that the four squares going in the opposite direction [belonging to the 4 corners], actually forms 4 LOOPS, one end feeding the other, sharing 2/3rds of their letters, moving counter clockwise.

Just saying that after that "Serpent Satan" loop, these loops should be checked for connections.

Think about curving the swastika, as we have seen in ancient art. What happens when you place one curved swastika upon another. You see a circle with a cross going horizontal and vertical. It is often seen depicted as a Halo.

Double check each compass before using, I thought I remembered that something needed to be fixed. //

The Tav ת

The Tav, or more correctly, Taw, is the 22nd letter of the Hebrew Aleph-Bet and has a numerical value of 400. The Paleo version of this letter looked like a cross or balance / scales.

Now consider the fact that the name of the letter (תו) Taw is a ruler of 2, owned by the (ו) Waw, or nail. The sign, linked to a Paleo-Hebrew balance/scales/cross and a nail. Now join that with "I am the Aleph and the Tav", or YHWH and the sign, cross, nail, covenant.

TOOLS :

Ruler of 2 :
(דת) decree, law, usage; religion
(לתת) to moisten grain
(שת) Buttocks, Posteriors; Foundation, Basis, Stay
(שתת) to flow gently, drip; to set, put, place, lay; to lay the foundation of, found, establish
(את) mark of the accusative (THE); with; plowshare; you, thou

Ruler of 3 :
(חות) to shrink from, loathe, abhor

The compass :
(אור) light, or to give light, shine; to air, ventilate; brightness, daylight; fire
(או) or
(רא) OSArab. to see
(רוא) To be feared, revered, or honored
(לקח) To take, buy, that which is received, learning, teaching, instruction.
(עקל) to attach (property), seize, foreclose, distrain. [Arab, 'aqila = he paid ransom]; to bend, twist, curve, make crooked ; to distort, pervert
(עלל) to accuse falsely
(קלל) to be light, be slight; to be swift; to be lightly esteemed, be despised
(חקל) lot, portion, share
(קח) he took
(חקק) to cut in, engrave, inscribe, decree
(חק) something prescribed, enactment, decree, statute, law, rule; Arab. obligation
(קעקע) to tattoo; to undermine, destroy
(על) yoke; on, upon, above; at, beside, towards; against, concerning, about; because of
(עלק) to suck
(קלע) to weave, plait, twist; to sling, hurl forth; slinger, marksman; to cut out, carve
(לעע) to talk wildly; to swallow, sip
(לקק) to lick, lap
(עלל) to insert, thrust in; to accuse falsely; to glean (grapes or olives); to act, to work

(קלח) Flow, spurt, stream, spout forth, flood
(חלק) to divide, share; to be smooth, be slippery; part, portion, share; lot, fate; tract of land
(עלל) to act, do, work; to glean (grapes or olives)
(לח) moist, fresh, new; freshness, vigor
(חל) rampart, wall; surrounding wall; something secular, profane, common
(קל) light; swift, fast; easy, not difficult
(לע) throat
(לעע) to swallow, sip
(אך) surely, truly; but, only, however

Now lets look at the compass letter combinations in another way :

PICK UP HERE. FINISH THIS. DO TOOLS

The ∧ compass (ע) (ק) (ל)
The ∨ compass (ק) (ל) (ח)
The > compass : (א) YHWH (כ) to make whole the dead with a gift of perfection (ו) a covenant of life and light, a present of equality in the sign of the nail.
The < compass א + ו = אלוף Aloph : (א) YHWH (ו) Covenant Son (ר) Son set apart to rule.

DO EVERYTHING OVER !!!!!!!!!!!!!!!!!!!!!!!!!!!!!!!!!!

Overlay Words :
(אד) mist, vapor, gas
(אדה) to bring about, to cause; to evaporate
(אדוק) attached to, fastened to; pious, devout, religious, observant
(אדק) to attach, fasten, connect
(אדש) to be indifferent; Aram. to be silent
(אה) to befit, to become; Aram. (f) beautiful
(אהה) wo!, alas!, ah!
(אהי) where
(אהיה) I AM
(או) or
(אוד) to bend; to brand, firebrand
(אוה) to desire, to long for
(אויה / אוי) woe!, alas!
(אוש) to make a noise, to shout
(אושש) to rustle
(אות) sign, signal, symbol, token; miracle; to consent, to agree, to signal
(אי) island; woe!, alas!; jackal; not; where?
(איד) to vaporize, to steam
(איה) hawk, falcon, kite; where?
(איש) man, husband, masculine, hero; everyone, each one, any one, anybody
(אית) to spell a word
(אקו) wild goat
(אש) fire; foundation

(אשד) to pour; waterfall, cascade; slope of a mountain

(אשה) woman, wife; burnt offering (offering made by fire)

(אשיה) pillar; foundation, base

(אשישה) cake made of dried, compressed grapes (something compact or solid)

(אשש) to strengthen; Arab. he founded, he established

(את) mark of the accusative (THE); with; plowshare; you, thou

(אתה) to come; you, thou

(אתיק) column, porch, gallery

(אתת) to signal

(דא) this

(דאה) to fly, glide in the air; bird of prey

(דד) breast, teat, nipple

(דדה) to move slowly

(דהה) to fade, to become dim

(דוד) uncle; a kettle, a large basket

(דודא) mandrake

(דודה) aunt

(דוה) to be ill, to be unwell, sick

(די) sufficiency; enough; who, which, that, of, about

(דיה) a bird of prey; the kite

(דיו) ink

(דיק) bulwark; siege wall; to be exact, to be precise

(דיש) threshing

(דית) to sweat; to exude; to ink

(דק) a thin curtain (the veil)

(דקדק) to examine minutely; to be strict

(דקק) to crush, to pulverize

(דשא) to sprout, shoot, grow; green grass, green herbage

(דשדש) to tread, to trample

(דשש) to tread, to trample, to pound

(דת) decree, law, usage, religion

(הא) lo, behold

(הד) a joyous shout

(הדא) this, that; that is what is written

(הדד) to reverberate

(הדהד) to reverberate

(הדק) to press together

(הו) ah!, alas!, woe!

(הוא) he, it

(הוד) **beauty**, splendor, glory, majesty; to resonate, to reverberate

(הוה) to fall; to be; destruction, ruin; desire

(הווי) present, actual

(הוי) ah!, alas!, woe!

(הות) to rely upon; to rush upon, to fall upon

(הידד) a joyous shout, cheer

(הידות) songs of praise

(היה) to be, to exist, to happen, to become; was, existed; came into being, became; he remained; it came to pass, it happened

(היות) to be
(השתה) putting, placing, setting
(התת) to rush upon
(ודא) to ascertain
(ודה) to confess
(וו) hook, peg, nail
(ותק) to praise; to become veteran
(יאה) to befit; to become
(יאש) to despair
(יד) hand, arm, foreleg
(ידד) to be friends, to become friends
(ידה) to give thanks, to confess; to throw, hurl, cast
(ידיד) friend, beloved
(ידידות) friendship
(יה) Yah (short for YHWH)
(יהד) to convert to Judaism (at a glance looks like Yah's door. "Judaism" was never an original word used to define the name of a religion. They were called Yahoo Millennia ago. . . now that has its roots in the יהו He/She/Creates image of YHWH.)
(יהו) He/She/Creates [יה = Yah + ו = Son // Gametria = 26 = אהיה "I AM"]
(יהוה) YHWH [simple breakdown יה = Yah + ו = Son + ה = to mediate // Yet also contains Man/Father in the Yud, Woman/Mother/Holy Ghost in the Hei, and the Covenant/Son/Creator in the Waw]
(יהודה) Judah [this may or may not apply as it is a name]
(יקד) to be kindled, to burn
(יקהה) obedience
(יקוד) hearth; burning
(יקוש) fowler, hunter, trapper
(יקש) to lay bait, to lay snares
(יש) there is, there are; possession, property
(ישיש) old man [structurally, יש shows a (י) man + my [possessive] + (ש) that which comes forth from the womb. To show this twice should be equivalent to grandfather, thus, old man]
(יתד) peg, pin, tent pin, nail; to peg, to wedge up
(יתוש) mosquito, gnat
(קא) what is vomited up, vomit
(קדד) to bow down, to bow ones head; to cut, bore, drill
(קדה) to bow
(קדוש) holy, holiness, sacred, saint, saintly
(קדיש) holy, sacred
(קדקד) head, crown of the head; vertex of an angle; to crow
(קדש) holy, sacred
(קהה) to be blunt, to be dull
(קו) a measuring line, line; voice
(קוה) to wait for; to collect (water); to call, to invoke; waiting for, hopeful
(קוקד) to draw a line of dots or dashes
(קוקו) to mark with lines, line, hatch
(קוש) to lay snares
(קיא) to vomit, to spit out; what is vomited up, vomit

(קיה) to vomit

(קיש) to compare, to draw analogous conclusions

(קש) straw, stubble, chaff

(קשה) to be hard, to be stiff; to be severe; difficult, cruel, fierce, violent

(קשוא) cucumber; gourd, vegetable marrow

(קשוה) a vessel for liberation; Arab. basket of palm leaves

(קשקש) to knock, to strike, to rattle; to hoe

(קשש) to gather, to assemble (esp. straw or stubble); to grow old

(קשת) rainbow, bow; bowman, archer

(ש) children of man, that which comes forth from the womb

(שאה) to make a din or a crash, to crash into ruins; to ruin, to lay waste; to wonder, to be astonished, to be amazed

(שאיה) desolation

(שאת) he lifted up, lifted up; elevation, strength, majesty, dignity; swelling, eruption; an elevated place; destruction, ruin, devastation

(שד) female breast; evil spirit; violence, havoc, devastation

(שדד) to plow, to harrow; to overpower, to destroy violently, rob, devastate, ruin; to despoil, ravage

(שדה) field, open country, land; a beautiful woman

(שדוד) devastated, destroyed, ruined, slain

(שדי) the Almighty

(שדידה) devastation, destruction, robbing

(שדש) six

(שה) (young) sheep, lamb; small cattle (sheep, goats)

(שהד) witness, to bear witness

(שהה) to tarry, linger, stay, delay, be late in coming

(שהק) to hiccup

(שו) equality

(שוא) lie, falsehood; nothingness, worthlessness, vanity; lifting up, rising, elation

(שואה) devastation, destruction, ruin

(שודד) robber

(שוה) to be like, be equal, be equivalent; to set, put, place; plain

(שוק) to be abundant; to drive, to run; to desire; market; street; leg, thigh

(שי) gift, present

(שיא) loftiness, pride

(שיש) to rejoice; white marble, alabaster

(שית) to set, put, place, lay; garment; thorn-bush

(שק) sack, bag, sackcloth

(שקד) to watch, to wake; to be almond-shaped, almond tree, almond

(שקה) to give to drink, to cause to drink, water

(שקוי) saturated

(שקשק) to make a noise; to shake, to move to and fro

(שקת) drinking trough

(שש) six, white marble; Egyptian linen

(ששה) six, to divide by six, to multiply by six

(ששי) sixth

(ששית) sixth, one sixth, the sixth part

(שת) posteriors, buttocks; foundation, basis, stay; he put, he placed

(שתה) to drink; to warp, to weave
(שתי) to warp on a loom
(שתיא) Aram., Syr., Arab. Satan
(שתיה) drinking
(שתק) to be silent, quiet
(שתת) to flow gently, to drip; to set, put, place, lay; to lay the foundation of, found, establish
(תא) A room, compartment (especially in the Temple) [Belongs to Aleph / YHWH]
(תאה) to mark out a boundary
(תאו) a wild sheep
(תאוה) desire, wish; passion, appetite; boundary, limit
(תהד) to resound
(תהה) to be astonished, to be amazed, to be dumbfounded; to meditate; to repent; to smell, to examine
(תהו) emptiness, waste, chaos, desert, confusion; vanity, nothingness, worthlessness
(תו) sign or mark
(תודה) thanksgiving; thank offering; thanksgiving choir, procession
(תוה) to make marks; to astonish, astound, amaze
(תושיה) advice, insight, wisdom
(תותו) to mark, to doodle
(תי) suff. my
(תיש) he-goat
(תקוה) cord; hope, expectation
(תשש) to be weak, feeble

(א) (ד) (ה) (ו) (י) (ק) (ש) (ת)

Individual letters :

Distilled definition : Sign or mark, light, instruction ; portion of his spirit which guides us ; balance, scales

Atbash Aleph : This is in the bottom of the same overlay

Tools :

Ruler of 2 :
(תא) cell, room, compartment (especially in the Temple)
(מא) what
(דא) this
(קא) what is vomited up, vomit
(פא) here ; name of the letter Peh
(בא) he who comes, he who arrives; coming, subsequent, next
(אבא) Father
(צא) go out!

Ruler of 3 :
(לדא) against this? / by this? / to this? / unto this? (Not in my dictionary)
(ספא) give to eat ; Palmyrene - feed, nourish

As there are four compass placements in this table, I have inserted symbols before each compass direction to help you follow along. I try to not list the same word
twice, so If a tool has already hit that letter combination, I will skip it. However, I
may have duplicates in here. It doesn't really matter.

< Compass :
(תף) drum
(פג) to grow cold, numb ; to evaporate, to become faint
(פת) their forehead ; morsel of bread ; piece of bread
(פתת) to break into pieces (especially bread), crumb, crumbled
(גפף) to embrace, caress, hug, cling
(גף) back, body, person
(גת) wine pit, wine press
(תגף) that you do not strike

> Compass :
(תל) mound, hill, heap
(תפל) to twist, to twine ; to be tasteless, unsalted, unsavory, vain, foolish ; to whitewash ; to smear, paste, plaster
(לתת) to moisten grain [Arab. mix flour with water - to knead dough]
(לפת) to twist, clasp, grasp with a twist ; to make tasty, to spice
(פתל) to twist, twine ; Aram., Syr. = twisted, distorted, perverted
(פלל) to judge, arbitrate, mediate ; to pray
(תלף) Arabic = to perish
(פלת) two Israelites

∧ Compass :
(עד) to, unto, up to, even to ; until, while ; eternity ; witness, testimony
(עדד) to count, reckon

(דע) knowledge, wisdom
(דעך) to go out, be extinguished ; to crush, trample
(דך) crushed, oppressed
(דכך) to crush, bruise, oppress
(כד) jug, pitcher, round end

V Compass :
(סד) stocks for torturing
(סך) large crowd ; thicket, hut
(כס) throne
(כסס) he pounded, ground, pulverized

NEW SQUARES:
   All I am doing in this edition is filling up the tools lists. These words have not yet been added to any of the texts.

Square 1 :
(אם) mother; matriarch; metropolis, large city; if, whether, when, on condition; nation, people
(אמת) stability, sureness; faithfulness; certainty; truth; to verify
(את) with; a cutting instrument (usually rendered plowshare); you, thou
(אתם) you, ye
(אתת) to signal
(מאת) from
(מם) Mem - name of letter (says PBH, but is it really?)
(מת) dead; a dead person, corpse
(מתם) wholeness, soundness; people, men
(מתת) gift
(תא) cell; room, compartment (esp. in the Temple)
(תאם) to be coupled together, be doubled, match, fit, be suitable; to bear twins; to be adjoining [one flesh?]; to adapt, adjust
(תם) was ended, was finished, was completed; complete, perfect; innocent, art-less; completeness, perfection; integrity; innocence
(תמם) to be finished, come to an end, be completed
(תת) he gave

Square 2 :
(אדק) to attach, fasten, connect
(דא) this
(דד) breast, teat, nipple
(דק) a thin curtain (the veil from position in the Temple within the grid)
(דקדק) to examine minutely, to be strict
(דקק) to crush, pulverize
(קא) what is vomited up, vomit
(קדד) to bow down, bow one's head; to cut, bore, drill
(קד) Syr. He tore, he cut away
(קדקד) head, crown of the head; to crow

Square 3 :
(אב) father; forefather, patriarch; ancestor, progenitor; head (of a family), leader, chief; God; master, teacher; important, great; young shoot, sprout
(אבא) father
(אבב) to bring forth shoots, sprout; the coming of spring
(אף) nose; anger; also, too
(אפף) to surround, encircle
(בא) he who comes; he who arrives; coming, subsequent, next
(בבא) Aram. gateway, entrance
(פא) here; name of letter פ Peh; mouth

Square 4 :
(אך) surely, truly; but, only, however
(אץ) hurrying, hastening
(צא) go out!
(צאצא) issue, offspring; produce, yield

Remember, this is old work and the new squares have not been added.

The theme in the word list :
two Israelites, witness(es), to perish, body, to grow cold, to evaporate, subsequent [second] coming, to crush, trample, wine press, to bruise, vain, foolish, perverted, twisted. Unto this, large crowd, room in Temple, throne, to judge, to mediate, to whitewash, to embrace, give to eat, morsel of bread, knowledge, wisdom, until, eternity.

Now what do we find for words beneath the Atbash Overlay :
(אב) father, forefather, ancestor, progenitor, patriarch, head of a family, leader, chief, God, master, teacher, important, great; a young shoot, sprout
(אבא) Father
(אבב) to bring forth shoots, sprout; the coming of spring
(אבק) to embrace, wrestle [become dusty]; dust, powder, shade of
(אך) surely, truly; but, only, however
(אם) mother, matriarch, metropolis, large city; if, whether, when, on condition; nation, people
(אמץ) to be strong; strength, might, courage, boldness; to close the eyes
(אמת) stability, sureness, faithfulness, certainty, truth
(אץ) hurrying, hastening
(את) with; plowshare; you, thou
(בא) he who comes, he who arrives ; coming, subsequent, next.
(בבא) Aram. - the gateway
(בך) in thee, in you
(בכא) a species of balsam tree
(בץ) mud, mire, silt
(בצבץ) also (בצץ) to squeeze out, to exude
(בקבק) to gurgle
(בקק) to be empty [destroyed, laid waste]; Arab. he cleft, split

(בת) daughter, girl, maiden, young woman; native inhabitant of; at the age of, worthy of, deserving

(כאב) to be in pain, pain

(כם) you, your

(כת) party, sect, group, class, herd

(כתב) to write, writing, document, letter

(כתבת) tattooing

(כתם) to stain; gold

(מאמץ) strength, effort, endeavor

(מאת) from

(מך) poor, lowly

(מכך) to be low, be humiliated

(מם) water

(מץ) oppressor

(מצא) to find

(מצב) standing place, station, position; garrison, placed, stationed

(מצמץ) to suck, lick; blink, wink

(מצץ) to suck

(מצק) to solidify

(מק) rottenness, decay

(מקק) to rot, decay

(מת) the dead

(מתם) wholeness, soundness

(צא) go out

(צאצא) the offspring

(צב) covered wagon, litter

(צבא) to wage war, army

(צבב) to cover

(צבת) to seize, to grasp; to plow crosswise; a bundle of sheaves

(צמא) to thirst, to be thirsty

(צמצם) to press, to reduce, to contract; JAram. he drew together, tied up, veiled

(צמת) to put an end to, exterminate, destroy; to join, attach, contract; to assign in perpetuity

(צתת) to kindle

(קא) what is vomited up

(קבב) to utter a curse; to be bent, crooked; to hollow out

(קבץ) to collect, gather, assemble, store

(קם) enemy, foe, adversary

(קמץ) to enclose with the hand; grasp, take a handful, to close, to shut

(קץ) end, destruction, ruin

(קצב) to cut off; to determine; form, shape; end, extremity

(קצץ) to cut off; to stipulate

(תא) cell, room, compartment (especially in the temple)

(תאב) to long for, to desire; to loathe, to abhor

(תאם) to be coupled together, be doubled, match, fit, suitable

(תך) oppression, violence

(תם) complete, perfect

Note : Overlay words complete.

The theme I get from the overlay :

When the master, faithful and true, comes the second time, the young woman, shall go out. Blink and decay [will] solidify. The [righteous] dead shall be kindled to be whole, sound, complete, and perfected.

Assemble the army to wage war, to utter a curse in strength and might. The waters shall squeeze out; they shall exude mud, mire, and silt to cut off and cover the enemy. The oppressor shall rot. The Adversary's end is destruction and ruin.

REMEMBER : We will be drawing letter-by-letter words from Atbash letter lists only.

So let's see what we find by looking in the Atbash tools lists only.

Since I have a bunch of words relating to a second coming, the dead rising, water from under the temple? . . . Just to make the job easier, I am going to inject the overlay words into the letter they would belong to according to the ruler of 2 rules wherever I can. That will help me to focus the words from each of the letters.

(א) two Israelites, witness(es), to perish, body, to grow cold, to evaporate. Subsequent [second] coming, to crush, trample, wine press, to bruise, vain, foolish, perverted, twisted. Unto this, large crowd, the offspring, room in Temple, the throne, the gate- way, to judge, to mediate, to whitewash, to embrace, give to eat, morsel of bread, knowledge, wisdom, until, eternity.

(ת) [At the] appointed time [the] decree, [of] power [shall] split open and break asunder, to kindle [the] dead kinsman.

(n) [HIS] people [shall be] whole, sound, complete [and] perfect

(צ) In the twinkling of an eye the daughter [of Zion] shall gather [From] the corruption of death and decay, to rise [through] the veil exalted

(ק) The love [of my] bosom, to glow, clothed in linen bright and pure

(כ) [A] tunic reaching to the palms and ankles. In the blink of an eye, to fly, to vault

(ב) rise, lift, gather, to be very high.

Let's put the word list, the overlay, and the letter-by-letter together. A more detailed description of this process will be found in your next overlay. However, for now, it is interesting to note the subtle changes once everything is combined.

The Atbash Aleph :

Two Israelites to perish and go out at my next coming.

The testimony, and the witness : Water to whitewash is only the gateway [for] the poor and lowly.

THE Master, faithful and true shall nourish with knowledge and wisdom. The woman to find a [white] tunic reaching to the palms and ankles. It is a thicket, [a hedge of protection] against the adversary. A room in the temple, linen to veil, in the side to whisper . . . [SORRY - OMITTING SOME TEXT - TO BE HAD ONLY IN THE TEMPLE -(n.ms.hg)] . . . drawn together, tied up and veiled, to be coupled together, unto eternity.

At the time appointed, my second coming, [I shall] rend the veil to kindle the dead kinsmen [that they may] go out. The rotten and decayed shall rise exalted and supreme, complete and perfect. In the twinkling of an eye the dead shall solidify, the offspring shall go out whole and sound. A numerous and strong [host], an army to wage war shall rise and gather to be inaccessibly high. Covered with clouds these glow bright and clear . . .

As a shattering hammer to strike and shock, a hill shall be split open, emptied . . the woman hastening to stand in the middle.

THE Master, mighty and strong, shall judge . . . and utter a curse!

For the blood guilt, [I shall] squeeze out to bubble, pierce and penetrate. Mud, mire, and silt [shall flow] to the sea west and the sea east to cover the enemy. To bruise the poisonous snake, the viper shall be cut off.

How about a riddle?

When you understand what is hidden by the first and the last, you will see that which is not seen under the heavens. What is this thing for travelers to dwell in? Look deeper. Chew on the fruits of the righteous dwelling and give a new name in accordance with its position. Add a dwelling beside it to cover the first, then let the second become something else. . . it shall become the least, and thus, the greatest. The glory of that which is eternal covers the aged eye which sees with clouds, that those traveling through the garden see not.

In order to see while on the earth, one must use a great nail to connect that which is above to that which is below. The whirlwind shall then tear away the veil from the first to the last. His law shall be laid bare in a string of pearls, unlocked by the Tree of Knowledge and Eternal Life, the Menorah.

There is so much more I would like to say . . .
For now, I'll have to let the Menorah speak for itself.

To my brethren the Jews :

You must know that this work was commissioned with you in mind. The times of the Gentiles are now fulfilled, and a day of darkness is upon us. Let the light of the Menorah guide you through the Day of YHWH.

I'm going to suggest a few things.

1. I have a HQ 300dpi print version on the website if you cannot obtain a book version in your location. So get a hard copy before the grid goes down for good.

2. I will post a few prophecies online so that you will understand me when I say, GET OUT OF NEW YORK CITY ASAP. You have three choices. (A) Stay in NYC and perish with the GOY. (B) Go to Israel. (C) Pray to the father of light to be guided to join the daughter of Zion, the thousands of Manasseh, and the ten thousands of Ephraim. I will see you there, and we will face what is coming together.

3. Do not delay. All I can tell you is that the days of tribulation are upon us. I can't even tell you where to go, lest we be overrun with the unclean. Ask our Father in Heaven for directions, and follow HIM.

Note : When I say "Go to Israel", it is NOT because you will escape Jacob's Trouble there. I say that because it is an escape from certain death. The prophecies which I will post do not give a day or an hour, and neither do I. However, I do say that Judgment Day [October 5th], is on our doorstep . . . and this one FEELS different. The pain is heartbreaking.

To the Gentiles who profess a belief in Yeshua :

You are entrenched in the traditions which your mother [The Whore] has taught you. What I have given you about what the early church actually believed, is a small amount of what I recognize in the Trees. Yet there is far more out there if you are willing to look and know that the "church" began fragmenting with different beliefs long before Rome came into the picture.

Most of you believe that on the day of Pentecost that authority was given to everyone because of a manifestation of the Holy Ghost. Go to that point in the scriptures and begin reading. They always need to call someone with authority, if not, his house would continually be divided against itself.

In the end, those who will hear HIS voice will find the way which leads to the narrow gate. Those who don't are not my concern. I'm not here trying to lead you anywhere. I'm telling you to open your eyes, ears, and heart and let the Creator lead you. Your destiny is in your own hands. Choose.

To the remnant of Joseph in the LDS Church :

I thought it was interesting to find that the Hopewell Indians had an X2a DNA linking them to Israel. There are a lot of remarkable evidences in archaeology which point to the Book of Mormons authenticity.

I was amazed to find that the mirrored bridal chamber with a mirror in front, and a mirror behind, is precisely what I see in the code. Joseph Smith said the symbols on the garments represented the ordinances of the Temple, and that is also found in the code. There is a lot of awesome decryption of sacred symbols in the menorah code. . .

However, those who wait for some "man" standing at the head of a 501.3c corporation to tell them what to do are trusting in the arm of flesh.

Those who follow the master's voice, will be far better off than those who flee with just what they can carry, or end up living in tents. If you can hear that voice, you would know that it is time. **Let the gathering begin**. You know where to go, but stay away from the fat valley [you don't want what they're having].

A curse remains to be played out continuously upon the fading flower, **until a leader is called by the spirit of prophecy, and written down as a revelation.**

The refuge of glory has become a refuge of lies [Is. 28] because of those who have transgressed the law, changed the ordinance, and broken the everlasting covenant [Is. 24]. Look it up now . . . read it. Tell me, is this a latter-day context in Is. 24? Who has the power to change the ordinance in the last days, or break the everlasting covenant, and what is the resulting curse.

Because of this, you will stumble and fall and be broken and snared and taken when you walk backwards. Your covenant with death and hell "as penalties" will be **dis**-annulled, and you WILL reap the fullness of that oath; your second endowment is but a sad delusion. Your one sided contract with no penalties will be made null and void in the hands of the Judge.

Let Jacob chapter 5 begin. Let the wild branches be cut off and cast into the fire while the natural branches begin to be grafted in. Let those who were called to his gospel and accounted as the salt of the earth be trodden under foot.

No way man, my patriarchal blessing says that I am of Ephraim. I'm not one of the "gentiles" being spoken of. . . Silly, little Nimrod. Search the Book of Mormon and the Doctrine and Covenants. The latter-day church is identified with the "gentiles" every single time.

"For then will I turn to the people a pure language, that they may all call upon the name of יהוה YHWH, to serve him with one consent."[see Zephaniah 3: 9,10]. This has been given to you in the Menorah, a pure language which will cause HIS people to act as one [because of the embedded doctrine]. I speak to you in another language, and I tell you that this is the rest, wherewith you may cause the weary to rest, and this is the refreshing, yet you will not hear. You will reject the fullness [3 Nephi 16: 10-15], and a house cleaning will see the 1845 Proclamation of the 12 fulfilled. I saw that meeting in vision, and there is something they left out. . . Oh that you could see what is coming.

I will be posting scriptures which speak about setting HIS house in order on the website.

For those who are entrenched in "the prophet could never lead you astray", we will show that that statement, from a "prophet", is as absurd as saying that the compass is to guide you to the north star, or that the square represents a square deal. Search the scriptures, all prophets are mortal and subject to error. The only thing that Joseph Smith ever said about the symbols on the garments was that they represented the ordinances of the Temple. . . And guess what, that is precisely what I see when they are placed into the Tree of Life.

So buckle your seat-belts, and be sure to take your vitamins, because you are about to see the actual result of going to Rome and joining hands with the mouth of the Serpent [Vati-Can]. . . The great and abominable church whose founder was the Devil   And how are those idols doing? Trying to be just like them? Well, they say that worshiping on "Sunday" is a mark of their authority over you. . . Interesting, because the Bible tells me that those who worship on YHWH's day [the Seventh day] have a mark on them, that they are HIS.

Well, it is the Seventh day breaking on the horizon. Let's see if it turns out to be YHWH's day. . . Remember "transgressed the law"? Yeah, the one written in stone to endure for all time. That's right, that little thing telling you to "REMEMBER" the Sabbath day and not to make graven images.

There will be no more millions of YHWH's money sent to U.N.HOLY organizations which sterilize mothers and abort their children. No more sanctioning a eugenics depopulation jab which cripples, kills, and causes still births or spontaneous abortions. . . the clergy response team is shedding innocent blood.

If every last child of the Almighty needs to be put through a tribulation which you can scarcely imagine, HE WILL have a people who can hear his voice and act as one... A people who are counted as Priests and Kings who are worthy of those titles. It's time to put on the full uniform of the full armor of Elohim that you may be able to withstand the evil day.

Trust this. My verbal rebuke is nothing compared to what is coming. If I could not feel the spirit guiding me, and telling me as an individual what was right, I would begin praying now. Pray for deliverance night and day. Repent for being a blind dumb donkey, rebellious and seeing only self interest in the moment. MOST of you are NOT going to make it.

If you cannot hear the master's voice, you will be counted as chaff.

The eternal iteration is more complex than you can currently understand, and there are parts that are hidden from me. However, let me bypass some of the details with their own rabbit holes and try to state these things simply.

Our first estate was not in spirit form. We existed on other planets, and the "war in the heavens" was actually in space. When Satan and his minions were cast down to the earth, it was literal. "enmity . . . between thy seed and her seed". Who's seed? Satan and his minions (see Gen. 3:15).

So, that war in the heavens was part of a test in and of itself. In the council of the Most High, Yeshua sat at the head of the table, and "jobs" were assigned to those who had passed a second estate test billions of years ago. This took place at a time we were between worlds, in spirit form. Messengers went out from the council to issue invitations to those who were deemed ready for a second estate test [they too were in spirit form, between worlds].

I was shown myself issuing one of these invitations to someone and telling them that I would help them on the earth. Yet the lengthy explanation necessary tells me that this knowledge was not had among first estate beings [they knew nothing about this]. That person had a choice of whether they would come here, or go to another place, yet the reward was not as great. I could tell by their apprehension or downright "fear" that it was a tough choice.

So the little children come to earth and are told to look up into the sky [שמים heavens]. [After the mini-nova 13,000 years ago] YHWH said, "Let their be light", and the sun returned to life. [The cold had created ice very quickly] So someone sent down some space rocks and cast a bunch of that ice into low earth orbit to create a terrarium. . . you get the point. The first six days [thousand years] was spent re-building the earth so that it might recover from the mini-nova and the sun blowing itself out for a bit. The word ברא "create" does NOT mean out of nothing.

This brings us to the test.

YHWH wants you to join his ranks in the Celestial Kingdom:

Job description includes being able to hear his voice and take directions while on a second estate test world. If you pass, you will understand the eternal iteration in the mirrored bridal chamber. You will come to places like this and help others in the great work of the Father, to bring to pass the immortality and eternal life of man. "Man" here is derived from the אדם Adam -> Man + Kindred, or kind, man-kind.

The work is more complex, but **those who have graduated from a second estate test have come here over and over and over**. They are taking part in the test, yet they are not here to be tested. They come to help the children in their assigned rolls [see Matthew 11: 11-15].

The perks are great in the Celestial Kingdom. Worlds without end where lesser beings could never go. No more eternal wars, slavery, injustice, or idiots. Beings raised to the same level of existence in the same kingdom as our Father and his Son. "we all with open face beholding as in a mirror the glory of YHWH, are changed into the same image from glory to glory, even as by the Spirit of YHWH." [see 2 Cor. 3: 18]

I was given a vision of something which took place in the council. I told my wife and she had the first and only vision which she has ever had. She saw the same thing, but noticed something else. The vision was then opened to me and I saw the same vision again, and saw what she was pointing out. Everyone at the table had a wife standing behind them with their hands on the shoulders of their husbands. Beyond that, I would rather not say more at this time.

The most powerful tool the accuser has in his arsenal is this lie: You are a sinner, unworthy, not good enough. . . but my brother, the perfect one, the one who is like El, gave us a gift. A sacrifice to nullify the power of the accuser. Cleanse yourself in the blood of the lamb and be born again; fresh and clean as the day you came to this planet. Then tell the devil, "I am a child of the Most High! Get thee hence, Satan."

Everybody stumbles and falls. It is part of the growth process. It is what happens when we forget who we are, and it is expected. HE wants people that will pick themselves up, dust themselves off, and drive-on. . . endure to the end.

www.ingramcontent.com/pod-product-compliance
Lightning Source LLC
LaVergne TN
LVHW051041080426
835508LV00019B/1642